PROGRESS IN COMPUTER-AIDED VLSI DESIGN

Volume 3

IMPLEMENTATIONS

edited by

George W. Zobrist
University of Missouri-Rolla

ABLEX PUBLISHING CORPORATION
NORWOOD, NEW JERSEY

Library of Congress Cataloging-in-Publication Data
(Revised for vol. 3)

Progress in computer-aided VLSI design.

    Includes bibliographies and indexes.
    Contents: v. 1. Tools. v. 3. Implementation.
    1. Integrated circuits—Very large scale integration—Design and con-
struction—Data processing. 2. Computer-aided design. I. Zobrist, George
W. (George Winston), 1934– .
TK7874.P765 1989   621.395   88-37022
ISBN 0-89391-540-8 (v. 3)

Ablex Publishing Corporation
355 Chestnut St.
Norwood, NJ 07648

TO MY WIFE—FREDI

Table of Contents

Series Editor's Preface

This is the third volume of a series concerned with state of the art developments in computer-aided VLSI design, analysis, and implementations. Contributions from researchers and practitioners are included. This volume is concerned with VLSI implementations useful in the VLSI community. Subsequent volumes will cover other topics of interest to the VLSI design community.

This Progress series is intended for those individuals professionally involved in VLSI research, design, developments, production, and scholars and managers.

The material contained in this volume discusses parallel algorithms and fundamental operations in cryptography with VLSI designs, two chapters on systolic arrays; one describes a systolic design simulator SYSIM2 and the other on multivalued VLSI logic implementations, synthesis of a pipelined data system, a tutorial on VLSI designs using Caesar and MOSIS, a chapter which discusses the utilization of semicustom arrays for quickly introducing new technologies through lower overhead in the design environment support, and a group of chapters on implementations in the CAD/CAM environment, a CMOS 16×16 parallel two's multiplier design, and the design and simulation of a RISC architecture.

The editor wishes to thank the contributing authors for making available the information contained in this book. Researchers interested in submitting manuscripts for future editions of this Progress series should contact: Dr. George W. Zobrist, Department of Computer Science, University of Missouri-Rolla, Rolla, MO 65401.

George W. Zobrist
University of Missouri–Rolla

1

Parallel Algorithms and Designs for Fundamental Operations in Cryptography

DAVID Y. Y. YUN
CHANG N. ZHANG

Department of Computer Science
Southern Methodist University

1. INTRODUCTION

Cryptography, as a means for sending secret information over insecure communication channels, is thousands of years old. In conventional cryptosystems, the sender and the receiver processors possess a joint key. The sender uses this key to encrypt the plaintext, while the receiver uses the same key in order to decrypt the ciphertext he gets. Suppose the messages sent are uniformly distributed random strings and the encryption is a permutation of these strings. In such an idealized cryptosystem it is impossible for an eavesdropper to infer any information about the identity of the messages or the key by just observing ciphertexts, no matter how much computing power he or she possesses. However, the situation changes greatly if the message space has a different distribution than the uniform one. Shannon [1] analyzed this problem quantitatively, introducing the tools of information theory. He showed that every additional ciphertext narrows down the key space, in the sense that certain keys become more and more likely. Ciphertext of sufficient length will determine the key uniquely (with high probability). Given a long enough ciphertext, the problem can thus be solved in principle.

Recently, the asymmetric encryption method, often called the public-key cryptosystem, has received much attention. These cryptosystems derive their name from the fact that of the two keys which are involved in encryption and in decryption, one is publicly known, and another is kept secret. This idea is due to Diffie and Hellman [2]. Two specific implementations were proposed: the first one was presented by Rivest, Shamir, and Adleman (RSA) [3]. This scheme is based on an observation that factoring a large integer is a considerably more difficult operation than testing the same number for primality. In 1979, Williams gave a modification of the RSA scheme [4], where it was proved that the factoring and the breaking of the code are computationally equivalent. The second implementation, developed by Merkle and Hellman [5], is based on the integer knapsack problem. Several other systems were proposed, including a public-key distribution system, based on the difficulty of finding logarithms over a finite field.

The problem involving the RSA scheme is that so far there is no proof that factoring is an NP-complete problem. In addition, it is now easy to factor 50-digit numbers, and a 67-digit number has recently been factored [6], while we soon may be able to factor 100-digit numbers perhaps in less than one year of computer time on special hardware [7]. However, factoring has been studied by mathematicians for thousands of years. There is still no known algorithm to factor a number in polynomial time, so encryption by this scheme is unbreakable for all practical purposes. The only secure way is to choose a key N of large length, where N is the product of primes p and q. Using N of length 200 digits, that is, both p and q of length approximately 330 bits, has been recognized as satisfactory. Such a requirement of large keys imposes several difficulties for this scheme, such as performing encryption and decryption efficiently, and implementing large circuits with current VLSI technologies.

A user B of the RSA cryptosystem creates his keys as follows:

   i. Choose at random two large prime numbers p and q.
  ii. Multiply them together to get the public modulus $N = pq$.
 iii. Choose at random a large integer D which has no divisors in common with $(p - 1)$ or $(q - 1)$ (e.g. GCD(D, $(p - 1)(q - 1)) = 1$).
 iv. Compute E as the multiplicative inverse of D modulo $(p - 1)(q - 1)$ (e.g., $E = D^{-1} \bmod (p - 1)(q - 1)$).
  v. Publish as the public key the pair (E, N) and keeps as the secret key the pair (D, N).

Anyone can then encrypt a message M for B using the public key of user B, resulting in the ciphertext C, using the equation:

$$C = M^E \pmod{N}$$

Similarly, B can decrypt the ciphertext C using the equation:

$$M' = C^D \pmod{N}$$

To show that $M' = M$, let us give some definitions.

Definition 1. Let N be a natural number. Z_N denotes the ring of integers modulo N, where addition and multiplication are done modulo N.

Definition 2. Let N be a natural number, Z_N^* denotes the group of integers which belong to Z_N and are relatively prime to N.

Theorem 1: (Chinese Remainder Theorem) Given a set of moduli $\{m_1, m_2, \ldots m_k\}$ and the a k-tuple $(c_1, c_2, \ldots c_k)$ where $GCD(m_i, m_j) = 1$ $(i \neq j)$, then there exists a unique integer C, $0 \leq C < \prod_{i=1}^{k} m_i$ so that
$$c_i = C \pmod{m_i} \ 1 \leq i \leq k.$$

To show $M' = M$ consider following two cases:

Case 1: $M \in Z_N^*$:

Since $DE = 1 \pmod{\Phi(N)}$, let $DE = S\Phi(N) + 1$, where S is an integer.

$$M' = M^{ED} \pmod M$$
$$= M$$

Case 2: $M \in Z_N$ but $M \notin Z_N^*$:

Let $DE = S\Phi(N) + 1$. Since $M \notin Z_N^*$ and $N = pq$, M must be either $M = cp$ or $M = cq$ where c is an integer.

If $M = cp$, it has $M^{ED} \pmod p = 0$ and $M^{ED} \pmod q = M$. If $M = cq$, it has $M^{ED} \pmod p = M$ and $M^{ED} \pmod q = 0$. So we have

$$M^{ED} \pmod p = M \pmod p = c_1 \quad \text{and}$$
$$M^{ED} \pmod q = M \pmod q = c_2$$

By the Chinese Remainder Theorem, there exists a unique integer X, $0 \leq X < pq$, so that

$$c_1 = X \pmod p \text{ and } c_2 = X \pmod q$$

Since $X = M$ satisfies these conditions, so it has

$$M^{ED} \equiv M \pmod N.$$

2. ALGORITHMS FOR COMPUTING M^E (mod N)

$M^E \pmod N$ is the basic function for both encryption and decryption of the RSA scheme and several other public-key systems [8]. Using the current conversional approach, the RSA cryptosystems are several orders of magnitude slower than other single key cryptosystems offering similar cryptosecurity, such as the Data Encryption Standard DES [9]. Assume N is a large integer, $N < 2^n$, and both E and M are in the range $(0, N - 1)$.

2.1. Linear Time Algorithm

The conventional method to calculate M^E (mod N) is first to compute $A = M^E$, then let A divide by N, and the remainder is the answer. This method is not practical, since it will expand the number A to be En bits. An alternative to avoid such difficulty is to do the following iterative algorithm:

> **Step 1:** Let S := 1;
> **Step 2:** Repeat S := S M (mod N) for E times;
> **Step 3:** Halt. S is result.

This approach requires E iterative loops. Each iteration computes one modular multiplication (AB (mod N)). This time delay is denoted by T_n (the basic time unit which will be used in the rest of Chapter 1), where n is the length of the operands. This algorithm has a time complexity of ET_n.

2.2. Binary Algorithm

A well known algorithm of computing M^E is the approach of repeating squaring and multiplications [10]. Since it is based on the binary representation of E, the algorithm is called the *binary algorithm*.

Binary Algorithm:

Let $E = e_{n-1} e_{n-2} \cdots e_0$ be the binary representation of E.

> **Step 1:** C := 1;
> **Step 2:** Repeat *step 2a* and *step 2b* for $i = n - 1, n - 2, \cdots 1, 0$;
> **Step 2a:** C := C^2 (mod N);
> **Step 2b:** C:= $\begin{cases} C \ M \ (\text{mod } N) & \text{if } e_i = 1 \\ C & \text{if } e_i = 0 \end{cases}$
> **Step 3:** Halt. C is the result.

An Example

Suppose one is going to compute M^E (mod N) where N = 13, M = 9 and E = 11. In the binary representation, E = 1011 ($e_0 = 1$, $e_1 = 1$, $e_2 = 0$, $e_3 = 1$)

> **step 1:** C = 1
> **step 2:** (loops):
>   i = 3: (step 2a) C = 1
>   (step 2b) C = 1×9 = 9
>   i = 2: (step 2a) C = C^2 (mod 13) = 3
>   (step 2b) C = C = 3
>   i = 1: (step 2a) C = C^2 (mod 13) = 9
>   (step 2b) C = 9×9 (mod 13) = 3
>   i = 0: (step 2a) C = 3^2 (mod 13) = 9
>   (step 2b) C = 9×9 (mod 13) = 3
> **step 3:** C = 3 is the result of 9^{11} (mod 15).

Theorem 2.   The *binary algorithm* is correct to compute the value of M^E (mod N) in time complexity of $2nT_n$.

Proof:

Let $E = \sum_{i=0}^{n-1} e_i\, 2^i$, and rewrite it by using Horner's rule as:

$$E = 2\,(\,\cdots\,2\,(2\,(0 + e_{n-1}) + e_{n-2}) + \cdots\, e_1)\ \text{to}\ e_0$$

To compute the value of E, let us define following iterative formula:

$$Y_n = 0 \text{ and}$$
$$Y_i = 2Y_{i+1} + e_i \quad i = n - 1, \cdots 1,0.$$

According to the above expression of E, it is easy to show that $Y_0 = E$. Similarly, one can define the iterative formula to compute M^E (mod N):

$$C_n = M^{Y_n} = 1 \qquad \text{and}$$
$$C_i = M^{Y_i}\ (\text{mod N}) \quad i = n - 1, \cdots 1, 0$$

$$= \begin{cases} (C_{i+1})^2\,M\ (\text{mod N}) & \text{if } e_i = 1 \\ (C_{i+1})^2\ (\text{mod N}) & \text{if } e_i = 0 \end{cases}$$

$$i = n - 1, \cdots, 1,0.$$

It is obvious that $C_0 = M^{Y_0}$ (mod N) = M^E (mod N), and this iterative loop is the exactly same as the *binary algorithm*. Since the *binary algorithm* requires n times of loops, each loop may need $2T_n$ time (twice modulo multiplications). So the total time is $2nT_n$ for its worst case. *Observation 1:* The total number of operations (modular multiplications) is $n + E_1$ where n is number of bits of E and E_1 is number of 1's of the binary representation of E. *Observation 2:* Since the first operation of Step 2a of the *binary algorithm* is to square unity (one times one), it is easy to modify the *binary algorithm* so that the maximum number of modular multiplications of the algorithm will be $2n - 1$.

Does this *binary algorithm* achieve the minimal number of operations (modular multiplications)? The answer is no. The smallest example is E = 15, when the binary algorithm needs six operations, yet one can calculate $Y = M^3 \pmod N$ in two operations and $M^{15} \pmod N$ $= Y^5 \pmod N$ in three more, achieving the desired result with only five operations. The approach discussed in the Knuth book [10] called factor method which is based on the factoring of the integer E. Although the factor method is better than the *binary algorithm* on the average [10], E may be very large and there is no existing method by which an integer can be factored in polynomial time. So the factoring approach cannot be applied to the RSA scheme.

2.3. Algorithm Based on the Recoding

Recall that the total number of operations executed by the *binary algorithm* is $n + E_1$, where n is number of bits of E, E_1 is number of 1's in the binary representation of E. Now let us consider how to reduce the total number of operations for computing $M^E \pmod N$.

Definition 3: The expression $E = \sum\limits_{i=0}^{n-1} e_i^* \, 2^i$ where $e_i^* \in \{0, 1, -1\}$ is

a redundant representation of E in base of 0, 1, −1.

The redundant representations of E can be viewed as the difference of two positive binary integers:

$E = \sum e_i' \, 2^i - \sum e_i'' \, 2^i$ where
$e_i' = e_i^*$ if $e_i = 1$ and $e_i'' = -e_i^*$ if $e_i^* = -1$.

In the following the notation $\bar{1}$ is to represent −1.

example: $E = 10\bar{1}\bar{1}0\bar{1}0 = 1010000 - 1010$.

Unlike the binary and other unique representations, there are more than one redundant representations for a given integer E.

example: $E = 101011 = 10110\bar{1} = 110\bar{1}0\bar{1}$.

If E is in the redundant representation, the following algorithm is a modification of the *binary algorithm* to compute M^E (mod N).
redundant binary algorithm:

$$(E = e^*_{n-1} e^*_{n-2} \cdots e^*_1 e^*_0 \qquad e^*_i \in \{1, \bar{1}, 0\})$$

Step 1: $C := 1$
Step 2: Repeat **Step 2a** and **Step 2b** for $i = n - 1, \cdots 1, 0$
  Step 2a: $C := C^2 \ (\text{mod } N)$

Step 2b: $C := \begin{cases} CM \ (\text{mod } N) & \text{if } e^*_i = 1 \\ CM^{-1} \ (\text{mod } N) & \text{if } e^*_i = \bar{1} \\ C & \text{if } e^*_i = 0 \end{cases}$

Step 3: Halt. C is the answer.

Theorem 3. The *binary redundant algorithm* is correct in computing the value of M^E (mod N) where E is in redundant representation.

Proof. The proving is very similar to the Theorem 2. The only difference is that here e^*_i has three possible values $(0,1,\bar{1})$ instead of two possible values $(0,1)$ in the *binary algorithm*.

Notice that the value M^{-1} (mod N) can be precomputed by the extended GCD algorithm. In fact, assume GCD(M, N) = 1, the extended GCD algorithm finds a pair of integers, X and Y, such that XM + YN = GCD(M,N) = 1, that is XM = 1 (mod N), X = M^{-1} (mod N). *Observation 3:* The total number of operations of *binary redundant algorithm* is n + r where n is length of E, r is total number of 1 or $\bar{1}$ in the redundant representation of E.

For a given integer E in the binary representation, it is possible to recode it into a redundant representation so that the number of non-zero's of the redundant form will be less than the number of 1's in its binary form.

For example 47 = 1011111 can be recoded as 47 = 1100001. To compute M^{47} (mod N), the *binary alorithm* require 13 operations but it only requires 10 operations by *redundant binary algorithm*.

In general, if there is a string of 1's in the binary representation, say $1 1 \cdots 1 \ (2^j + 2^{j+1} + \cdots 2^i, i > j)$, one can recode it as $100 \cdots \bar{1} \ (2^{i+1} - 2^j)$.

In the following, two converting rules are introduced and shown that the result of applying these two rules to any binary integers is optimal.

For any string of 1's in the binary representation of E (E $< 2^n$) $11 \cdots 1$ ($2^j + 2^{j+1} + \cdots 2^i \geq j$).

rule 1: if i $\neq$ n − 1 and i − j > 1 then recode it as $100 \cdots \bar{1}$ ($2^{i+1} − 2^j$).

Notice that in the case of i − j > 2, it will always reduce the number of nonzero elements for this particular string. In the case i − j = 2, after applying rule 1, the string will be $10\bar{1}$ ($2^{j+1} − 2^j$). Although this does not reduce the number of nonzero elements of the string, it changes the (i + 1)-th bit from 0 to 1, so it may propagate a 1 to the next string.

rule 2: if i = n − 1 and i − j $\geq$ 4 then recode it as $100 \cdots \bar{1}$ ($2^n − 2^j$).

This rule is for the case of the 1's string starting from the most significant bit. It is obvious that if the length of the 1's string is less than 4, then it will not reduce any operations for this particular string. The following algorithm is based on those two rules:

example 1:
   E = 101110111101
     = $11000\bar{1}000\bar{1}01$
example 2:
   E = 111101111
     = $1000\bar{1}000\bar{1}$

Theorem 4. For a given integer E, $2^{n-1} \leq$ E 2^n in binary representation, if E* is the result of applying the *recoding* rules to E, then the number of operations is minimized by applying *redundant binary algorithm* to E*.

Proof. Suppose E** is a redundant representation of E, such that the number of operations of E** executed by the *redundant binary algorithm* is less then the operations corresponding to E*.

Let E** = $e_s^{**} e_{s-1}^{**} \cdots e_1^{**} e_0^{**}$ where $e_i^{**} \in \{0,1,\bar{1}\}$, s = n or n − 1, e_s^{**} = 1. Screening this expression of E** from the left to right by checking if there is a pattern $10 \cdots 0\bar{1}$ ($2^i − 2^j$, i > j). If there is, it is replaced by the equivalent string $011 \cdots 1$ ($2^j + 2^{k+1} + \cdots 2^{i-1}$). Continuing this process until no such patterns exists, it finally will get a binary representation of E**. It is clear that this binary representation must be E, since for a certain number, its binary representation is unique.

Notice that this converting from a redundant representation into an equivalent binary representation is the inverse conversion by applying the *recoding* rule 1 and rule 2, except that rule 1 and rule 2 have some constraints which guarantee that the result will not increase the number of operations. So, the number of operations of E^{**} must be equal or less than the ones of E^* found by execution of the *redundant binary algorithm*. This contradicts the above assumption. Therefore, Theorem 4 holds.

Observation 4:   for any given integer E, $E < 2^n$, the time complexity of computing M^E (mod M) is $\left(n + \left\lceil \dfrac{n}{2} \right\rceil + 1 \right) T_n$ by applying the *recoding* rules and *redundant binary algorithm*.

Suppose E is the integer randomly distributed in the range of 2^{n-1} and $2^n - 1$. It is easy to figure out that the average number of 1's for the integers between 2^{n-1} and $2^n - 1$ is $\left(\dfrac{n}{2} + 1 \right)$.

The average number of nonzero's after applying the *recoding* algorithm for the integers distributed in the range of 2^{n-1} and $2^n - 1$ can be calculated by the following equation:

$$n_2 = \frac{\displaystyle\sum_{i=0}^{2^{n-1}-1} f(i)}{2^{n-1}}$$

where f(i) is the number of nonzero's after execution the *recoding* rules to the integer $2^{n-1} + i$ ($i = 0, \cdots 2^{n-1} - 1$).

Table 1.1 shows the comparison of the number of nonzero elements between the original integer and the recoded one.

Formally it can be proved that the ratio of $\dfrac{n_1 - n_2}{n_2}$ is greater than

Table 1.1. Comparison of Number of Nonzero's Between Binary Representation and Recoded Representation.

n number of bits	Before recoding number of 1's n_1	After recoding number of nonzero's n_2	$\dfrac{(n_1 - n_2)}{n_1}$
10	6	4.44	26.0%
15	8.5	6.11	28.1%
20	11	7.77	29.4%
25	13.5	9.44	30.8%

$\frac{1}{3}$ when n $\geq$ 25. Notice that in practice, E is very large, and one may need to compute a series of computations of M_i^E (mod N) i = 1,2, $\cdots$ m. Therefore the total saving is m $\times$ ($n_i - n_2$) on average.

2.4. Parallel Binary Algorithm

It was known that one way to speed up the computation of the algorithm is to make the operations of the algorithm as parallel as possible. The algorithm may be computed in a shorter period of time than the previous one by the use of two or more parallel processors. In the following algorithm, it is shown that a modification of the *binary algorithm* to use two parallel processors results in the performance of the same computation of M^E (mod N) almost twice as fast as the *binary algorithm*.

Parallel Binary Algorithm

Let E = $e_{n-1} e_{n-2} \cdots e_0$ be the binary representation of E.

> **Step 1:** $C_A := M$ and $C_B := 1$;
> **Step 2:** Repeat Step 2a for i = 0,1, $\cdots$ n $-$ 1;
> **Step 2a:** $C_A := C_A^2$ (mod N) and
>
> $$C_B := \begin{cases} C_B \, C_A \text{ (mod N)} & \text{if } e_i = 1 \\ C_B & \text{if } e_i = 0 \end{cases}$$
>
> **Step 3:** Halt. The value of C_B is the result.

Notice that in this *parallel binary algorithm*, it uses the "and" instead of ";" to imply the parallelism of computations between two processors (A and B).
Example: Applying the *parallel binary algorithm* to the same example as the one used before (9^{11} (mod 13)).

> **Step 1:** $C_A = 9$ and $C_B = 1$.
> **Step 2:** (loops)
>   (i = 0) $C_A = 9^2$ (mod 13) = 3 and $C_B = 9$ ($e_0 = 1$)
>   (i = 1) $C_A = 3^2 = 9$ and $C_B = 9 \times 3$ (mod 13) = 1 ($e_1 = 1$)
>   (i = 2) $C_A = 9^2$ (mod 13) = 3 and $C_B = 1$ ($e_2 = 1$)
>   (i = 3) $C_A = 3^2$ (mod 13) = 9 and $C_B = 1 \times 3 = 3$ ($e_3 = 1$)
> **Step 3:** $C_B = 3$ is the result of 9^{11} (mod 13).

Theorem 5.   The *parallel binary algorithm* correctly computes M^E (mod N) in n steps by two parallel processors.

Proof:

The problem of M^E (mod N) can be viewed as the modulo product of two subterms:

$$M^E \text{ (mod N)} = A B$$

where $B = M^{\sum_{i=0}^{n-1} 2^i e_i}$ (mod N) and $A = M^{2^{n-1}}$ (mod N)

Let:

$$Y_0 = 0 \text{ and}$$

$$Y_i = \begin{cases} Y_{i-1} + 2^i & \text{if } e_i = 1 \\ Y_{i-1} & \text{if } e_i = 0 \end{cases}$$

It is easy to prove that

$$Y_{n-1} = E = \sum_{i=0}^{n-1} e_i \, 2^i$$

Let $C_{A_0} = M$ and $C_{B_0} = M^{y_0} = 1$

$$C_{A_i} = (C_{A_{i-1}})^2 \text{ (mod N) and}$$

$$C_{B_i} = M^{Y_i} = \begin{cases} C_{B_{i-1}} C_{A_{i-1}} \text{ (mod N)} & \text{if } e_i = 1 \\ C_{B_{i-1}} & \text{if } e_i = 0 \end{cases}$$

It is obvious that $C_{B_{n-1}} = M^{Y_{n-1}}$ (mod N) $= M^E$ (mod N). The *parallel algorithm* actually computes M^E (mod N) in n steps using two parallel processors.

3. VLSI DESIGNS FOR RSA CRYPTOSYSTEM

3.1. A Double Linear Systolic Array Design

Recall that in the RSA encryption, E and N are fixed (for decryption, use constant D instead of E) and M stands for the message. It is reasonable to assume that people want to encrypt (decrypt) multiple messages. In the following section, a double linear systolic array structure is to be developed. This structure consists of 2n processing elements (PE's) and uses a pipeline structure to reduce the computation time on average. The proposed double linear systolic array can compute the M_j^E (mod N) (j = 1,2, $\cdots$ m) in asymptotically constant time on average.

Figure 1.1 shows the processing element and its function, which has two data inputs, A and B, and one control signal e, and one data output C. If control signal e = 0, then output C just passes the data B. If e = 1, then the processor computes modulo multiplication A B (mod N), and sends the result out according to C, N is a constant stored in each PE.

The whole pipeline network to compute sequence of M_j^E (mod N) is shown in Figure 1.2. It consists of 2n PE's configured as a double linear systolic array. The left side of the network computes the sequence of the power of M modulo N and is synchronized with the right side of the network by a common clock. The inputs of the right side of the network are always 1's, while the sequence of the messages (M's) is sent to the left side of the network and also synchronized by the common clock. The outputs are interleaved from the right top PE as shown in Figure 1.2. It takes n time units delay to get the first result from the time of the first message sent in, and then the following results will be obtained in each subsequent time unit delay. The average time delay per message, $\hat{t}_n$, is

$$\hat{t}_n = \left(\frac{m + n - 1}{m} \right) T_n = \left(1 + \frac{n - 1}{m} \right) T_n.$$

If m = 1, than $\hat{t}_n = n\, T_n$, which is the case of implementing by two PE's. If m = n − 1, then $\hat{t}_n = 2\, T_n$. If m >> n, then $\hat{t}_n \approx T_n$.

Notice that the left-top PE is not useful (computes M^{2n}), and the right-bottom PE is just to pass 1 or M (depends on the value of e_0) which can be implemented by a simple circuit. Hence this pipeline network can be simplified to have 2 (n − 1) PE's.

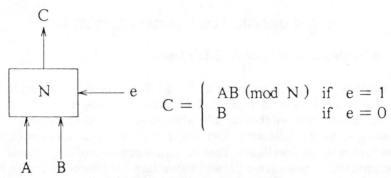

$$C = \begin{cases} AB \text{ (mod } N \text{)} & \text{if } e = 1 \\ B & \text{if } e = 0 \end{cases}$$

Figure 1.1. Basic Function of PE.

$$M_j^E \pmod{N}$$

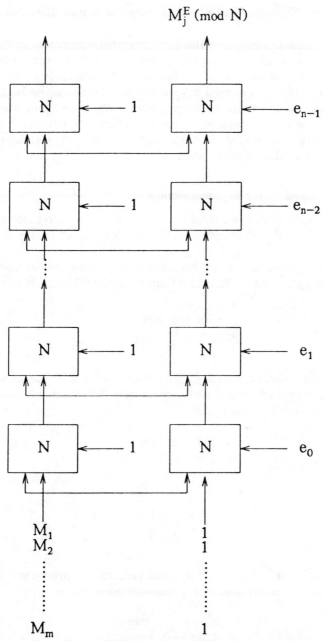

Figure 1.2. A Pipeline Network for RSA Public-key System.

3.2. A Fast Modular Multiplication Algorithm and VLSI Design

Modular multiplication is the fundamental operation in RSA and several other public-key cryptosystems. To obtain reasonable cryptosecurity, the moduli must be hundreds of bits long.

The algorithm presented by Brickell [11] combines the binary multiplication with division (remainder) into one procedure and achieves the $(n + 7)$ steps to compute the product modulo M of n bits. This algorithm is fast since each step requires only a delayed carry addition (a modified carry save addition).

3.2.1. Delayed Carry Representation

Delayed carry adder is a modification of the carry-save adder developed by Norris and Simmons [12] which is used in the Brickell's algorithm.

In a carry-save adder, the accumulator consists of a sum register S and a carry register C. To add a binary number B to the accumulator, one computes,

$$s_i := s_i \oplus c_i \oplus b_i$$
$$c_{i+1} := s_i c_i \ V \ s_i b_i \ V \ c_i b_i$$

for all i.

In a delayed carry adder, the accumulator still consists of two registers, T and D. To add a binary number B to the accumulator, one forms in a single clock cycle.

$$s_i := t_i \oplus d_i \oplus b_i$$
$$c_{i+1} := t_i c_i \ V \ t_i b_i \ V \ b_i d_i$$

and then

$$t_i := s_i \oplus c_i$$
$$d_{i+1} := s_i c_i$$

for all i.

The important property of the delayed carry representation which is different from carry-save representation is:

$$d_0 = 0 \qquad \text{and}$$
$$d_{i+1} t_i = 0 \quad \text{for all i.}$$

Figure 1.3 shows the diagram of the delayed carry adder which consists of a half-adder and a carry-save adder.

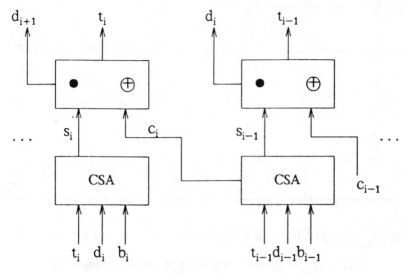

Figure 1.3. Diagram of delayed Carry Adder.

3.2.2. Brickell Algorithm

Let A and B be two delayed carry integers of length n and $N = 2^n - K$. The Brickell algorithm can be written as follows:

Step 1: $D := 0$ and $t_1 := 0$ and $t_2 := 0$
Step 2: *For* $j = 1$ to $n + 10$ *do*
Step 3: *begin*
Step 4: $B^* := \alpha_{n-1} B + \alpha_n 2B;$
Step 5: $K^* := t_2 2^{11} K + t_1 2^{10} K;$
Step 6: $D := 2 (D + B^* + K^*);$
Step 7: $A := 2A;$
Step 8: *Add* the top 4 bits of D to the top 4 bits of 2^{10} K
    if there is an overflow of 2^{10} and $t_2 = 0$
      then $t_1 := 1$ *else* $t_1 := 0$
    end;

3.2.3. Hardware Implementation

Figure 1.4 shows a logic diagram of the hardware design for the Brickell algorithm. The 5 to 2 delayed carry adder (DCA) is used to compute the statement of $D := 2 (D + B^* + K^*)$ which can be implemented by cascading five half adders, as shown in Figure 1.5. The number B^* is also in delayed carry from and is stored in two registers, β^* and δ^*. Notice that for $i > n$, δ_i^* and β_i^* are 0. So the first 5 bits

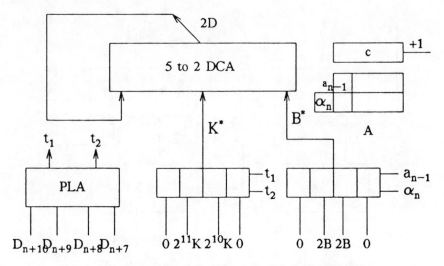

Figure 1.4.   Diagram of Hardware for Brickell's Algorithm.

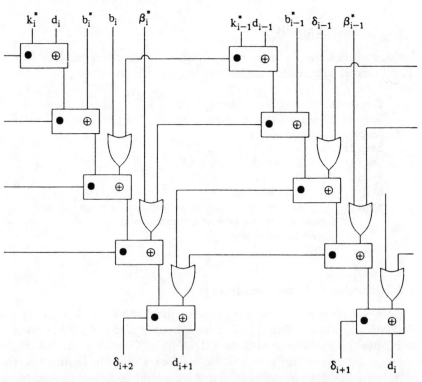

Figure 1.5.   5 to 2 DCA Computing D: = 2 (D + B* + K*) 0 = i ≤ n.

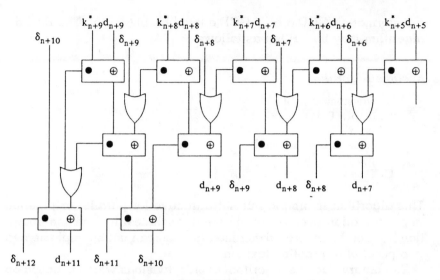

Figure 1.6.   5 to 2 DCA for i ≥ n + 5.

of 5 to 2 DCA to compute $D := 2(D + B^* + K^*)$ is different from the others. Figure 1.6 shows this design. Delayed carry register A actually contains n bits for register α, and n + 1 bits for register α, so α can be stored after the left shift of A ($A := 2A$). The counter C is used to control the number of loops. The statements $B^* := (\alpha_{n-1} B + \alpha_n 2B)$ and $K^* := t_2 2^{11} K + t_1 2^{10} K$ are realized by two selectors. t_1 and t_2 are determined by the top four bits of the D and K^* which can be implemented by the same circuit of Figure 1.5 or a PLA.

4.   INTEGER GCD COMPUTATION

Let us now describe the algorithms for computing the integer greatest common divider (GCD), extended integer GCD, and parallel VLSI hardware designs.

The basic operation of the key generator in the RSA cryptosystem is the extended GCD computation. This operation also arises when performing exact computations and factorization in a symbolic math system.

4.1. Euclid's Algorithm and Binary Euclid's Algorithm

The Euclid's algorithm and its variants are widely used for GCD computations [10]. Euclid's algorithm is based on GCD preserving transformation $GCD(a,b) = GCD(a \pmod b, b)$ $(a \geq b)$. The Euclid's algorithm may be written as follows.

Euclid's Algorithm:

```
      {assume a ≥ b}
   while b ≠ 0 do
     begin
       a := b; b := a (mod b);
     end;
     GCD := a.
```

This algorithm is simple but not attractive for parallel or pipeline implementation because the interloop includes the division operation "$a \pmod b$" which takes time $\omega(n)$, and can not be implemented in a parallel or pipeline fashion.

The binary Euclid's algorithm avoids divisions which is based on magnitude tests ("is $a > b$") and on GCD preserving transformations $(GCD(a,b) = GCD(a,b-a))$. The binary Euclid's algorithm can be written as follows.

Binary Euclid's Algorithm:

```
      {assume a and b are odd}
   t := |a − b|;
   while t ≠ 0 do
     begin
       repeat t := t div 2 until odd(t);
       if a ≥ b then a := t else b := t;
       t := |a − b|;
     end;
     GCD := a.
```

These are performed in an O(n) long sequence of iterations where n denotes the number of bits in the two inputs. The next iteration can not start before the previous iteration has terminated. Thus, it is not at all clear whether any attempt to parallelize the Euclid's algorithm could go beyond O(n) parallel time.

4.2. Purdy's GCD Algorithm

In contrast to the Euclid's algorithm, which operates on the most significant bit first, G. B. Purdy [13] proposed a different way to compute integer GCD's which requires no whole-word comparisons. The key idea of Purdy's GCD algorithm is to use the GCD preserving

transformation of GCD(a,b) = $\left| \text{GCD} \left(\dfrac{a + b}{2}, \dfrac{a - b}{2} \right) \right|$.

Purdy's GCD algorithm:

```
while a ≠ 0 and b ≠ 0 do
   begin
      repeat a := a div 2 until odd(a);
      repeat b := b div 2 until odd(b);
```
$$a := \frac{(a + b)}{2} ;$$

$$b := \frac{(a - b)}{2} ;$$
```
   end;
   GCD := |a + b|.
```

The advantage of Purdy's algorithm is that it provides a possible way to speed up the period of each iteration by using a carry-save technique. However, it requires $O(n^2)$ iterations in its worst case, where n denotes the number of bits of the inputs.

4.3 PM Algorithm

Brent and Kung [14] presented their plus-minus (PM) GCD algorithm. The tests used in the PM algorithm are parity tests ("is b even", "is

$\dfrac{b + a}{2}$ even", and "is $\dfrac{b - a}{2}$ even") and the GCD preserving trans-

formations are: GCD(a,b) = GCD $\left(a, \dfrac{b}{2} \right)$ for a odd, b even, and

GCD(a,b) = GCD $\left(a, \dfrac{b \pm a}{2} \right)$ for a, b odd, while the number of it-

erations is still $O(n)$. The advantage of this approach is that the next iteration can start as soon as the least significant bits from the previous iteration are known. In particular, this gives a linear time implementation on a systolic array [14].

The code for *PM algorithm* is as follows.

PM algorithm
(assume A and B are odd, B $\neq$ 0, 0 $\leq$ A, B < 2^n.)
Step 1: [initialization] $\delta := 0$ and $\alpha = n$ and $\beta := n$ and $\alpha := B$ and $b := B$; {$\delta = \alpha - \beta$}
Step 2: [iterations]
  repeat
    while EVEN (b) do

$b := \dfrac{b}{2}$ and $\delta := \delta + 1$ and $\beta := \beta - 1$; {operation of type 1, b is odd,

$|b| \leq 2^\beta$, $\delta = \alpha - \beta$}
    if $\delta \geq 0$ then
      swap (α,b) and swap (α,β) and $\delta := -\delta$; {operation of type 2, $\alpha \leq \beta$, $\delta = \alpha - \beta$, $|\alpha| \leq 2^\alpha$, $|b| \leq 2^\beta$, a,b are odd}

    if EVEN $\left(\dfrac{\alpha + b}{2} \right)$ then

$b := \dfrac{b + \alpha}{2}$ {operation of type 3} else

$b := \dfrac{b - \alpha}{2}$; {operation of type 4}

    until b = 0;
Step 3: [output] return with GCD:= α.

This algorithm return the GCD of its inputs, A and B, provided that A and B are odd. Its correctness under this condition follows from the

fact that if b is even and a is odd, then GCD(a, b) = GCD $\left(\alpha, \dfrac{b}{2} \right)$

while if both a and b are odd then GCD(a, b) = GCD $\left(\alpha, \dfrac{\alpha + b}{2} \right)$

= GCD $\left(\alpha, \dfrac{\alpha - b}{2} \right)$. In every repeat loop, the sum $\alpha + \beta$ decreases

by at least 1. It has been proved that the upper bound of number iterations is [3.1105n] [14].

Note that α and β are not necessary for the actual execution of the *PM algorithm*. It is sufficient to keep δ and remember that $\delta = \alpha - \beta$. The algorithm uses a signed number δ to guide the direction so that both numbers in register α and b will balance to be reduced.

4.4. Two-bit PM Algorithm

The PM algorithm can be modified to achieve more high degree of parallelism [15]. The basic idea of the modified algorithm is to pack two consecutive transformations of *PM algorithm* into one parallel phase and to avoid the swap operations during the iterations to achieve a higher parallelism. It has been proved that for any two n-bit integers, the number of iterations of the modified algorithm is less than 1.56 n + 1 which is almost half what of the *PM algorithm*. **Observation 5:** The swap operation (swap(a,b)) (operation of type 2) is not necessary.

Instead, the sign bit of δ can be used to determine which argument (a or b) should be replaced next.

Observation 6: During the repeat loop after execution of type 3 and

type 4 $\left(b := \dfrac{b + a}{2} \text{ and } b := \dfrac{b - a}{2} \right)$ at least one operation of type 1

must follow.

In fact, before the execution of an operation of type 3 or type 4, both a and b are odd. Table 1.2 shows all possible combinations of the two least significant bits of a and b and the corresponding two least significant bits of b + a and b − a.

From Table 1.2, one can see that either b + a or b − a must be divisible by 4. Therefore the operation of type 3 or type 4 and opera-

tion of type 1 can be combined together as one operation; $\dfrac{b + a}{4}$ or

$\dfrac{b - a}{4}$.

Having removed all powers of two shared by A and B, GCD of A and B is odd. the *two-bit PM algorithm* is as follows.

Two-bit PM algorithm:
Step 1: [initialization] $\delta := 0$ and a := A and b := B;
Step 2: [iterations]

$$\text{Case 1} \left(\text{ EVEN } \left(\frac{a}{2} \right) \text{ \& EVEN(a) } \right) : a := \frac{a}{4} \text{ and } \delta := \delta - 2;$$

Table 1.2. The Two Least Significant Bits of a, b, b + a and b − a.

a	b	b + a	b − a
01	01	10	00
01	11	00	10
11	01	00	10
11	11	10	00

Case 2 $\left(\overline{\text{EVEN}} \left(\dfrac{a}{2} \right) \text{ \& EVEN}(a) \right)$: $a := \dfrac{a}{2}$ and $\delta := \delta - 1$;

Case 3 $\left(\text{EVEN} \left(\dfrac{b}{2} \right) \text{ \& EVEN}(b) \right)$: $b := \dfrac{b}{4}$ and $\delta := \delta + 2$;

Case 4 $\left(\overline{\text{EVEN}} \left(\dfrac{b}{2} \right) \text{ \& EVEN}(b) \right)$: $b := \dfrac{b}{2}$ and $\delta := \delta + 1$;

Case 5 $\left(\delta \geq 0 \text{ \& EVEN} \left(\dfrac{(b+a)}{2} \right) \right)$: $a := \dfrac{(b+a)}{4}$ and $\delta := \delta - 1$;

Case 6 $\left(\delta \geq 0 \text{ \& EVEN} \left(\dfrac{(b-a)}{2} \right) \right)$: $a := \dfrac{(b-a)}{4}$ and $\delta := \delta - 1$;

Case 7 $\left(\delta < 0 \text{ \& EVEN} \left(\dfrac{(b+a)}{2} \right) \right)$: $b := \dfrac{(b+a)}{4}$ and $\delta := \delta + 1$;

Case 8 $\left(\delta < 0 \text{ \& EVEN} \left(\dfrac{(b-a)}{2} \right) \right)$: $b := \dfrac{(b-a)}{4}$ and $\delta := \delta + 1$;

Step 3: [finished ?] if $a = 0$ or $b = 0$ then return with GCD := b or a else go to step 2.

Theorem 6: $(1.56n + 1)$ iterations are sufficient to compute GCD of any two n-bit integers A and B.

Proof: It had been proved that $N^* \leq 3.1105n$ by Brent and Kung [14], N^* denotes the total number of iterations required by *PM algorithm*. Let a' and b' be the new values of arguments a and b after perform one iteration. The result can be expressed as follows:

$$N^* = \sum_{i=1}^{6} p_i^* \leq 3.1105n \text{ where } p_i^* \text{ is the number of operations corre-}$$

sponding to the Case i in the *PM algorithm*:

Case 1: $a' = \dfrac{a}{2}$, $b' = b$

Case 2: $a' = a$, $b' = \dfrac{b}{2}$

Case 3: $a' = \dfrac{a+b}{2}$, $b' = b$

Case 4: $a' = \dfrac{b-a}{2}$, $b' = b$

Case 5: $a' = a$, $b' = \dfrac{a+b}{2}$

Case 6: $a' = a$, $\quad b' = \dfrac{b - a}{2}$

Notice that here it is assumed that the swap operation does not take time and one can combine the swap operation with its following operation for easy comparison. In *two-bit PM algorithm* it has:

$$N = \sum_{i=1}^{8} p_i$$

where N denotes the total number of operations, p_i denotes the total of operations in Case i:

Case 1: $a' = \dfrac{a}{4}$, $\quad b' = b$

Case 2: $a' = \dfrac{a}{2}$, $\quad b' = b$

Case 3: $a' = a$, $\quad b' = \dfrac{b}{4}$

Case 4: $a' = a$, $\quad b' = \dfrac{b}{2}$

Case 5: $a' = \dfrac{b + a}{4}$, $\quad b' = b$

Case 6: $a' = \dfrac{b - a}{4}$, $\quad b' = b$

Case 7: $a' = a$, $\quad b' = \dfrac{b + a}{4}$

Case 8: $a' = a$, $\quad b' = \dfrac{b - a}{4}$

Comparing these two algorithm carefully, one finds that:

$$p_5 = p_3^{\cdot}, \; p_6 = p_4^{\cdot}, \; p_7 = p_5^{\cdot} \text{ and } p_8 = p_6^{\cdot}$$

$$p_1 + p_2 \leq \lceil \frac{(p_1^{\cdot} - p_3^{\cdot} - p_4^{\cdot})}{2} \rceil$$

$$p_3 + p_4 \leq \lceil \frac{(p_2^{\cdot} - p_5^{\cdot} - p_6^{\cdot})}{2} \rceil$$

So it has

$$N = \sum_{i=1}^{8} p_i$$

$$\leq p_3^* + p_4^* + p_5^* + p_6^* + \left[\frac{(p_1^* - p_3^* - p_4^*)}{2} \right] + \left[\frac{(p_2^* - p_5^* - p_6^*)}{2} \right]$$

That is, $2N \leq \sum_{i=1}^{6} p_i^* + 2$. Therefore $N \leq 1.56n + 1$.

Notice that if both a and b are odd, one of $(a + b)$ and $(a - b)$ must divisible by 2^2, but may not be divisible by 2^3. So the three-bit PM algorithm (i.e., check the three lowest bit and shift three bits at one time) will not reduce the upper bound on the number of iterations.

4.5. Extended GCD Algorithm

For given positive integers A and B, the extended GCD problem is to find integers X and Y, so that

$$AX + BY = GCD(A,B).$$

There are many applications of the extended GCD, for example, in error correcting codes and integer factorization. A common case is that $GCD(A,B)$ is known to be 1 (A and B are relative prime) and one wants to compute a multiplicative inverse modulo B, that is, compute X such that $AX = 1 \pmod{B}$.

The *two-bit PM algorithm* can be expressed by follow transformation: Let $a_0 = A$ and $b_0 = B$, a_i and b_i be the contents of arguments a and b after the i-th iteration of the loop. It has the form

$$\begin{bmatrix} a_k \\ b_i \end{bmatrix} = T_k \begin{bmatrix} a_{k-1} \\ b_{k-1} \end{bmatrix}, \quad \text{for} \quad k = 1,2,\cdots,$$

until $a_m = 0$ or $b_m = 0$ for some $m > 0$. The transformations T_k can be represented by 2×2 matrices of the following eight forms corresponding to the 8 cases of the two-bit *PM algorithm*:

$$M_1 = \begin{bmatrix} 1/4 & 0 \\ 0 & 1 \end{bmatrix} \qquad M_2 = \begin{bmatrix} 1/2 & 0 \\ 0 & 1 \end{bmatrix}$$

$$M_3 = \begin{bmatrix} 1 & 0 \\ 0 & 1/4 \end{bmatrix} \qquad M_4 = \begin{bmatrix} 1 & 0 \\ 0 & 1/2 \end{bmatrix}$$

$$M_5 = \begin{bmatrix} 1/4 & 1/4 \\ 0 & 1 \end{bmatrix} \qquad M_6 = \begin{pmatrix} -1/4 & 1/4 \\ 0 & 1 \end{pmatrix}$$

$$M_7 = \begin{bmatrix} 1 & 0 \\ 1/4 & 1/4 \end{bmatrix} \qquad M_8 = \begin{bmatrix} 1 & 0 \\ -1/4 & 1/4 \end{bmatrix}$$

If $b_m = 0$, then $|a_m| = $ GCD(A, B).

The extended GCD algorithm proceeds in the same manner as the *two-bit PM algorithm*, but maintains a sequence of integer matrices

$$U_k = \begin{bmatrix} X_k & Y_k \\ Z_k & W_k \end{bmatrix} \qquad \text{such that}$$

$$U_k \begin{bmatrix} a_0 \\ b_0 \end{bmatrix} = \begin{bmatrix} a_k \\ b_k \end{bmatrix}$$

Thus, after m transformations

$$X_m A + Y_m B = \text{GCD}(A, B).$$

Clearly it starts with

$$U_0 = \begin{bmatrix} 1 & 0 \\ 0 & 1 \end{bmatrix}$$

Assuming that before the k-th transformation, it has (by induction on k):

$$U_{k-1} \begin{bmatrix} a_{k-1} \\ b_{k-1} \end{bmatrix} = \begin{bmatrix} a_0 \\ b_0 \end{bmatrix}$$

and $\text{GCD}(a_{k-1}, b_{k-1}) = \text{GCD}(a_0, b_0)$ $(a_0 = A, b_0 = B)$. The transformation T_k is determined by the *two-bit PM algorithm*,

$$\begin{bmatrix} a_k \\ b_k \end{bmatrix} = T_k \begin{bmatrix} a_{k-1} \\ b_{k-1} \end{bmatrix}$$

It is to be shown that one can always choose the integers of X_k, Y_k, W_k and Z_k of the matrix U_k corresponding to the specific form of the matrix T_k.

First consider the Case 1: $T_k = M_1 = \begin{bmatrix} 1/4 & 0 \\ 0 & 1 \end{bmatrix} \left(a_k := \frac{1}{4} a_{k-1}, b_k := b_{k-1} \right)$.

Let $Z_k = Z_{k-1}$ and $W_k = W_{k-1}$ it has

$$\begin{bmatrix} X_k & Y_k \\ Z_{k-1} & W_{k-1} \end{bmatrix} \begin{bmatrix} a_0 \\ b_0 \end{bmatrix} = \begin{bmatrix} a_k \\ b_k \end{bmatrix}$$

So

$$X_k \, a_0 + Y_k \, b_0 = a_k \tag{1}$$

$$Z_{k-1} \, a_0 + W_{k-1} \, b_0 = b_k \tag{2}$$

Since $Z_{k-1} \, a_0 + W_{k-1} \, b_0 = b_{k-1}$ and $b_k = b_{k-1}$, equation (2) holds. One wants to choose the integers X_k and Y_k such that equation (1) holds.

Notice that a_{k-1} is divisible by 4, so the last two bits of a_{k-1} must be 00. a_{k-1} is the sum of two products ($a_0 X_{k-1}$ and $b_0 Y_{k-1}$), so there are only three possible combinations of the last two bits of these two products: 00 + 00 or 01 + 11 or 10 + 10. Because both a_0 and b_0 are odd, there are only three combinations for X_{k-1} and Y_{k-1}: i. both X_{k-1} and Y_{k-1} are divisible by 4 ii. both X_{k-1} and Y_{k-1} are even but not divisible by 4 iii. both X_{k-1} and Y_{k-1} are odd. For each of the three cases one always can choose proper integers X_k and Y_k such that the equation (1) holds. i. both X_{k-1} and Y_{k-1} are divisible by 4:

Let $X_k = \dfrac{1}{4} x_{k-1}$ and $Y_k = \dfrac{1}{4} Y_{k-1}$. Since $X_{k-1} \, a_0 + Y_{k-1} \, b_0 = a_{k-1}$, so

$\dfrac{1}{4} X_{k-1} \, a_0 + \dfrac{1}{4} Y_{k-1} \, b_0 = \dfrac{1}{4} a_{k-1}$. That is $X_k \, a_0 + Y_k \, b_0 = a_k$. ii. X_{k-1} and Y_{k-1} are even but not divisible by 4: Let $X_k = \dfrac{\left(\dfrac{X_{k-1}}{2} + b_0\right)}{2}$ and

$Y_k = \dfrac{\left(\dfrac{Y_{k-1}}{2} + a_0\right)}{2}$. Since X_{k-1} is even but not divisible by 4 and b_0 is

odd so $\dfrac{X_{k-1}}{2} + b_0$ is even, that is, X_k is an integer. For the same reason Y_k is an integer too. It is easy to see that the equation (1) holds. iii. both X_{k-1} and Y_{k-1} are odd: consider the terms of $(X_{k-1} + b_0)$, $(X_{k-1} - b_0)$, $(Y_{k-1} + a_0)$ and $(Y_{k-1} - a_0)$. Because $X_{k-1} a_0 + Y_{k-1} b_0$ is divisible by 4, only one of the following two cases occurs:

$$\text{case 1: even} \left(\frac{X_{k-1} + b_0}{2} \right) \text{ and even} \left(\frac{Y_{k-1} - a_0}{2} \right)$$

$$\text{case 2: even} \left(\frac{X_{k-1} - b_0}{2} \right) \text{ and even} \left(\frac{Y_{k-1} + a_0}{2} \right)$$

$$\text{Let } X_k = \begin{cases} \dfrac{X_{k-1} + b_0}{4} \text{ if even } \dfrac{X_{k-1} + b_0}{2} \text{ \& even } \dfrac{Y_{k-1} - a_0}{2} \\[2ex] \dfrac{X_{k-1} - b_0}{4} \text{ if even } \dfrac{X_{k-1} - b_0}{2} \text{ \& even } \dfrac{Y_{k-1} + a_0}{2} \end{cases}$$

and

$$\text{let } Y_k = \begin{cases} \dfrac{Y_{k-1} - a_0}{4} \text{ if even } \dfrac{X_{k-1} + b_0}{2} \text{ \& even } \dfrac{Y_{k-1} - a_0}{2} \\[2ex] \dfrac{Y_{k-1} + a_0}{4} \text{ if even } \dfrac{X_{k-1} - b_0}{2} \text{ \& even } \dfrac{Y_{k-1} + a_0}{2} \end{cases}$$

It is not difficult to see that the equation (1) holds and that X_k and Y_k are integers. The rest of the cases of the *two-bit PM algorithm* can be proved by a method similar to the one in Case 1.

Notice that the types of the operations to compute X_k, Y_k, Z_k and W_k are addition (subtraction) and shift. Examination of the two least significant bits of the previous results and the two constants a_0 and b_0 are sufficient to determine the next operation. Suppose that there are total of s kinds of operations. Those operations can be implemented by a PLA circuit as shown in Figure 1.7, where the Case 1 through the Case 8 are the eight Cases of the *two-bit PM algorithm*, x, y, z, w, a, b are the registers corresponding to the arguments of X,

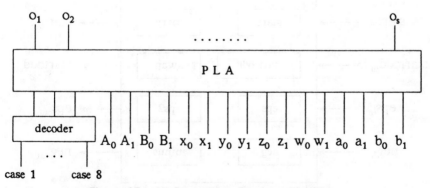

Figure 1.7.   All Operations Produced by PLA.

Y, Z, W, a, b. x_1 and x_0 are the two least significant bits of x. y_1, y_0, z_1, z_0, w_1, w_0, a_1, a_0, b_1, b_0 are the two least significant bits of y, z, w, a and b. A_1 and A_0 are the two least significant bits of input A, B_1 and B_0 are the two least significant bits of input B.

4.6. Systolic Array Design

Brent and Kung proposed a systolic array design [14] to implement their *PM algorithm*. This design is based on the following three facts:

i. The next iteration can start as soon as the two least significant bits from the previous iteration are known.
ii. The upper bound on the number of iterations for the inputs of n bits is $\lceil 3.1105n \rceil$.
iii. Once b becomes zero (a becomes GCD of A and B), the remaining operations of the iterations will not change values of a and b at all.

Figure 1.8 shows the processing element of this systolic array which has six inputs and six outputs.

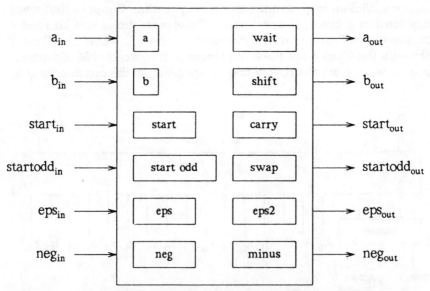

Figure 1.8.   The Processing Element of the Systolic Array for PM Algorithm.

The linear systolic array for the *PM algorithm* consists of $\lceil 3.1105n \rceil$ PE's. Assuming that A and B are represented in 2's complement; enter the array with the least-significant bit first.

The *two-bit PM algorithm* combines two operations into one, while still satisfying the above three conditions (facts). Therefore it can also be implemented by a systolic array. This systolic array consists of $\lceil 1.56n \rceil + 1$ processing elements. The processing element of this systolic array is only slightly different from one of Brent-Kung's design. For example, it needs two flip-flops to represent the two different shift cases, that is, one bit or two bits.

Notice that this systolic design uses the upper bound of a number of iterations to compute any inputs, no matter how many iterations it actually requires.

Table 1.3 shows the average number of operations and upper bound of operations of the PM and the *two-bit PM algorithms* corresponding to several different input lengths randomly distributed in the range $(2^{n-1} + 1, 2^n - 1)$.

From the Table 1.3, one can see that the average number of operations executed by the *two-bit PM algorithm* is about $2/5$ of the upper bound of the *two-bit PM algorithm* and $1/5$ of the upper bound of the PM algorithm.

Table 1.3.   Number of Operations Required for n-bit Inputs.

n (number of bits)	1	2	3	4
10	31.11	16.55	10.07	5.39
11	34.22	18.11	12.09	6.20
12	37.33	19.66	12.98	6.59
13	40.44	21.22	14.14	7.77
14	43.55	22.77	16.06	8.18
15	46.66	24.33	17.55	8.70
16	49.77	25.88	19.01	9.09
17	52.88	27.44	20.64	10.36
18	55.99	28.99	21.28	10.64
19	59.00	30.50	21.91	11.01
20	62.21	32.10	23.68	11.89
21	65.32	33.66	25.29	12.69

1. Upper bound of number of operations of the *PM algorithm*
2. Upper bound of number of operations of the *two-bit PM algorithm*
3. Average number of operations of the *PM algorithm*
4. Average number of operations of the *two-bit PM algorithm*

4.7. Borrow-save Implementation

Since the primitive operations of the *two-bit PM algorithm* are binary addition, subtraction, and shift, the use of redundant number representation may be advantageous in avoiding the delay of carry or borrow propagations. In the carry-save representation, a number R is represented as two-bit strings R^c (set of carries) and R^p (place value) such that $R = R^c + R^p$. In the borrow-save representation, a number R is represented as the two strings, R^b (set of borrows) and R^p (place value) such that $R = R^p - R^b$. Recall that the *two-bit PM algorithm* requires a check for $b = 0$ or $a = 0$ to determine the termination of the algorithm. In the carry-save form, it is difficult to check whether number R is equal to zero or not, since it requires a standard binary addition. However, in the borrow-save representation, R is zero then, if and only if $R^p = R^c$. Figure 1.9 shows the logic design of a zero detector. Here both registers of R^p and R^c are length of 4. The principle idea can be used for the register R with arbitrary length.

Addition and subtraction of two operands in borrow-save form can be performed in a bit-wise fashion. Figure 1.10 shows the logic diagram of a subtractor which computes $R := R - A$, where R is in borrow-save representation and A is a binary number.

Table 1.4 shows the truth table for the outputs of r_i^p and r_{i+1}^b of this borrow-save subtractor.

It only remains to consider how to identify one of the eight cases during the loop of the *two-bit PM algorithm* if both a and b are in borrow-save representation. It is to be shown that examining the two

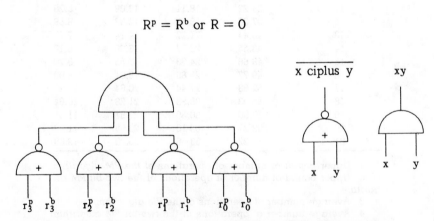

Figure 1.9.   Zero Detector of R in Borrow-save Representation.

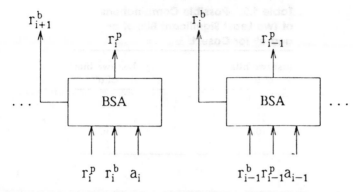

Figure 1.10. Logic Diagram of Subtractor in Borrow-save Form.

least significant bits of a and b is sufficient to determine which of the eight cases applies.

Case 1: EVEN $\left(\dfrac{\alpha}{2} \right)$ and EVEN (α)

Since $\alpha = \alpha^p - \alpha^b$, the two least significant bits of α^p and α^b should be equal. Table 1.5 shows the all possible combinations of the two least significant bits of α^p and α^b for the Case 1.

Case 2: EVEN (α) & $\overline{\text{EVEN}} \left(\dfrac{\alpha}{2} \right)$

Table 1.4. Truth Table of r_i^p and r_{i+1}^b of the Borrow-save Subtractor.

Inputs			Outputs	
r_i^p	r_i^b	α_i	r_i^p	r_{i+1}^b
0	0	0	0	0
0	0	1	1	1
0	1	0	1	1
0	1	1	0	1
1	0	0	1	0
1	0	1	0	0
1	1	0	0	0
1	1	1	1	1

**Table 1.5. Possible Combinations
of Two Least Significant Bits of a^p
and a^b for Case 1.**

last two bits of a^p	last two bits of a^b
00	00
01	01
10	10
11	11

Since $a^p - a^b$ is even, but not divisible by 4, all possible combinations of the two least significant bits of $a^p - a^b$ are $00 - 10$, $11 - 01$, $01 - 11$, or $10 - 00$. Table 1.6 shows those combinations:

Case 3 is similar to Case 1. Case 4 is similar to Case 2. Case 5, Case 6, Case 7 and Case 8 are determined by the two least significant bits of both a and b. The following shows the all combinations of the two least significant bits of a and b for Case 6.

$$\text{Case 6: EVEN} \left(\frac{b - a}{2} \right) \ \& \ \delta \geq 0. \ \text{(Since } \delta \text{ is a flip-flop, it is easy to detect.)}$$

The possible combinations of the two least significant bits of a and b such that $b - a$ is divisible by 4 and both a and b are odd are $11 - 11$ or $01 - 01$. Also one should consider all possible combinations of the two least significant bits of a^p, a^b and b^p, b^b such that $a^p - a^b$ is divisible by 1 and 3, and $b^p - b^b$ is divisible by 1 and 3. Table 1.7 shows those possible combinations of the two least significant bits of a^p, a^b, b^p, and b^p for the Case of 6.

**Table 1.6. Possible Combinations
of Two Least Significant Bits of a^p
and a^b for Case 2.**

last two bits of a^p	last two bits of a^b
00	10
11	01
10	00
01	11

Table 1.7.   All Combinations of Two Least Significant Bits of a^p, a^b, b^p, b^b for Case 6.

last two bits of a^p	last two bits of a^b	last two bits of b^p	last two bits of b^b
11	00	11	00
11	00	00	01
11	00	10	11
11	00	01	10
00	01	11	00
00	01	00	01
00	01	10	11
00	01	01	10
10	11	11	00
10	11	00	01
10	11	10	11
10	11	01	10
01	10	11	00
01	10	00	01
01	10	10	11
01	10	01	10
01	00	01	00
01	00	10	01
01	00	11	10
01	00	00	11
10	01	01	00
10	01	10	01
10	01	11	10
10	01	00	11
11	10	01	00
11	10	10	01
11	10	11	10
11	10	00	11
00	11	01	00
00	11	10	01
00	11	11	10
00	11	00	11

The Case 5, Case 7 and Case 8 are similar to the Case 6. Therefore, all those eight cases can be produced by a PLA as shown in Figure 1.11 with the two least significant bits of registers a^p, a^b, b^p and b^b as its inputs. The outputs of the PLA correspond to Case 1 through Case 8.

Figure 1.12 shows a logic diagram of hardware design for the *two-bit PM algorithm* using borrow-save representation, where a^p, a^b, b^p and b^b are n-bit registers that can shift either one or two bits. Initially, $a^p = A$, $a^b = 0$, $b^p = B$, and $b^b = 0$. BSS is a 4 to 2 borrow-save

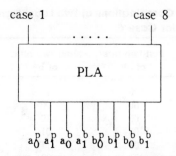

Figure 1.11.   A PLA Producing Eight Cases.

subtractor of length $n + 1$ which is constructed by cascading two 3 to 2 borrow-save subtractors. The result of the BSS always right-shift two bits to registers a^p, a^b or b^p, b^b depending on the different cases. Cases 1 through 8 are produced by a PLA with the two least significant bits of a^p, a^b, b^p, and b^b as its inputs. The counter δ can either increment or decrement by one or two according to the control signals which are formed by Cases 1 through 8 and the sign of the δ (δ_s). The two zero detectors check the termination of the loop: "$a = 0$" or "$b = 0$". Whenever one of them occurs, the computation will stop. The result is in the registers a^p and a^b or register b^p and b^b depending "$b = 0$" or "$a = 0$". To get the final result in binary representation, an additional binary adder is required to convert the borrow-save representation into binary representation.

4.8. Cascading

The above hardware design of the *two-bit PM algorithm* can be cascaded. Suppose one has the above GCD chips for computing GCD of two n-bit integers, and one now wishes to compute the GCD of the 2n-bit integers. It can be done by simply cascading these two n-bit GCD chips together with a few additional circuits and links between the two chips as shown in Figure 1.13.

Notice that since the time delay of the BSS is a constant; so the new GCD unit resulting from the cascading of two smaller GCD chips can work by the same clock as the single one. Also notice that the basic operations and the controls of the two-bit PM extended GCD algorithm are similar to the *two-bit PM algorithm*. Hence one can add additional registers and control components (PLA's) to the above design to implement the extended two-bit PM algorithm.

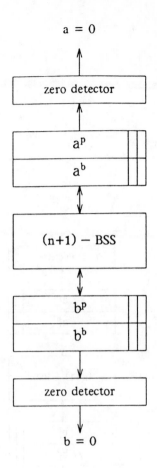

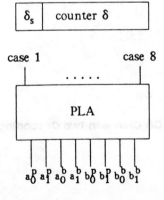

Figure 1.12. Logic Diagram of Hardware Design for Two-bit PM Algorithm.

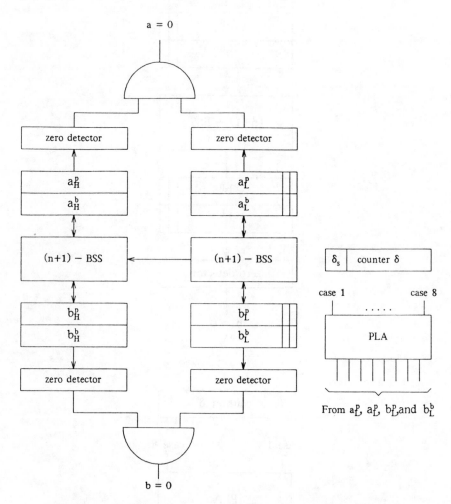

Figure 1.13.   A GCD Chip with Two Cascading Smaller Chips.

REFERENCES

1. C.E. Shannon, "Communication Theory of Secrecy Systems," *Bell System Technical Journal*, 1949, pp. 656–715.
2. W. Diffie and M.E. Hellman, "New Direction in Cryptography," *IEEE Transactions on Information Theory IT-23* (6), November 1978, pp. 644–654.
3. R.L. Rivest, A. Shamir and L. Adleman, "A Method for Obtaining Digital Signatures and Public Key Cryptosystems," *Communications of ACM*, Vol. 21, February 1978.
4. H.C. Williams, "A Modification of the Public-key Encryption Procedure," Scientific Report, No. 92, Dept. of Computer Science, University of Manitoba, Canada, July 1979.
5. R.C. Merkle and M.E. Hellman, "Hiding Information and Signature in Trapdoor Knapsacks," *IEEE Transactions Information Theory IT-24 (3)*, September 1978, pp. 525–530.
6. I. Peterson, "Faster Factoring for Cracking Computer Security," *Science News*, Vol. 125, 1984.
7. M.C. Wunderlich, "Recent Advances in the Design and Implementation of Large Integer Factorization Algorithms," *Proceedings of Symposium on Security and Privacy*, 1983.
8. S. Pohlig and M.E. Hellman, "An Improved Algorithm for Computing Algorithm in GF(p) and Its Cryptographic Significance," *IEEE Transactions on Information Theory IT-24*, January 1978, pp. 106–110.
9. R.W. Roberts, "Encryption Algorithm for Computer Data Encryption," *Federal Register* National Bureau of Standards, Vol. 40, No. 52, March 1975, pp. 12134–12139.
10. D.E. Knuth, *Art of Computer Programming*, Vol. 2, Addison-Wesley, Reading, MA, 1981.
11. E.F. Brickell, "A Fast Modular Multiplication Algorithm with Applications to Cryptography," *Advances in Cryptography: Proceedings of Crypto 82*, Plenum Press, NY, 1983.
12. M.J. Norris and J.F. Simmons, "Algorithms for High-speed Modular Arithmetic," *Congressus Numeratium*, Vol. 31, 1981.
13. G.B. Purdy, "A Carry-free Algorithm for Finding the Greatest Common Divisor of Two Integers," *Computer and Mathematics with Applications*, Vol. 9, 1983, pp. 311–316.
14. R.P. Brent and H.T. Kung, "A Systolic Algorithm for Integer GCD Computation," *IEEE Proceedings of the 7th Symposium on Computer Arithmetic*, June 1985, pp. 118–125.
15. D.Y.Y. Yun and C.N. Zhang, "A Fast Carry-free Algorithm and Hardware Design for Extended Integer GCD Computation," *ACM International Conference on Symbolic and Algebra Computation*, July 1986, pp. 82–84.

2
Designing Systolic Processors Using SYSIM2

TAO LI

Department of Computer Science, University of Adelaide, South
Australia

BRENT E. NELSON

Department of Electrical and Computer Engineering, Brigham Young
University

1. INTRODUCTION

Systolic array design has become one of the important approaches in
VLSI systems development [1,2]. Systolic arrays have the advantages
of the compact layouts, the synchronized operation, the simplicity of
cell structures, and the high speed of parallel processing. All these
have made systolic arrays the very popular choices in the design of
special purpose parallel architectures.

In the design of VLSI systems, designers often use the method of
simulation to verify the correctness of a design. Therefore, simulation tools are needed. However, most of the simulation tools available are for low-level circuitry. Electrical simulation such as SPICE2
and switch level simulation [3] are of too fine granularity for the
simulation of interactions among large cells. On the other hand,
systolic arrays often employ regular connection patterns rather than
arbitrary connection patterns. The connection patterns of systolic
arrays can be easily specified by simple routing functions. Therefore, it would be convenient to have a simulator which supports
higher level constructs, regular connection patterns, and synchronous communication protocols. A network of synchronous communicating processes [4,5] would best model the operation of a sys-

tolic array. These considerations have motivated the implementation of a hierarchical simulation tool for systolic array design.

A simulator, SYSIM, was implemented for systolic arrays [6]. The implementation of SYSIM used fixed connections among cells and was not very flexible. In addition, the implementation was not efficient due to the complexity of the built-in structures. Also, SYSIM does not allow the specification of flexible routing functions (it does not incorporate the concept of routing functions). SYSIM was used to simulate several systolic arrays and the experience gained indicated that SYSIM is not very powerful and not flexible. To overcome the problem of SYSIM, the development of the SYSIM2 simulator was initiated. Along with the implementation of the SYSIM2 simulator, a top-down approach to the design of systolic VLSI processors is also being developed. This top-down approach of systolic array design is similar to the stepwise refinement of software development.

The simulation language of SYSIM2 is general purpose and has a similar syntax with the programming language C. The specification of a systolic array in the simulation language of SYSIM2 is first translated into a program in C (with the addition of declaration tables and the simulator kernel). The simulator kernel is table-driven and allows interactive simulation. Therefore, SYSIM2 supports hierarchical definition of cells and arrays, clock signals can also be hierarchically defined, and input data streams can be defined to feed the systolic arrays. The movements of data among the array cells and between the cells and the data streams are accomplished by using the routing functions. Registers in the cells can be declared as local variables. The simulation language also supports a powerful and flexible definition of routing functions. Both high-level and low-level programming constructs are supported in the simulation language because the language resembles C. This facilitates the top-down design and simulation of systolic arrays.

This section is a brief introduction of the SYSIM2 systolic simulator. The important features of the SYSIM2 simulation language will be discussed in section 2. Several examples will be used to show the simulation of systolic arrays and the top-down development approach in section 3. The fastest approach to learning about the simulator is perhaps through examples. Some important features for user-simulator interactions will be presented in section 4. Section 5 contains a discussion about the synchronized communicating processes. The implementation details will be given in section 6. A summary and future research directions will be included in section 7. The grammar of the simulation language will appear in the Appendix.

2. SIMULATION LANGUAGE FEATURES

The important programming constructs of the SYSIM2 simulation language are discussed here. The functionality of the constructs will be explained. These constructs can be divided into several groups such as the cell definition and array definition constructs, data and input/output constructs, synchronization constructs, and ordinary programming language constructs. The syntax of the simulation language is given in the appendix.

The following constructs are employed in defining the cell and the array structures of systolic processors. These include the CELL and ARRAY constructs as described below.

- *CELL.* This construct is used to define the structure and operation of systolic cells. The cell definition has the following format.

    CELL cell-name (io-ports)
         io-port-declarations;
         internal-registers;
         { variable-definition;
         cell-body
           }

A cell has a name, cell-name—which also defines a data structure—and several input/output ports. The types of the i/o ports are declared through the *io-port-declarations*. The storage elements (internal registers) are declared through the *internal-registers*. The cell body defines the operations to be performed by the cell. There is a communication register associated with each i/o port. The input/output ports are declared in the same way as procedure parameters. Temporary variables are declared in *variable-definition*. The values of the temporary variables are lost after each activation of the cell. The values of the communication registers and the internal registers are memorized after each activation. The *cell-body* specifies the functionality of the cell and consists of compound statements in programming language C and the *clocked* statements (which will be explained later).

- *ARRAY.* Systolic arrays are defined by using this construct. The definition of a systolic array has the following format.

    ARRAY cell-type array-name [dimensions]
         = { initialization }

The *cell-type* must be a cell defined by the *CELL* construct. The cells in the array are of the type *cell-type*. The *array-name* is the name for the systolic array and can be used for cell reference. The sizes and the dimensions of a systolic array are defined in *dimensions*. The *initialization* part is optional. An array can be initialized in the same style as in programming language C. To initialize an array, the values of all i/o ports and all internal registers must be given.

- *CONNECT*. This construct is used to specify the routing functions for systolic arrays. The format for specifying a routing function is shown as follows.

      CONNECT conn-name (parameters)
              parameter-declaration;
              { variable-definition;
               conn-body
              }

The *conn-name* identifies a specific routing function. A routing function may have parameters and the parameters are declared in the *parameter-declaration*. Local variables for a routing function are declared in *variable-definition*. The *conn-body* specifies the routing function operations and may contain any ordinary construct in programming language C such as iterative loops, conditional statements, and compound statements. The *clocked* statements can also be included in *conn-body*. The cells in a systolic array are linked by some routing functions. The routing functions may also link input and output streams with systolic array cells. The routing functions provide not only the interconnection pattern of systolic arrays but also the actual data movements among the cells.

Several routing functions can be specified for the interconnection of a systolic array and for the linkage between the array and the data streams. The use of routing functions in the simulation of systolic arrays is particularly suitable and extremely powerful.

Two constructs are included for generating data streams and for synchronizing operations. They are described as follows.

- *STREAM* sname(start-time,clock)[dimension] = sequence. The *sname* is the name of the stream and the *start-time* indicates when this stream will be available to the systolic arrays. The *[dimension]* indicates the width of the stream. In other words, a stream can generate a vector at a time. The user may optionally initialize a stream by specifying a *sequence* which is a regular expression. A *sequence* has the form *(init-value, v1, v2, . . . , vn, final-value)*. Before the *start-time*, the stream always assumes the *init-value*. After *v1* through *vn* have been generated in a sequence, the stream always assumes *final-value* until the end of this simulation run.

* CLOCK *cname* = *pattern*. The *name* uniquely identifies a clock signal. The *pattern* specifies the clock pattern with respect to the system clock cycles. This pattern is repeatedly generated.

The simulation language also features all the constructs in programming language C and the *clocked* compound statements. These are described as follows:

* *Variables*. An internal variable in a cell definition represents a local register. The meaning of an ordinary variable is the same as in the language C. A variable may be of predefined type such as *int, char, float, array* and any structured type defined by *struct*.
* *Arithmetic Operators*. Ordinary arithmetic operations such as addition, subtraction, multiplication, quotient, and remainder can be used in cell definitions and function definitions.
* *Boolean Operators*. AND, OR, XOR, NOT, are also provided. When used with bytes, integers, and floats, these are bit wise operations.
* *Relational Operators*. Such as greater-than, less-than, equal-to, and other combinations of these. These operations can be performed on any basic type of data.
* *Expressions and Statements*. These are the same as in the programming language C. Ordinary statements in cell definitions and in routing functions are executed on every system clock cycle.
* *Clocked compound statements*. A clocked compound statement has the following format.

ON clock-expression
{
Statements
}

The clock expression determines when the statements should be activated. The statements are executed only when the clock expression is evaluated to be true.
* *Functions and Procedures*. These are the same as in the programming language C. The use of recursive functions is discouraged because of the difficulty in hardware realization.

- *Macro.* Same as macro definitions in programming language C.
- *Loops and Conditionals.* Same as corresponding control structures in C.

The special and the ordinary constructs of the SYSIM2 simulation language provide a suitable environment for the behavioral specification of systolic arrays. Such a programming environment is also very powerful and very convenient.

3. EXAMPLES OF SYSTOLIC ARRAY DESIGN

In this section, several examples are given to demonstrate the specification of systolic arrays in the simulation language of SYSIM2. The use of the language features is nicely captured in the examples. These examples are taken from some well-known systolic algorithms to help readers understand SYSIM2.

3.1. Examples of Simulation Specification

The use of the systolic simulation language to specify systolic arrays is discussed here. Two examples are given to show the specification of typical systolic arrays. Only the top-level specification of the systolic algorithms is given. The top-down design and step-wise refinement will be demonstrated later.

Example 1. The specification of a matrix multiplier [7] is given here to demonstrate the basic features of SYSIM2. The purpose of the systolic array is to compute the elements of the product matrix given below.

$$\begin{bmatrix} c_{11} & c_{12} & c_{13} \\ c_{21} & c_{22} & c_{23} \\ c_{31} & c_{32} & c_{33} \end{bmatrix} = \begin{bmatrix} a_{11} & a_{12} & a_{13} \\ a_{21} & a_{22} & a_{23} \\ a_{31} & a_{32} & a_{33} \end{bmatrix} \times \begin{bmatrix} b_{11} & b_{12} & b_{13} \\ b_{21} & b_{22} & b_{23} \\ b_{31} & b_{32} & b_{33} \end{bmatrix}$$

The rectangular systolic array for matrix multiplication is shown in Figure 2.1. A single cell computes the functions

$$a_{out} = a_{in}$$
$$b_{out} = b_{in}$$
$$c_{out} = c_{in} + a_{in} \times b_{in}$$

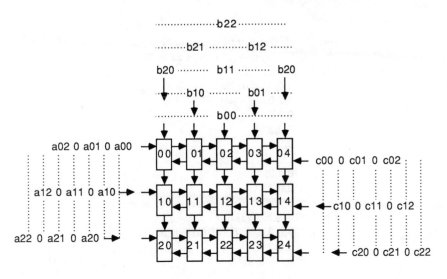

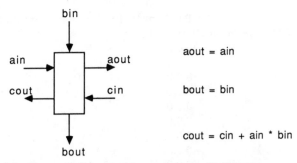

Figure 2.1.   The systolic array for matrix multiplication.

The cell structure, the systolic array, and the data streams are specified as follows.

```
DEFINE arraysize 3;
CLOCK clock0 = 10;
CLOCK clock1 = 01;
CELL multcell(ain,aout,bin,bout,cin,cout)
    int ain,aout,bin,bout,cin,cout;
    {
    ON(clock0)
    {
    aout = ain; bout = bin;
    cout = cin + ain*bin
```

```
            }
        } /* End of cell definition multcell */
    ARRAY multarray[arraysize][2*arraysize − 1];
    STREAM input a(1,clock0)[3] =
                    {0,0,0,  /* initial value of stream a */
                     3,0,0,
                     0,6,0,
                     2,0,9,
                     0,5,0,
                     1,0,8,
                     0,4,0,
                     0,0,7,
                     0,0,0} /* final value of stream a */
    STREAM input b(3,clock0)[5] =
                    {0,0,0,0,0,  /* initial value of stream b */
                     0,0,3,0,0,
                     0,6,0,2,0,
                     9,0,5,0,1,
                     0,8,0,4,0,
                     0,0,7,0,0,
                     0,0,0,0,0} /* final value of stream b */
    STREAM input c(1,clock0)[3] =
                    {0,0,0,
                     0,0,0,
                     0,0,0,
                     0,0,0,
                     0,0,0,
                     0,0,0,
                     0,0,0,
                     0,0,0,
                     0,0,0}
    CONNECT multconn()
            { int i,j;
              ON(clock1)
                {
                    for(i=1; i⟨arraysize; i++) /* move bij elements */
                    for(j=0; j⟨(2*arraysize−1); j++)
                        multarray[i][j].bin = multarray[i−1][j].bout;
                    for(i=0; i⟨arraysize; i++) /* move aij elements */
                    for(j=1; j⟨(2*arraysize−1); j++)
                        multarray[i][j].ain = multarray[i][j−1].aout;
                    for(i=0; i⟨arraysize; i++) /* move cij elements */
                    for(j=0; j⟨(2*arraysize−2); j++)
                        multarray[i][j].cin = multarray[i][j+1].aout;
                    /* fetch elements from stream a */
                    for(i=0; i⟨arraysize; i++)
                        multarray[i][0].ain = a[i];
```

```
        /* fetch elements from stream c */
        for(i=0; i<arraysize; i++)
            multarray[i][2*arraysize-1].cin = c[i];
        /* fetch elements from stream b */
        for(i=0; i<(2*arraysize-1); i++
            multarray[0][i].bin = b[i];
    }
} /* End of routing function multconn */
```

The data streams in this example are defined to implement those as shown in Figure 2.1. There is a one-one mapping between the data streams specified in the example and those in Figure 2.1. The two clock signals clock0 and clock1 are alternately turned on. On clock0 the cells execute their functions. On clock1 the routing function transfers data items among the cells according to the predefined network topology. The definition of the cell is self-evident and the routing function is annotated. Therefore, no further explanation is given here. Next an example for computing graph transitive closure is given to show other features of SYSIM2.

Example 2.   This example simulates a systolic array which computes the transitive closure of a graph. The graph is represented by its adjacency matrix. The details of this algorithm can be found in [8]. The systolic array for this algorithm is shown in Figure 2.2. The systolic algorithm [8] for computing transitive closure is described as follows.

Algorithm Transitive:

Input: two copies of the adjacency matrix, one vertical copy and one horizontal copy, as shown in Figure 2.2.

1. During each cycle, the horizontal and the vertical copies advance by one to the right and down, respectively. Each cell "ands" the data coming to it from the left and from above, and "ors" it into its local accumulator. A single cell is also shown in Figure 2.4.
2. Normally, a cell passes the data coming from the left to its right, and that from above downwards.
3. When an element of the horizontal copy passes its "home location" in the cell array (data item d_{ij} passes cell C_{ij}), it updates itself to the value of the accumulator at that location. The same update process must also be applied to the elements of the vertical copy.

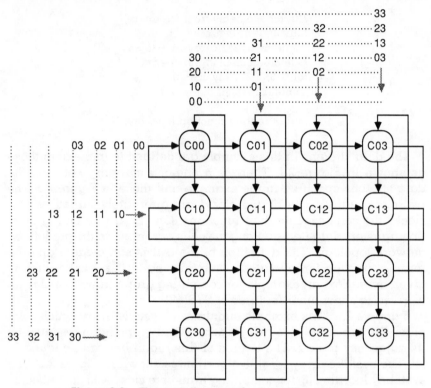

Figure 2.2. The systolic array for transitive closure.

4. As the horizontal copy starts coming out at the right end of the cell array, it is immediately fed back in at the left side using the end-around connections. As the vertical copy starts coming out at the bottom, it is immediately fed back in at the top.

5. After the two copies have cycled three times through, the accumulators of the cells contain the transitive closure of the graph.

Synchronization signals, denoted by "syn," are used to identify the home location of a matrix element. The "syn" signals travel with the diagonal elements of the two copies. The horizontal "syn" signals identify the home locations for the vertical copy elements and the vertical "syn" signals identify the home locations for the horizontal copy elements. When the "syn" signals passes through a cell, the corresponding output is updated to the value in the accumulator. The *flip* signals are entered into the switch cell arrays when every

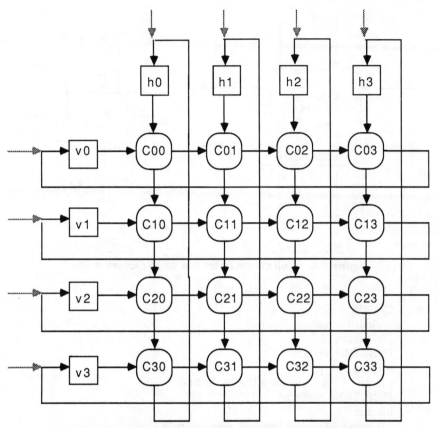

Figure 2.3.   Specific implementation of transitive closure.

element of the initial adjacency matrix has been entered into the array (the first pass is over).

The specific implementation described below uses a row and a column of switch cells to alter the data flow after the first pass. As shown in Figure 2.3, the row of switch cells, identified as $h_0, \ldots, h_3$, is located on the top of the array. A cell in this array is shown in Figure 2.4. The column of switch cells, identified as $v_0, \ldots, v_3$, is located on the left of the array. The systolic array for the transitive closure is specified below.

```
DEFINE size = 4;
DEFINE zero = 0;
DEFINE one = 1;
TYPEDEF bit = (zero, one);
```

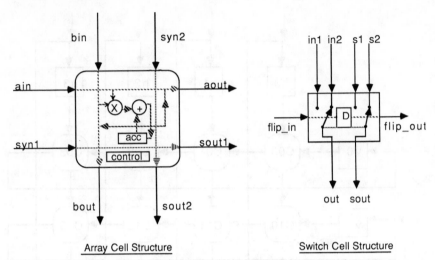

Array Cell Structure   Switch Cell Structure

Figure 2.4.   Cell structure for transitive closure array.

```
CLOCK
    clock0 = 10;
    clock1 = 01;
FUNCTION or(a,b)
bit a,b;
{ if a==1 || b==1 return(1) else return(0) }
FUNCTION and(a,b)
bit a,b;
{ if a==1 && b==1 return(1) else return(0) }
CELL trans(ain,aout,bin,bout,syn1,syn2,sout1,sout2)
bit ain,aout,bin,bout,syn1,syn2,sout1,sout2;
INTERNAL bit acc;
{
    ON(clock0)
    {
        acc = or(ain,and(bin,acc));
        if syn1==one aout = acc else aout = ain;
        if syn2==one bout = acc else bout = bin;
        sout1 = syn1; sout2 = syn2;
    }
}
CELL switch(in1,in2,out,syn1,syn2,sout,flip_in,flip_out)
bit in1,in2,out,syn1,syn2,sout,flip_in,flip_out;
INTERNAL bit s;
{
    if s==zero
    { out = in1; sout = syn1 }
```

```
        else
        { out = in2; sout = syn2 }
        ON(clock0)
        {
           if flip_in==one s = one;
           flip_out = flip_in;
        }
}
ARRAY trans transmat[size][size];
ARRAY switch h_switch[size],v_switch[size];
CONNECT transconn()
            { int i,j;
                ON-CLOCK(clock1)
                { /* connections to side switches */
                   for(i=0;i<size;i++)
                   { /* horizontal wrap-around connection */
                     h_switch[i].in2 = transmat[size-1][i].bout;
                     h_switch[i].s2 = transmat[size-1][i].sout2;
                     /* vertical wrap-around connection */
                 v_switch[i].in2 = transmat[i][size-1].aout;
                 v_switch[i].s2 = transmat[i][size-1].soutl;
                 /* horizontal stream inputs to array */
                 h_switch[i].inl = h_stream[i];
                 h_switch[i].sl = h_syn_stream[i];
                 /* vertical stream inputs to array */
                 v_switch[i].inl = v_stream[i];
                 v_switch[i].sl = v_syn_stream[i];
                    }
                   /* connections within internal cells */
                   for(i=1;i<size;i++)
                   for(j=1;j<size;j++)
                   {   transmat[i][j].ain = transmat[i][j-1].aout;
                       transmat[i][j].bin = transmat[i-1][j].bout;
                       transmat[i][j].synl = transmat[i][j-1].soutl;
                       transmat[i][j].syn2 = transmat[i-1][j].sout2;
                   };
                   /* connections from switch cells to array cells */
                   /* and connections among border cells of array. */
                   for(i=1;i<size;i++)
                   { /* from horizontal switch cell */
                     transmat[0][i].bin = h_switch[i].out;
                     transmat[0][i].syn2 = h_switch[i].sout;
                     /* between horizontal border cells */
                     transmat[0][i].ain = transmat[0][i-1].aout;
                     transmat[0][i].synl = transmat[0][i-1].soutl;
                     /* from vertical switch cell */
                     transmat[i][0].ain = v_switch[i].out;
```

```
                    transmat[i][0].syn1 = v̄_switch[i].sout;
                    /* between vertical border cells */
                    transmat[i][0].bin = transmat[i−1][0].bout;
                    transmat[i][0].syn2 = transmat[i−1][0].sout2;
             }
             transmat[0][0].ain = v_switch[0].out;
             transmat[0][0].bin = h̄_switch[0].out;
             transmat[0][0].syn1 = v̄_switch[0].sout;
             transmat[0][0].syn2 = h̄_switch[0].sout;
      }
}
```

To completely understand the routing function, one should refer to Figure 2.3 and Figure 2.4. The data streams are shown in Figure 2.2. However, the "syn" signals are not shown there. Readers should bear in mind that the (horizontal and vertical) "syn" signals always accompany the diagonal elements of each copy of the adjacency matrix. These two examples should be sufficient to illustrate the specification of systolic arrays in the SYSIM2 simulation language.

3.2. Top-Down Design of Systolic Processes

The simulation tool has been successfully used in the design of systolic processors. The use of the simulation tool in designing systolic arrays has several advantages. First, the design phase and the verification phase are combined. This reduces design errors and speeds up the design process. Second, the hierarchical structure of the simulator facilitates the top-down refinement of a design.

When a designer is developing a systolic processor, he or she may start with a high level of abstraction. High-level functions may be defined for systolic cells. Only the high-level clocks need be incorporated. This simplifies the simulation and debugging of the design. When the high level design is simulated, the designer may refine the design by decomposing of the high-level structures. The decomposition is a refinement of the previous design and contains more details. This decomposition and refinement process may continue several times until a physically realizable systolic processor is designed.

The building of a systolic pattern matching circuit [9] is taken as an example to illustrate the design process. The structure of a single cell and a linear array for matching the pattern "BANANA" is shown in Figure 2.5. A stream of characters is to be searched to match against some patterns. To design such a circuit, one might begin by

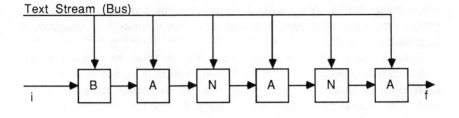

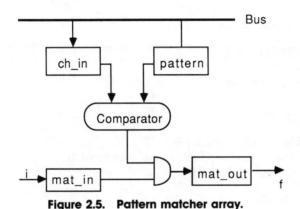

Figure 2.5. Pattern matcher array.

specifying a cell which compares the stored character with the input character. This cell can be defined as

```
CELL match(cn_in,mat_in,mat_out)
char ch_in[8];
bit mat_in,mat_out;
{INTERNAL char pattern[8];
  ON(clock0)
  {
    if (strcmp(ch_in,pattern) && mat_in==1)
      mat_out = 1 else mat_out = 0
  }
}
```

A linear array of such cells is used as a pattern matcher. If the character stored in a cell matches the current input character and the previous input characters form a prefix of the pattern, the output *mat_out* should be 1 to indicate a match for this cell. The structure of the array is specified elsewhere and so is the routing function. Notice that the cell comparison is on the character level, but the details of the comparator is not specified. Typically, the comparator is implemented as a parallel one. One may also use a bit-serial comparator in a cell.

Now assume that a parallel input interface (eight bits are input each time) is used. If a bit-serial comparator is adopted in the design, only some clock signals and the cell definition need be modified. The array definition, the routing functions, and some other things do not have to be changed. This corresponds to a decomposition on the cell level. The bit-serial cell is defined as follows.

```
CELL match(_in,mat_)
byte ch_in;
bit mat_in,mat_out;
INTERNAL byte pattern;
INTERNAL bit mat;
{ mat = 1;
  ON(clock10)
  {
     if (pattern[0]==ch_in[0])
        mat = and(mat,1) else mat = and(mat,0);
     shift(reg); shift(ch_in)
  }
  ON(clock0)
  {
     if (mat_in==1 and mat==1)
        mat_out = 1 else mat_out = 0
  }
}
shift(reg)
byte reg;
{ int i;
   for(i=0;i<8;i++) reg[i] = reg[i+1];
}
```

The timing diagram of the two clock signals clock0 and clock10 are shown in Figure 2.6. Clock10 controls the shifting and bit comparison. Clock0 controls the output of the cell. The variable *mat* is a flip-flop which indicates if there is a mismatch.

When each decomposition is accomplished, the designer can simulate the operation of the systolic array with more details. Because each level is a refinement of the previous level, the effort involved in decomposition and simulation can be minimized. In addition, the top-down design may involve many levels of decomposition and simulation may be performed after each decomposition. The repeat-

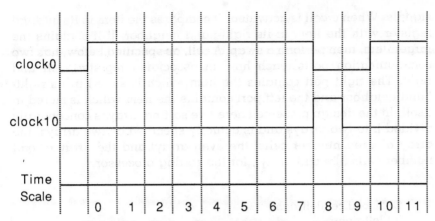

Figure 2.6.   Timing diagram for pattern matcher.

ed simulation and verification also minimizes the design errors and the final design will be highly reliable.

This top-down approach to the development of systolic arrays has been used in the design of several systolic processors. The simulation tool provided significant help to the designers. In the following, a complete example of systolic array design and step-wise refinement is given.

Example 3.   A systolic array for odd-even transposition sorting is to be designed in this example. Details of the algorithm can be found in [1]. The essential idea of odd-even transposition sorting is to divide a linear array, each cell of which holds an item to be sorted into odd-numbered cells and even numbered cells as shown in Figure 2.7. The odd and the even cells are alternately activated by two clock

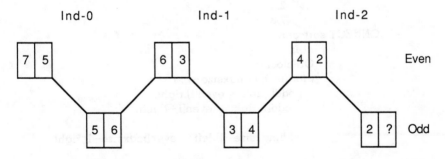

Odd-even transposition sort of six numbers: 7,5,6,3,4,2.
(Initial   Configuration)
Figure 2.7.   Odd-even transposition sort array.

signals. When a cell is activated, it compares the item in its internal register with the item in its right-hand neighbor. If it contains the larger item, then perform a swap. A cell, as specified below, has two communication ports (each has an associated register), left and right. The right port contains the item which is stored in its right-hand neighbor and the left port contains the item which is stored in itself. In the design presented here, the sorting array is conceptually divided into two arrays and is actually specified as two arrays, the array of even number cells (the even array) and the array of odd number cells (the odd array), for the sorting processor.

```
CELL odd_cell(left,right)
int left,right;
{
    ON(clock2)
    { if (left > right) swap(left,right) }
}
    CELL even_cell(left,right)
int left,right;
{
    ON(clock0)
    { if (left > right) swap(left,right) }
}
ARRAY odd-cell odd[maxsize] =
            { 5,2,
              4,7,
              3,inf };
ARRAY even-cell even[maxsize] =
            { 6,5,
              2,4,
              7,3 };
CONNECT sortconn();
        { int i;
          ON(clock1)
          { for (i=0; i<(maxsize−1); i++)
            { odd[i].left = even[i].right;
              odd[i].right = even[i+1].left;
            }
            odd[maxsize−1].left = even[maxsize−1].right
          }
          ON(clock3)
          { for (i=1; i<maxsize; i++)
            { even[i].left = odd[i−1].right;
              even[i].right = odd[i].left;
            }
```

```
            even[0].right = odd[0].left
    }
}
```

Notice that the data transfers in this example are accomplished by the "sortconn" routing function. Let us assume that intercell communication uses parallel interface, that is, a number is transmitted on each clock cycle.

Assume that the bit-serial comparator and the bit-serial swap circuit (a circular shifter) as shown in Figure 2.8 are adopted in the design. Also assume that an integer consists of eight bits. The cell needs a redesign. The original definition of the cell can be kept unchanged. However, the comparator > function and the swap function are further decomposed to reflect the bit-serial organization. These functions are specified together with the cell definition shown below.

```
CELL odd-cell(left,right)
byte left,right;
{
    ON(clock2)
    { if greaterp(left,right) swap(left,right) }
}
```

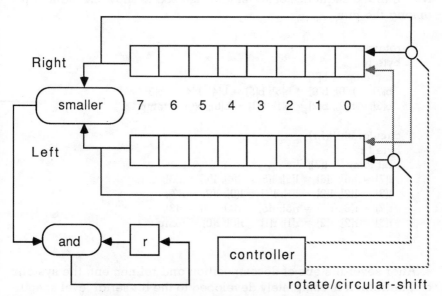

Figure 2.8.   Comparator and shifter circuits.

```
greaterp(left,right)
byte left,right;
{ int compclock;
   bit r = 1;
   for(compclock=0; compclock<8; compclock++)
   {
      r = and(smaller(left[7],right[7]),r);
      rotate(left); rotate(right); /* rotate one bit */
   }
}
swap(left,right)
byte left,right;
{ int compclock;
   for(compclock=0; compclock<8; compclock++)
      circular_shift(left,right);
}
```

Both *greaterp* (the comparator) and the *swap* circuits use a local clock signal *compclock*. This clock is implicit and is not executed on the system level. The *rotate* function and the *circular_shift* function are not specified above. In a further refinement, these two function are specified. Other definitions of the systolic array do not have to be changed.

The further refinement of *rotate* and *circular_shift* is given below. Notice that a sequence of statements is used to show the static links among the bits.

```
rotate(b)
byte b;
{ bit temp = b[7];
   b[7] = b[6]; b[6] = b[5]; b[5] = b[4]; b[4] = b[3];
   b[3] = b[2]; b[2] = b[1]; b[1] = b[0]; b[0] = temp
}
circular_shift(l,r)
byte l,r;
{ bit temp = l[7];
   l[7] = l[6]; l[6] = l[5]; l[5] = l[4]; l[4] = l[3];
   l[3] = l[2]; l[2] = l[1]; l[1] = l[0]; l[0] = r[7];
   r[7] = r[6]; r[6] = r[5]; r[5] = r[4]; r[4] = r[3];
   r[3] = r[2]; r[2] = r[1]; r[1] = r[0]; r[0] = temp
}
```

After several steps of decomposition and refinement, the systolic cell definition is completely developed to the bit-serial level specification. The above definition of bit-serial operations closely corresponds to the cell structure as given in Figure 2.8. This level of specification can be easily mapped into a VLSI layout. This example should be sufficient to illustrate the top-down design style and the step-wise refinement.

4. USER-SIMULATOR INTERACTIONS

In addition to the simulation language, SYSIM2 also provides users with interactive simulation features. A set of commands are used to facilitate user-simulator interaction. The basic interactive simulation commands are described below.

- *TRACE.* This command allows the user to monitor a specific cell. The contents of a traced cell will be displayed after the execution of some simulation steps.
- *UNTRACE.* This command inverts the effect of TRACE.
- *STEP.* This command initiates a single step of simulation in the system clock cycle.
- *CYCLE clock-name.* Initiates a new cycle of simulation in the given clock.
- *LOADCMD [file-name].* Loads a file containing a sequence of simulation commands. The sequence of commands will be executed when the file is loaded.
- *LIST.* This command gives a summary of cell definitions, routing functions, and array definitions. The command may take argument to list specific items.
- *RESET.* This command brings the simulation process to the original environment, ready for a new round of simulation.
- *RUN.* To start simulation in the current environment, use this command.
- *EXIT.* To finish simulation, use this command.

These commands are useful when the user wants to observe the details of simulation. They also serve as good debugging tools. With the help of these commands, SYSIM2 becomes a powerful and very useful tool for the design of systolic arrays.

5. SYNCHRONOUS PROCESSES AND ROUTING FUNCTIONS

In this section, the concepts of synchronous communicating processes and systolic arrays are discussed. The application of synchronous communicating processes to modeling systolic arrays and the implementation of SYSIM2 are also addressed in this section.

Let us consider the set of names of events, $E_i = e_1^i, e_2^i, \ldots, e_n^i$, which are relevant to an object O_i. E_i is called the *alphabet of O_i*. Any event with name e_j^i where $1 \le j \le n$ may occur to object Oi. If the events occur at only discrete (finite or enumerable) points in time, then the event space is a discrete-time space; otherwise, the event space is a continuous-time space. If the events occur at only multiples of a time period τ_i, then the event space is a periodic-time space.

The dynamic behavior of an object O_i is a *process*, denoted by P_i. If the object O_i has a continuous-time event space, the corresponding process P_i is an *asynchronous* process. If the object O_i has a discrete-time event space, the corresponding process P_i is a *semi-synchronous process*. If the object O_i has a period-time event space, the corresponding process P_i is a *synchronous* process.

A communicating process P_i may have a set of input/output ports. P_i may receive messages from its input ports and send messages to its output ports. A set of processes P_i, $1 \le i \le k$, may communicate with each other through their input/output ports by sending messages. A *synchronous communicating process* is a communicating process with synchronous event space. In this chapter, the discussion is confined to synchronous communicating processes since such processes can model VLSI systolic arrays. In addition it is assumed that associated with each communication port, there is also a communication register to store the messages temporarily.

Ideally it would be appropriate to allow the processes to communicate with each other in a more flexible manner, maybe even to generate and to link processes dynamically. However, VLSI systolic arrays often need fixed interconnection topology. For purpose of simulation, a systolic array is defined as follows:

1. A network of some types of synchronous communicating processes. Each process has a small storage space, normally several registers.
2. The number of different types of processes is small.
3. The interconnection topology is regular and is stable with respect to time. These imply that regular interconnection patterns such as rectangular connection, triangular connection, and hexagonal connection are included and that the interconnection pattern will not change in a short period of time.

Since fixed and regular interconnection patterns are used for systolic arrays, one should take advantage of this fact to simplify the design of systolic processors as well as to simplify the simulator itself. Therefore the concept of routing functions are adopted for the specification of interconnection patterns among the cells of a systolic array. Not only do the routing functions specify the interconnection patterns, they also perform the actual data transfer among the cells. The routing functions are called on each clock cycle and are checked for executable *clocked* statements. In addition to specifying the connections among cells, the routing functions also specify the transfer of data from input streams to cells and from cells to output streams. The routing functions in SYSIM2 are a generalized concept of those which are used in specifying multiprocessor interconnection topology.

Another advantage of using the routing function is the reduction in the number of copies for the same type processes. A single copy of the executable code is needed for each type although an array of the data structure must be allocated. The routing function is one of the most important features of SYSIM2.

6. IMPLEMENTATION ISSUES

The simulator builds a data structure for each user-defined systolic processor and the simulation process utilizes the data structure. The communication paths among the systolic cells are realized by the CONNECT functions which are executed on the corresponding clock cycles.

A data structure is defined for each systolic cell declaration. The communication ports and the internal registers are all allocated storage space in the data structure. To model synchronous operation and to keep the results from the previous step, a temporary storage is also associated with each communication port and each internal register.

A 1D or a 2D array of systolic cells is defined as an array of structures as defined by the cell declaration. For the cells which are in the same array, a common evaluation procedure is defined. This evaluation procedure is used to perform the specified operations for every cell in the array and to update the register values in the cell.

Example 4.   The data structure for a cell of the odd-even transposition sorting array is shown below and so is the evaluation function of the array.

```
Cell structures:
  struct odd_cell {
    int left,right;
```

```
        int left_temp, right_temp
    };
  struct even-cell {
    int left,right;
    int left_temp,right_temp
  };
Evaluation Functions:
  odd_cell_eval(ocell)
  odd_cell ocell;
  {
    if clock0=1 swap(ocell.left_temp, ocell.right_temp);
    ocell.left = ocell.left_temp;
    ocell.right = ocell.right_temp;
  }
  even_cell_eval(ecell)
  even_cell ecell;
  {
    if clock2=1 swap(ecell.left_temp, ecell.right_temp)
    ecell.left = ecell.left_temp;
    ecell.right = ecell.right_temp;
  }
```

The routing functions are also translated to reflect the movements of data from cell to cell. The routing function of the odd-even transposition array is translated into the following form.

```
Routing Function:
  sortconn()
  { int i;
    if clock1=1        /* ON(clock1) */
    {
      for (i=0; i<(maxsize-1); i++)
      {
        odd[i].left_temp = even[i].right;
        odd[i].right_temp = even[i+1].left;
      }
      odd[maxsize-1].left_temp = even[maxsize-1].right_temp;
    }
    if clock3=1        /* ON(clock3) */
    {
      for (i=1; i<maxsize; i++)
      {
        even[i].left_temp = odd[i-1].right;
        even[i].right_temp = odd[i].left;
      }
      even[0].right_temp = odd[0].left;
    }
  }
```

The simulator uses the following algorithm to simulate systolic array operations. The interactive simulation features are not included in the algorithm for clarity and brevity.

Algorithm SIMULATE:

Inputs: Current elements of input data streams S_0, S_1, . . . , S_k (the current element of each stream S_i is stored in a buffer B_i), systolic cell/array definitions $C_0(dim0)$, $C_1(dim1)$, . . . , $C_p(dimp)$ (dim0 . . . dimp are dimensions of the arrays), and the routing functions R_0, R_1, . . . , R_n.

1. (Initialization). Allocate memory space to systolic data structures. Set all clocks $\{clk_0, clk_1, . . . , clk_m\}$ to 0. Initialize all the data streams. Set system clock *sysclk* to 0.
2. *sysclk* ← *sysclk* + *1*.
3. FOR each $clk_i \in \{clk_0, clk_1, . . . , clk_m\}$ DO
    IF *last_cycle_of*(clk_i) THEN clk_i ← clk_i + *1*.
4. FOR each $S_i \in \{S_0, S_1, . . . , S_k\}$ DO
    execute S_i and store the result in B_i.
5. FOR each $C_i \in \{C_0, C_1, . . . , C_p\}$ DO
    FOR j:=0 TO dim0 DO
    execute the cell function with parameter $C_i(j)$, i.e., $f_i(C_i(j))$, where f_i is the operation procedure defined for cell type C_i.
6. FOR each $R_i \in \{R_0, R_1, . . . , R_n\}$ DO
    execute R_i.
7. IF *end_of_simulation* THEN halt
    ELSE IF reset THEN go to step 1
    ELSE go to step 2.

There is also a top-level driver to SIMULATE. This driver interacts with the user to provide data for simulation. The driver also handles the display of results and accepts user commands. The simulation language translation process is not specified but readers can readily derive the translation from the grammar of the simulation language.

7. SUMMARY AND FUTURE RESEARCH

A simulator for systolic array design has been discussed in this chapter. The cells in a systolic array may communicate with each other through input/output channels rather than through shared variables. This resembles the network of communicating processes. Since the systolic arrays are synchronous circuits, the implementation corresponds to synchronous communicating processes. The simulation language of SYSIM2 takes advantages of the regular structure of systolic arrays to develop efficient implementation. Instead of the traditional static linkages among the cells of an array, routing functions are used to specify the interconnection paths and to carry out data movement.

Several systolic algorithms [10,11] have been specified using the simulation language of SYSIM2. The top-down refinement method reduces design errors and helps the designers to build their confidence. This approach of design, although inherited from software engineering, has been quite powerful and extremely helpful for the development of systolic arrays.

For future research, the consistency checking and the verification of timing and data movements in systolic arrays will be investigated. This will help the users in debugging their designs. Another subject of interests is the translation of high level specifications, such as in temporal logic, into SYSIM-2 specifications and the relevant optimization techniques.

APPENDIX: THE SIMULATION LANGUAGE SYNTAX

In the following syntactic description of the SYSIM2 simulation language, *function*, *procedure*, *statement*, and *expression* are the same as in the programming language C. Also, *declaration* is the same as in C. The double braces enclose an optional item. Words in bold face letters are reserved words. Parantheses and single braces are also terminal symbols. Alternatives are separated by the symbol |.

⟨cell-definition⟩   :: = *cell* ⟨name⟩ (⟨parameters⟩)
                           ⟨sysim-declarations⟩
                           { ⟨sysim-comp-statement⟩ }

⟨array-definition⟩   :: = *array* ⟨name⟩ [⟨dimension⟩]
                           { = ⟨initialization⟩ }

⟨conn-definition⟩   :: = *connect* ⟨name⟩ (⟨parameters⟩)
                           ⟨sysim-declarations⟩
                           { ⟨sysim-comp-statement⟩ }

⟨sysim-declarations⟩   :: = ⟨declaration⟩ ; ⟨sysim-
                           declarations⟩
                           | *internal* ⟨declaration⟩ ⟨sysim-
                           declarations⟩

⟨sysim-comp-statement⟩   :: = ⟨statement⟩ ⟨sysim-comp-
                           statement⟩

		⟨clocked-statement⟩ ⟨sysim-comp-statement⟩
⟨clocked-statement⟩	: : = ⟨clock-expression⟩ ⟨compound-statement⟩
⟨clock-expression⟩	: : = on (⟨clock-list⟩)
	| ⟨clock-expression⟩ && ⟨clock-expression⟩
	| not ⟨clock-exprssion⟩

REFERENCES

1. H.T. Kung, "The Structure of Parallel Algorithms," *Advances in Computers*, Academic Press, New York, 1980, pp. 65–112.

2. H.T. Kung, "Why Systolic Architecture?" *IEEE Computer Magazine*, Vol. 15, No. 1, January 1982, pp. 37–46.

3. R. Bryant, *A Switch-Level Simulation Model for Integrated Logic Circuits*, Ph.D. Dissertation, MIT, Cambridge, MA, 1981.

4. C.A.R. Hoare, *Communicating Sequential Processes*, Prentice Hall, Englewood Cliffs, NJ, 1986.

5. G. Kahn and D. McQueen, "Coroutines and Networks of Parallel Processes," *Proceedings of the IFIP 77*, North-Holland, Amsterdam, 1977, pp. 993–998.

6. T. Li, "SYSIM: A Simulation Tool for Systolic Processors," *INTEGRATION*, Vol. 5, 1987, pp. 73–76.

7. J.D. Ullman, *Computational Aspects of VLSI*, Computer Science Press, Rockville, MD, 1984.

8. L.J. Guibas, H.T. Kung and C.D. Thompson, "Direct VLSI Implementation of Combinatorial Algorithms," *Proceedings of the Caltech Conference on VLSI*, 1979, pp. 65–90.

9. A. Mukhopadhyay, "Hardware Algorithms for Nonnumeric Computation," *IEEE Transactions on Computers*, Vol. C-28, No. 6, June 1979, pp. 384–394.

10. T. Li and K.F. Smith, "An Equilateral-Triangular Architecture for Computing Divided Differences," *Proceedings of the International Conference on Computer Design/VLSI (ICCD84)*, October 1984, pp. 539–542.

11. T. Li and K.F. Smith, "Exploiting Triangular Architecture for VLSI Systolic Implementation," *Journal of Microprocessing and Microprogramming* (forthcoming).

3

Multiple-Valued VLSI and Systolic Array with CCD Realization*

JIA-YUAN HAN

Department of Electrical Engineering
Southern Illinois University

1. INTRODUCTION

The binary number system and the two-valued logic are used in nearly all of our computer systems today. The two-valued logic has a big advantage of high accuracy and noise-tolerance over analog circuits. Besides their application in computers, binary digital systems are widely applied in communications, control systems, and even video and audio systems. Even though in the early days when the two-valued electronic circuits and components were developed, the scientists and engineers noticed the functions of multiple-valued logic (MVL) which has three or more logic values. Compared with the two-valued logic, information in the multiple-valued form can be more quickly processed using less ALU hardware, more compactly stored using less memory chips, and more efficiently transferred using less communication lines and less time. Another positive aspect of the MVL is that it keeps the good properties of the two-valued logic to a certain degree, that is, high accuracy and noise-tolerance. Multiple-valued logic has been the object of much research for more than a decade. The research topics of the multiple-valued logic range from theoretic representations and manipulations to hardware implementation and applications. During the last decade, various

*The author wishes to thank Dr. Jia-Liang Han for his time in discussing and preparing this chapter. The author greatly appreciates Mr. Peter Jovanovich, Mr. D. Chidambarakrishnan and Ms. C. Y. Wang for helping in the preparation of the figures. He would also like to deeply thank Mrs. Laura Thomas and Miss Lisa Swisher for their excellent typing and their patience with revisions. Without their help, this chapter would never have been completed.

67

integrated circuit technologies have been applied to implement multiple-valued logic functions, such as, CMOS, NMOS, MESFET, I²L, TTL, ECL, and CCD technology. These technologies make the application of the MVL to LSI or VLSI possible.

The rapid development of VLSI technology makes hardware cheaper and cheaper. Various powerful microprocessors and large amount of memory cells have been fabricated in single chips. To use chip area efficiently and to limit the number of pins, various design and implementation approaches are developed. A multiple-valued variable has three or more logic levels, which contains more information than a binary variable. Because of this, the same amount of information can be transferred using less interconnection lines within the chip. The use of multiple-valued logic can reduce the chip area of VLSI design and also can reduce the number of required pins for exchanging information among chips.

Systolic array processors are the result of advances in semiconductor technology and of applications that require extensive throughput. Since Kung and Leiserson [1] introduced the concept of a systolic array, much research has been done on this topic. The application of systolic arrays ranges from matrix arithmetic computation, non-numerical computations, to signal and image processing and pattern recognition [2]. Parallel and pipeline computing takes place along all dimensions of a systolic array and results in very high computational throughput. Multiple-valued systolic arrays which are extension of binary systolic arrays have been found to be more efficient in many applications [3,4,5,6].

The CCD (Charge-Coupled Devices) technology is one of the approaches to implement multiple-valued logic. In recent years, it has attracted a lot of attention. Much research and applications in the CCD have been completed [7]. In practice, the CCD read/write memories for multiple-valued logic have been efficiently realized [8]. The CCD is a MOS-based technology which is compatible with the chips used in today's computers and other digital devices. Therefore, the CCD circuits are good candidates for interfacing circuits between existing devices and future MVL circuits and devices. As is well-known, the CCD technology has been successfully used in video camera. For computer vision and image processing, the CCD technology could also be a potential technology.

Multiple-valued logic VLSI and systolic arrays are introduced in this chapter. Since CCD technology has found its way in efficiently implementing MVL [9] and has potential in direct processing of image and computer vision, the CCD realizations of MVL VLSIs and systolic arrays are chosen as examples. The organization of this chapter is as follows. Basic CCD gates and their implementation and limitations are discussed in Section 2. Three CCD synthesis approaches are introduced in Section 3. Then some basic operations are realized using basic CCD gates as applications of the synthesis approaches. The realized basic operations can be utilized as elementary blocks in the later design. In Section 4, first a general radix converter is designed as interfaces between binary logic and MVL or among MVLs. Then a radix-r systolic array processor is realized as an example of a natural extension from binary logic to MVL. Fault-tolerance is an important research topic in systolic array processor. Algorithm-based fault-tolerance is implemented in an MVL CCD systolic array processor. At the end of this section, MVL VLSI systems for fuzzy inference in expert systems are addressed and their CCD realization is shown. Future research topics are suggested in Section 5.

2. BASIC CCD GATES, IMPLEMENTATION, AND LIMITATIONS

2.1. Introduction

The charge-coupled device was invented by Boyle and Smith at Bell Research Laboratories in 1970 [10]. Since then, much research and applications of CCDs have been conducted [11]. The CCD technology has matured and many application areas—such as filtering, imaging, memories, and digital signal processing—have been reported [12]. The principle of the CCD is illustrated in several books, such as [12,13,11]. The logic functions of basic CCD gates will be described in this section. The logic completeness of CCD gates and two basic concepts related to timing and cost are also addressed.

2.2. Basic CCD Gates

Four basic CCD gate configurations: constant, addition, overflow, and inhibit were reported in [14]. These four gates can be used to realize any multiple-valued logic and are discussed in detail here.

Constant gate or charge generation gate generates a constant charge which is often used in the input section of CCD circuits to convert input voltages into discrete charge packets. Whenever the total amount of output charge exceeds the total amount of input charge in a CCD circuit, charge generation is needed. The mechanism used in this gate is the fill and spill technique [11]. The symbol

Symbols	Logic Function	Relative Cost
1. Constant 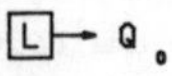 $\boxed{L} \rightarrow Q_0$	$Q_0 = L$ $L = 1, 2, \cdots$	1
2. Addition 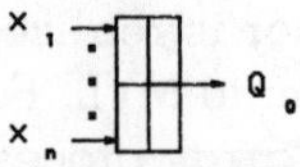 $x_1 \cdots \atop x_n$ $\rightarrow Q_0$	$Q_0 = \sum_{j=1}^{n} x_j$	$2n - 2$
3. Fixed Overflow 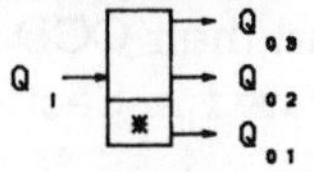 $Q_1 \rightarrow$ Q_{03} Q_{02} Q_{01} $* = \{ C1, C2, C3 \}$	$Q_{01} = \min(Q_1 , C_1)$ $Q_{02} = \min(Q_1 - C_1 , C_2)$ $Q_{03} = \min(Q_1 - C_1 - C_2 , C_3)$	4
4. Inhibit 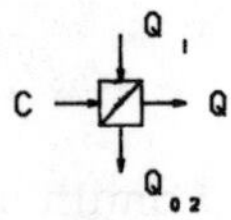 Q_1 $C \rightarrow \not\!\square \rightarrow Q_{01}$ Q_{02}	$Q_{01} = \begin{cases} Q_1 & \text{if } C \neq 0 \\ 0 & \text{Otherwise} \end{cases}$ $Q_{02} = \begin{cases} Q_1 & \text{if } C = 0 \\ 0 & \text{Otherwise} \end{cases}$	6 if $Q_1 \leq 2$ 18 if $Q_1 \geq 3$
5. Delay 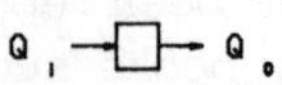 $Q_1 \rightarrow \square \rightarrow Q_0$	$Q_0 (t) = Q_1 (t - 1)$	2

Figure 3.1. Basic CCD Gates.

of constant gate is shown in Figure 3.1(1). Its logic function is expressed as

$$Q_0 = L$$

where $L = 1, 2, \ldots$

Charge addition is the simplest gate configuration in CCD technology. In this gate, the input charges are transferred into a common storage well where they are merged together. The function of charge addition is to combine two or more input charge packets representing two or more variables in the charge domain. The symbol of charge addition is shown in Figure 3.1(2). The logic function is expressed as

$$Q_0 = \sum_j x_j$$

where x_j's are input charge packets and the resulting output charge Q_0 is the analog sum of the input charge packets x_j's.

Charge overflow gate configuration distributes an input charge Q_i over a number of storage wells one by one. Every storage well has a fixed charge capacity. If the input charge to the i-th well exceeds its handling capacity, the excess charge will pass to the (i+1)-th well. No charge will be passed to the next well if the input charge is less than or equal to the handling capacity of the current well. Charge overflow gate is an important logic gate to split the impact charge into a number of charge packets for further manipulation. The symbol of fixed charge overflow is shown in Figure 3.1(3). The logic function is expressed by

$$Q_{01} = \min (Q_i, C_1)$$

$$Q_{02} = \min (Q_i - C_1, C_2)$$

$$Q_{03} = \min (Q_i - C_1 - C_2, C_3)$$

where C_1, C_2, and C_3 are fixed handling capacities of the well 1, 2, and 3, respectively; Q_i is the input charge, Q_{01}, Q_{02}, and Q_{03} are the outputs of the three wells. In order to avoid a serious degradation in speed, the number of outputs is usually limited to three in quaternary logic [9].

Inhibit gate: Whether the outputs of this gate are equal to the input Q_i depends on the control input C. The input charge Q_i is exclusively routed to the output Q_{02} whenever the control input C is zero, otherwise the input charge Q_i is exclusively routed to the output Q_{01}. This gate is also named binary programmable overflow [15], which plays an important role in the synthesis of multiple-valued logic. It is implemented by replacing a barrier gate in fixed overflow configuration by the barrier gate of a floating gate [16]. The symbol of the inhibit gate is shown in Figure 3.1(4). The logic function is expressed by

$$Q_{01} = \begin{cases} Q_i & \text{if } C \neq 0 \\ 0 & \text{otherwise} \end{cases}$$

$$Q_{02} = \begin{cases} Q_i & \text{if } C = 0 \\ 0 & \text{otherwise} \end{cases}$$

Delay gate: In order to synchronize the operation in a systolic array, especially in the fault-tolerant design appearing later in this chapter, delay gates are used quite often. As a matter of fact, the delay gate is not an independent logic gate in the functionally complete set. However, it is very convenient to have it for systolic array design. The delay gate can be easily implemented using an addition gate or a fixed overflow gate. Its symbol is shown in Figure 3.1(5). The logic function is expressed by

$$Q_0(t) = Q_i(t - 1)$$

where t is the current clock period and $t - 1$ is the previous clock period.

2.3. Functional Completeness and Other CCD Gates

As is well known in binary logic, AND and NOT or OR and NOT are functionally complete sets. Functional completeness is also important in multiple-valued logic. In order to construct any MVL function, the set of basic gates must be functionally complete. As is known, the existing operators: minimum, maximum, literal, and successor form a functionally complete set [17]. Starting from the analysis of the existing operators, the corresponding mathematical expressions of these operators were derived by using the basic gates in Section 2.2 [14,18]. Therefore, the basic gates described in Section 2.2 are functionally complete.

There is another gate called linear programmable overflow in CCD technology [15]. It has been shown that the following two sets of basic CCD gates are functionally complete [15].

1. Addition, constant, linear programmable overflow
2. Addition, constant, fixed overflow, inhibit

In this chapter, set (2) is chosen to implement any MVL functions because the fixed overflow and inhibit are more basic, more flexible for design, and more cost-effective than linear programmable overflow.

2.4. Cost Factors and Depths of Basic Gates

In many function decomposition techniques, some kind of minimization procedure is usually incorporated. For example, in the Allen-

Givone Algebra, a minimization of the number of literals was suggested [17] to reduce the number of components in IC technology. A different cost criterion from IC technology was proposed for CCDs by Kerkhoff [15]. The relative cost factors were derived based on the chip-area consumption, the number of different power-supply and data lines, as well as the sensitivity to typical process and voltage variations of a gate configuration. In order to compare different designs for multiple-valued functions, the relative cost factors are used through this chapter. The cost factors of basic CCD gates are listed in Figure 3.1. The cost factor of a CCD realization is defined as follows.

Definition 1. The *cost factor* of a CCD realization of a function is a measure of the chip area occupied by the set of basic gates needed to implement the function.

One of the most important issues in sequential binary logic is the timing on synchronization. In CCD realization, timing is still an important issue in the design. The delay between the input and output charge of the basic gates in Section 2.2 is always one clock period. The unit delay gate is also one clock period. If a delay of more than one clock period is needed, a cascade of unit delay gates can be used to form any number of delay clock periods as required. The concept of depth of a CCD realization is defined below for determining the clock cycles elapsed by the realization.

Definition 2. The *depth* of a CCD realization of a function is defined as the number of clock cycles elapsed from the time the input is presented until the output becomes available. It is equal to the maximum number of basic gates in series in any path from input to output.

2.5. Realization and Limitations

There are several specific CCD properties which must be taken care of during the circuit realization. For example, the input and output signals of a complete CCD circuit are voltage signals, while the logic operations are all performed in charge domain. Within the CCD circuit, direct copying of charge packets is impossible. To get a copy of charge packets, the inhibit gate with constant gates must be used. The following aspects for designing CCD realization must be carefully followed:

1. For the voltage controlled inputs of a complete CCD circuit, the copying of the input charge is freely possible.

2. In the rest of the realization, a fan-out facilitator must be used to copy the charge packets when they are needed.
3. In order to maintain an acceptable operation speed, the feedback of signals are prohibited.

The major limitation of CCD technology is the low speed of CCD gates. However, with the development of the technology, the speed of the CCD gates is improving. The CCD technology has the inherent advantages of low power consumption, high packing density, and MOS compatibility. These advantages are very suitable for VLSI implementation.

3. SYNTHESIS APPROACHES AND SOME BASIC OPERATIONS

In binary logic, there are many approaches to minimize a Boolean function, such as the Karnaugh map and the Quine-McCluskey's tabulation method to minimize product-of-sums or sum-of-products expressions of a Boolean function [19]. These approaches are effective to reduce the complexity for binary logic implementation. Similar to the binary logic design, the synthesis approaches are of vital importance for the development of multiple-valued logic integrated circuits. In the past decades, numerous techniques have been proposed to decompose a multiple-valued function into a set of logic operators from a mathematical point of view. Unfortunately, these techniques were difficult to implement electronically. The Allen-Givone algebra is an implementation-oriented algebra, which links the basic operators (minimum, maximum, and literal) to all current IC technologies. However, the implementation of complex MVL functions in IC technologies based on this algebra is still not very efficient. Several synthesis techniques for I^2L technology were developed [20,21]. As a matter of fact, there is a distinct tendency to develop synthesis techniques for multiple-valued logic circuit from basic transistor configurations.

Since Kerkhoff developed the basic gates for CCD MVL and their application to MVL circuits, three main approaches have been developed for the synthesis of 4-valued functions using CCDs [11,22,23,7]. The three approaches are reviewed in this section.

3.1. Kerkhoff's Approach

Because the similarities between the logic operation in charge-mode and the current-mode devices, McCluskey's method for I^2L was modified to adapt to the synthesis of CCD MVL [15]. This modified method has successfully applied to CCD MVL. However, the cost factors of CCD gates are quite diverse from gates to gates. This is quite different from I²L technology where each basic transistor is considered to have equal complexity and equal sensitivity in its performance. A synthesis approach based on the cost minimization was developed by Kerkhoff [11]. The main idea of this approach and one example are given as follows.

First, the decomposition for one-variable functions in CCD technology is addressed. The configuration of the CCD MVL circuit consists of one input with free copying of the input charge, a number of parallel strings, and one output from an additional gate (Figure 3.2 [15]). The output from an inhibit gate is also possible, but this will not be discussed here. Forty-five elementary strings of basic CCD gates are defined and tabulated in the order of increasing costs [18]. Suppose that the MVL function to be decomposed is $F(x)$. Let $R_0(x) = F(x)$.

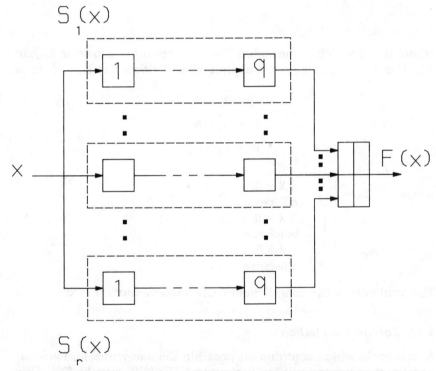

$S_1(x)$

X

$F(x)$

$S_r(x)$

Figure 3.2. General Scheme of Kerkhoff's Decomposition. From H. G. Kerkoff and H. A. Robroek, "The Logic Design of Multiple-Valued Logic Functions Using Charge-Couple Devices," *Proceedings of the 12th International Symposium on Multiple-Valued Logic,* © 1982 IEEE.

The decomposition procedure can be expressed as the following recursive formula:

$$R_j(x) = R_{j-1}(x) - S_j(x) \qquad (j = 1, \ldots, n)$$

where the $R_j(x)$ denotes a non-negative rest function and $S_j(x)$ is a string with the lowest cost in the table. The procedure terminates when $R_n(x) = 0$. The total cost of the decomposition is the sum of the costs in the parallel strings and the cost of the final addition.

This approach can be used for two or more input variables, but the cost table will be much more complex and must be generated by a computer. The modification of the above approach has been made to use only a 24-entry table instead of a 45-entry table. The result has been shown to yield a lower cost implementation for some functions [22].

An example of CCD MVL to complement a quaternary variable X is described. The logic function is to complement the input X

$$\overline{X} = (R - 1) - X$$

where R = 4 which is the radix. The logic circuit is shown in Figure 3.3. The design procedure is explained as follows. Let $R_0 = \overline{X}$, then

$$R_1 = R_0 - S_1$$
$$R_2 = R_1 - S_2$$
$$R_3 = R_2 - S_3$$

where
$$S_1 = \begin{cases} 1 & \text{if } X = 0 \\ 0 & \text{otherwise} \end{cases}$$
$$S_2 = \begin{cases} 1 & \text{if } X = 0, 1 \\ 0 & \text{otherwise} \end{cases}$$
$$S_3 = \begin{cases} 1 & \text{if } x = 0, 1, 2 \\ 0 & \text{otherwise} \end{cases}$$

The total cost of the complement CCD implementation is 29.

3.1.1. Tabulation Method

A cost table which contains all possible 256 one-variable, four-valued functions was built for designing CCD MVL circuits [22]. This table is quite longer than the previous two tables (45 and 24 one-variable, four-valued functions). However, it is a universal cost table

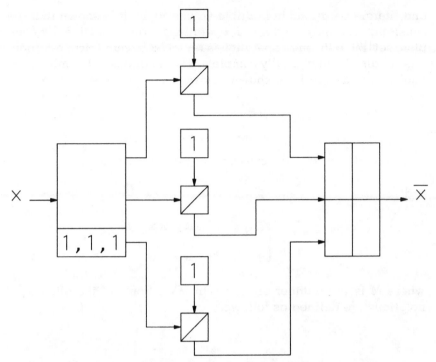

Figure 3.3. 3's Complement Circuit for One Digit Quaternary Number.

which can be used just through a table-look-up approach instead of a combination of decomposition and table-look-up. The lowest-cost design can be achieved using the universal table.

Since the table size would increase exponentially with the number of variables, a direct extension of the cost table technique is nearly impossible for the number of variable n ≥ 2. For four-valued two-variable functions, the cost table would have $4.3*10^9$ entries [22]. One approach to extend the tabular method is to decompose a two-variable function into four one-variable functions. One of the variables can be considered as a control variable which can be chosen as 0, 1, 2, 3 and the others are independent variables.

3.2. Realization Using CCD PLA's

As is well-known in binary logic, PLAs can be used to implement a Boolean function in sum-of-product form. A PLA-type circuit was developed from the basic CCD gates in [23]. Similar to the AND and OR operations in binary logic, there are maximum, minimum, constant, and literal operations in multiple-valued logic. It is shown that the constant, min, max, and literal operations form a functionally complete set [17]. If the max operation is replaced by numerical addition. The set also is functionally complete. The notations of the min, max, addition, and literal are shown below

$$\max(x,y) = x + y$$

$$\min(x,y) = x.y$$

$$\text{sum}(x,y) = x \overset{o}{+} y$$

and

$$
\overset{a\ b}{x} = \begin{cases} 0 & \text{if } x < a \text{ or } x > b \\ M - 1 & \text{if } a \le x \le b \end{cases}
$$

where M is the number of values in MVL. Some of the often used notations are defined as follows.

$$
\overset{a,b,c}{x} = \overset{a\ a}{x} + \overset{b\ b}{x} + \overset{c\ c}{x}
$$

$$
\overset{a,b}{x} = \overset{a\ a}{x} + \overset{b\ b}{x}
$$

A product term $r*\phi(x_1,x_2, \ldots ,x_n)$ is defined to be the min of a set of literals, where any variable x_i can appear at most once, and r is a constant. It was shown that any four-valued function can be expressed in sum-of-product (max-of-min) form. An expression of a four-valued function $f(x)$ using the max operation is called *minimal*, if there is no other expression of $f(x)$ using the max operation that has fewer product terms than the given expression. The Allen-Givone implementation and related topics can be found in [17,24].

Just as for a binary PLA, a four-valued CCD PLA consists of a product level and a sum level. The product level of the four-valued CCD PLA can be constructed by a series of n inhibit gates with a constant gate of r controlled by the literals $L^1(x_1)$, $L^2(x_2)$, . . . , $L^n(x_n)$ and a so-called Universal Inhibit Control Processing Circuit (UICPC) as shown in Figure 3.4 [24] and 3.5 [24], respectively. The sum level can be realized by either addition gates with some other gates or max gate with some other gates.

Example. A two-variable function is given and its Q-map is

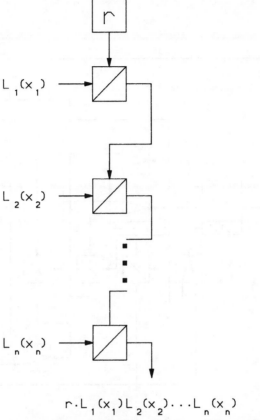

Figure 3.4. Realization of A Product Term. From P. Tirumalai and J. T. Butler, "On the Realization of Multiple-Valued Logic Functions Using CCD PLA's," *Proceedings of the 14th International Symposium on Multiple-Valued Logic,* © 1984 IEEE.

shown in Figure 3.6a [24]. Using the max-of-min form expression, the function may be written as

$$f(x_1, x_2) = 1.^0 x_1^1.^2 x_2^3 + 2.^1 x_1^2.^1 x_2^2 + 3.^3 x_1^3.^0 x_2^0$$

or in the sum of min form

$$f(x_1, x_2) = 1.^0 x_1^1.^2 x_2^3 \overset{\circ}{+} 1.^1 x_1^1.^3 x_2^3 \overset{\circ}{+} 2.^1 x_1^2.^1 x_2^2 \overset{\circ}{+} 3.^3 x_1^3.^0 x_2^0$$

The PLA implementation of this function is shown in Figure 3.6b [24], which consists of two UICPC's for $L^1(x_1)$ and $L^2(x_2)$, four series of

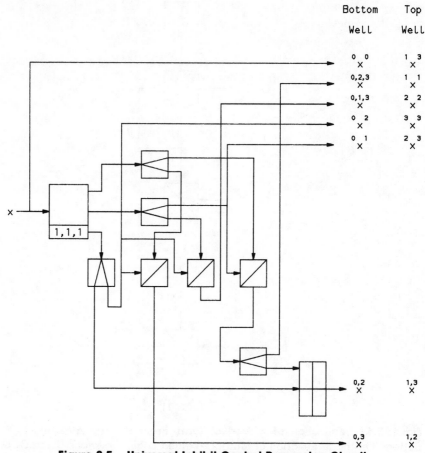

Figure 3.5.   Universal Inhibit Control Processing Circuit.

inhibit gates for product terms, and one addition gate for the sum. Recently, Kerkhoff and Butler [25] developed a multiple-valued PLA using profiled peristaltic CCD technology. The design of the PLA is highly modular and includes DRAM-type sense-amplifier circuits. The CCD PLA circuits can operate at high speed.

3.3. Synthesis of Multivalued Multithreshold (MVMT) Functions

The previous approaches to realize MVMT functions do not take into account the constraints inherent in the CCD technology. The constraints include the difficulty to generate a negative weight and charge transfer inefficiency. Four techniques for the decomposition of MVMT functions and realization using CCD were investigated in [7]. After designing modulo-r adder, multiplier, multiplexer, single-threshold element, and multithreshold element using CCD, the CCD realization based on the four decomposition techniques was addressed. The cost factors and depths of the realizations of several MVMT function using the four techniques were compared. Readers may find the detailed description and design in [7].

3.4. Some Basic Operations

Some basic operations are used very often in CCD circuit design. Applying the above synthesis approaches, one can design the following four basic operations and derive their depths and cost factors. The circuits designed are for three-valued or four-valued logic, but they can be extended to any valued logic.

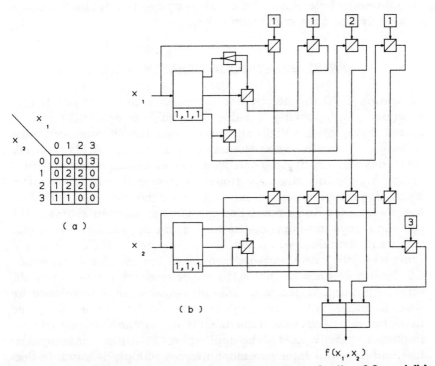

Figure 3.6.(a) Q-map for the Function of Example in Section 3.2; and (b) CCD PLA Realization of Example in Section 3.2.

- *Fan-Out Facilitator*. As mentioned earlier, charge quantities are representative of logic levels in MVL CCD. This fact limits the fan-out of the signals to one. However, the fan-out may be increased when the fan-out facilitator (Figure 3.7) is used [23,7]. The fan-out facilitator shown is for four-valued logic. From one charge b_j the facilitator generates many b_j's. The depth of this circuit is 3 and the cost factor is 61 m + 4, where m is the number of duplicates.
- *Multiplier*. A radix-4 multiplier is shown in Figure 3.8. The inputs are α and c and the output is p = α*c. The depth is 3 and the cost factor is 65.
- *Modulo-3 Adder*. A four digit modulo-3 adder with carry-in and carry-out is shown in Figure 3.9. For each digit, the depth of the sum is 4, the depth of the carry-out is 2, and the cost factor is 16.
- *Complement Element*. A 3's complement element for one digit of a modulo-4 number is shown in Figure 3.3. The input is a single digit of a modulo-4 number and the output is the 3's complement which corresponds to 1's complement in binary number. A 4's complement of a modulo-4 number can be easily designed using the complement elements and addition gates. The depth of the element is 3 and the cost factor is 29.

4. VLSI AND SYSTOLIC ARRAY IN MVL-CCD

As known, CCD technology has the advantage of low power consumption, high-packing density, and MOS compatibility, which makes it suitable for VLSI implementation. The MOS compatibility allows CCD circuits to be potential interfaces between MVL devices and today's binary devices and good bridges among different valued MVLs. A general radix converter is discussed first in this section. Binary logic systolic arrays have attracted the attention of VLSI researchers since Kung published his pioneer work in 1978 [1]. MVL systolic arrays are supposed to have more processing power, less communication lines within chips, and less pins in VLSI packages. A radix-r systolic array processor using CCD is addressed in Section 4.2. Fault tolerance is one of the major research topics in systolic array. Algorithm-based fault tolerance was recently developed for systolic arrays. A ternary, fault-tolerant systolic array is discussed in Section 4.3. Because of huge amount of computation and real time implementation in most of the applications in artificial intelligence, fast and powerful inference machines are in high demand. In Section 4.4, VLSI and systolic array processors for fuzzy inference in expert systems are proposed and designed.

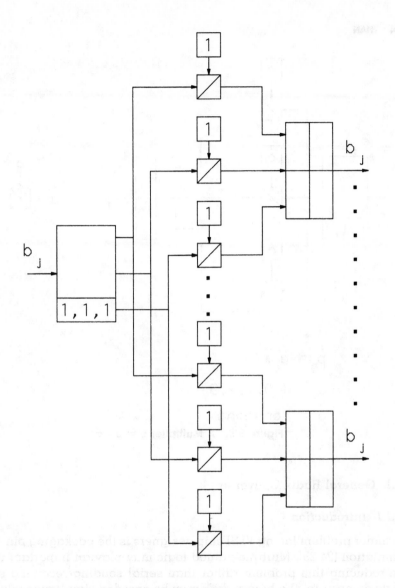

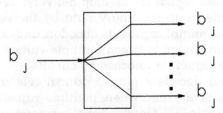

Figure 3.7. A Fan-Out Facilitator.

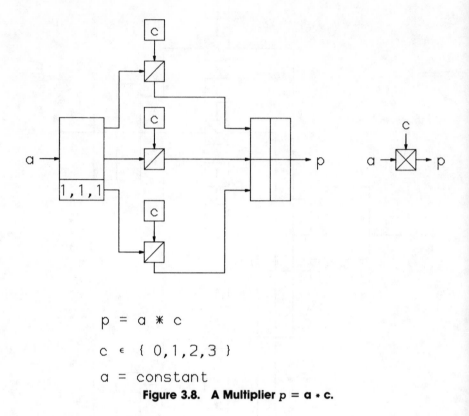

$$p = a * c$$

$$c \in \{ 0,1,2,3 \}$$

$$a = \text{constant}$$

Figure 3.8.   A Multiplier $p = a * c$.

4.1. General Radix Converter

4.1.1. Introduction

A major problem facing VLSI chip designers is the packaging pin-out limitation [24,29]. Multiple-valued logic may play an important role in reducing this problem rather than serial sending/receiving signals on one pin, the binary data may be encoded simultaneously as a multiple-valued signal for off-chip delivery. The multiple-valued signal is decoded into its binary data by the receiving chip [26]. Therefore it is essential to provide encoders and decoders to perform the required conversion between multiple-valued signal on the bus and the binary signals in processing circuits.

Encoders and decoders play a critical role in multiple-valued memories. This is one area where multiple-valued devices are commercially available [27]. Conventional memories store one bit of information in the memory cell as two states. If two bits of information

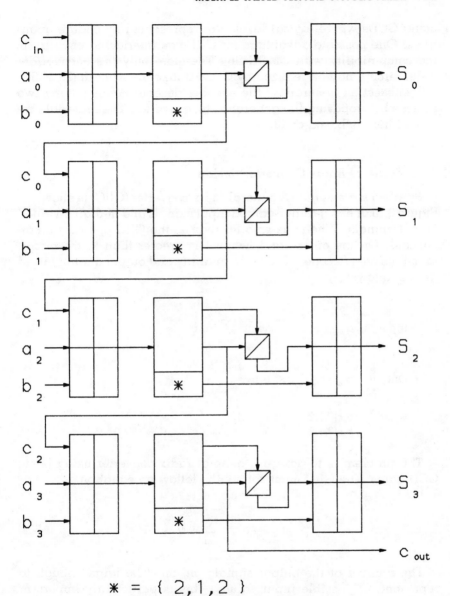

$$* = \{ 2, 1, 2 \}$$

Figure 3.9.   4 Digit Modulo-3 Adder with Carry.

that represent four states are encoded in a single memory cell, the storage capacity of the memory is doubled [28].

Several encoder/decoder circuits have been proposed and implemented for various technologies [29,26,30]. This subsection presents another approach for designing a general radix converter (GRC) using CCDs where logical levels are represented by charge quantities. One possible advantage for CCDs as interfacing circuitry is the compatibility with CMOS [16]. Therefore only the encoder/decoder circuit may be realized by CCD. Unlike the work in [29,26,30], this subsection generalizes the encoder/decoder circuit to any two radices by proposing the general radix converter. The material presented here is based on [31].

4.1.2. General Radix Converter Design

Problem statement. A general radix converter (GRC) is shown in Figure 3.10. It has n-digit r-valued input signals and m-digit k-valued output signals. When r is smaller than k, the GRC operates as an encoder. On the other hand, when r is greater than k, the circuit functions as a decoder. The input quantity and output quantity used are as follows:

$$\text{Input:} \quad a_{n-1}a_{n-2}\dots a_1a_0 = \sum_{i=0}^{n-1} a_i . r^i$$

$$\text{Output:} \quad b_{m-1}b_{m-2}\dots b_1b_0 = \sum_{j=o}^{m-1} b_j k^j$$

where $a_i \epsilon \{0,1,2,\dots,r-1\}$
         $b_i \epsilon \{0,1,2,\dots,k-1\}$

The problem is to design a general radix converter using basic CCD gates. The GRC must satisfy the following equation:

$$\sum_{i=1}^{n-1} a_i r^i = \sum_{j=1}^{m-1} b_j k^j \tag{3.1}$$

The number of the output signals, m, must be large enough to represent all possible input values. This is particularly important when the circuit is operating as a decoder. In general, the value of m is given by

$$m = \lceil \log_k (r^n - 1) \rceil \tag{3.2}$$

where $\lceil x \rceil$ is the least integer containing x.
Assumption. In this subsection, we assume that the largest al-

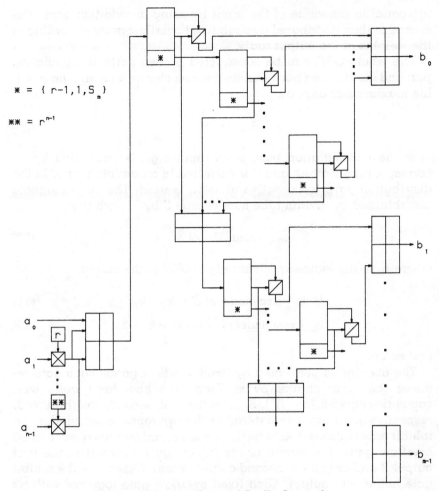

$* = \{ r-1, 1, S_m \}$

$** = r^{n-1}$

Figure 3.10.   The General Radix Converter.

lowable charge in basic CCD gates can be equal to the total input or
output quantity:

$$S = \sum_{i=1}^{n-1} a_i r^i = \sum_{j-1}^{m-1} b_j k^j \qquad (3.3)$$

However, if the largest allowable charge is less than S, the basic
design principle developed here can still be applied. The only
change is to divide the input into several groups.

GRC design. The basic design idea is to obtain a charge quantity equal to the value of the input by using an addition gate. The charge is then distributed through fixed overflow gates according to the weights of the output radix.

The whole GRC can be constructed by two parts: accumulation part and distribution part. Denote the sum charge by S and the possible maximum charge by

$$S_{max} = r^n - 1 \tag{3.4}$$

In the accumulation part, each input digit is multiplied by its corresponding weight, and S is collected in an addition gate. In the distribution part, the iterative division is used. The output signals are obtained by dividing the sum charge S by k, such that:

$$b_0 = \text{remainder of } S \div k \tag{3.5}$$

where b_0 is the least significant digit (LSD) of the output:

$$b_1 = \text{remainder of } \lceil S \div k \rceil \div k \tag{3.6}$$

$$b_2 = \text{remainder of } \lceil \lceil S \div k \rceil \div k \rceil \div k \tag{3.7}$$

and so on.

The division is performed by fixed overflow gates; each gate reduces the input charge by k. Each gate has three wells with capacities equal to $(k - 1)$, 1, S_{max} for the first, second, and third well, respectively. In order to determine the appropriate remainder, an inhibit gate is connected to the first and second outputs of each fixed overflow gate. The output of the inhibit gate is equal to the first output if and only if the second output is zero. Otherwise the inhibit gate has a zero output. Each fixed overflow gate together with its inhibit gate are referred to here as a unit.

As shown in Figure 3.10, l_1 units in series are required for the LSD b_0:

$$l_1 = \left\lfloor \frac{S_{max}}{k} \right\rfloor \tag{3.8}$$

where $\lfloor x \rfloor$ is the largest integer contained by x. The outputs of the l_1 units are collected in an addition gate which has an output equal to

b_0. The result of the division $\dfrac{S}{k}$ is collected in another addition gate so as to be used in determining the second digit b_1. For b_1, l_2 units are needed.

$$l_2 = \left\lfloor \frac{l_1}{k} \right\rfloor \qquad (3.9)$$

Again, the outputs of the l_2 units are collected in an addition gate so as to form b_1. In general,

$$l_i = \left\lfloor \frac{l_{i-1}}{k} \right\rfloor \qquad (3.10)$$

The above procedure continues until l_m, that generates the most significant digit (MSD) b_{m-1}, is reached. In general, the times which the above division repeats are:

$$m = \lceil \log_k(r^n - 1) \rceil \qquad (3.11)$$

4.1.3. Illustrative Examples

In this subsection, four illustrative conversions using the GRC are presented: Quintuple-to-ternary; ternary-to-quintuple; binary-to-quaternary; quaternary-to-binary. Only the quintuple-to-ternary is discussed with some detail.

Quintuple-to-ternary conversion.   Consider a 2-digit quintuple (5-valued) input and a ternary (3-valued) output. In other words, the values of r, n, and k, are equal to 5, 2, and 3, respectively. The maximum value of the sum charge, from Equation (3.4) is equal to 24. From Equation (3.2):

$$m = \lceil \log_3 24 \rceil = 3$$

Therefore, there are 3 3-valued output lines, and l_1 through l_3 are determined according to Equation (3.10)

$$l_1 = \left\lfloor \frac{24}{3} \right\rfloor = 8,$$

$$l_2 = \left\lfloor \frac{8}{3} \right\rfloor = 2, \text{ and}$$

$$l_3 = \left\lfloor \frac{2}{3} \right\rfloor = 0.$$

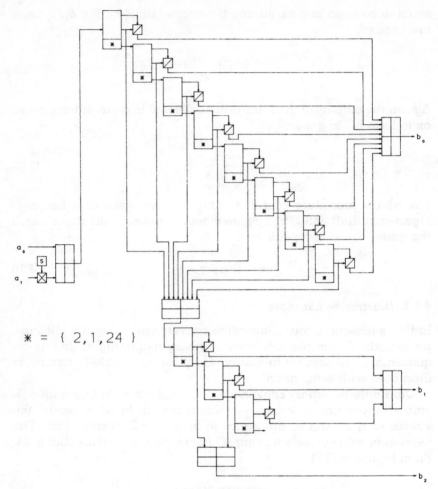

$$* = \{ 2, 1, 24 \}$$

Figure 3.11. Quintuple-to-Ternary Conversion.

Figure 3.11 shows a GRC operating as a 2-input 3-output quintuple-to-ternary decoder.

Other examples.

- *Ternary-to-quintuple conversion.*
  Specified parameters: r = 3, n = 2, k = 3
  Determined parameters: $S_{max} = 8$, m = 2, $l_1 = 1$, $l_2 = 0$.

Figure 3.12 shows the GRC operating as an encoder.

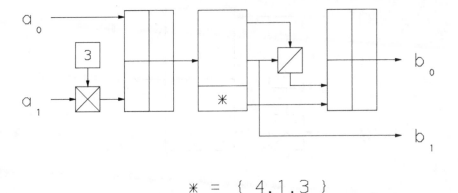

$$\ast \; = \; \{ \; 4, 1, 3 \; \}$$

Figure 3.12.   Ternary-to-Quintuple Conversion.

- *Binary-to-Quaternary* conversion.
  Specified parameters: $r = 2$, $n = 2$, $k = 4$
  Determined parameters: $S_{max} = 3$, $m = 1$, $l_1 = 0$

Figure 3.13a shows the complete diagram.

- *Quaternary-to-Binary* conversion.
  Specified parameters: $r = 4$, $n = 1$, $k = 2$
  Determined parameters: $S_{max} = 3$, $m = 2$, $l_1 = 1$, $l_2 = 0$

Figure 3.13b shows the complete diagram. The converters between binary number and quaternary number are suitable interfaces between MVL RAMs or MVL ROMs and binary computers.

4.2. Radix-r Systolic Array Processor Using CCD

Recent development in VLSI research and implementation makes it possible to design various kinds of special purpose array processors, such as processors for matrix manipulation, signal processing, and FFTs in VLSI chips [32,33]. In order to carry out multiple-valued array processors, a ternary inner product step processor designed using basic CCD gates was developed in [34]. However, the ternary CCD step processor was quite slow and could not be easily extended to other based multiple-valued logic. In order to deal with general radix-r computation, a general radix converter using CCD was designed in [31]. This subsection is based on the material in [5].

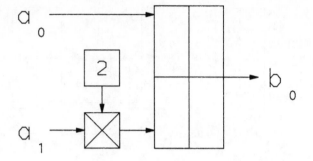

Figure 3.13a.   Binary-to-Quaternary Conversion.

4.2.1. Inner-product Step Processor

The systolic architectural concept was developed by Kung and his colleagues [1,33]. Since then, various systolic array processors have been designed, such as one-dimensional linear arrays, two-dimensional square arrays, and hexagonal arrays which are often applied to matrix computations. The hexagonal array architecture is used in the proposed radix-r systolic array processor. The structure of the array processor is the same as in [33].

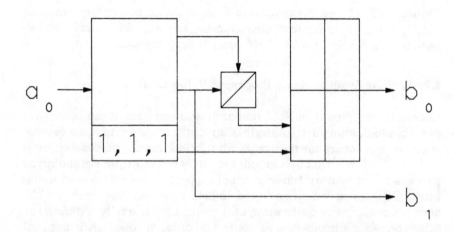

Figure 3.13b.   Quaternary-to-Binary Conversion.

The core of a systolic array processor is the inner-product step processor. This step processor can implement the desired computations:

$$R = A * B + D$$

However, the number of clock periods, where the computations of the components of the result R take, are different. In order to implement a desired step processor, as shown in Figure 3.14, one must have

$$C_{out}^{k+1} = C_{in}^k + A_{in}^k * B_{in}^k, \qquad (3.12)$$

$$A_{out}^{k+1} = A_{in}^k, \text{ and} \qquad (3.13)$$

$$B_{out}^{k+1} = B_{in}^k \qquad (3.14)$$

where A_{in}^k, B_{in}^k, and C_{in}^k are inputs of the step processor at step k and A_{out}^{k+1}, B_{out}^{k+1}, and C_{out}^{k+1} are outputs of the step processor at step k. In order to explain the design method, a quaternary-logic step processor is chosen as an example.

First of all, a single digit unit called full-multiply-add element (FMA) for computing $r_j = c_{1j} + \ldots + c_{mj} + a_j * b_j$ is designed and shown in Figure 3.15. In order to convert the results r_j into quaternary number, a radix-4 base converter is designed based on the same principle used in the last subsection where $r = 4$.

The step processor is designed by using FMAs, converters, delay elements, and fan-out facilitators. The block diagram is shown in Figure 3.16. In the Figure 3.16, the blocks with character C are radix-4

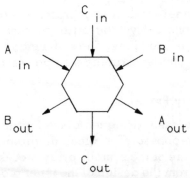

Figure 3.14. Step Processor in a Hexagonal Array Processor.

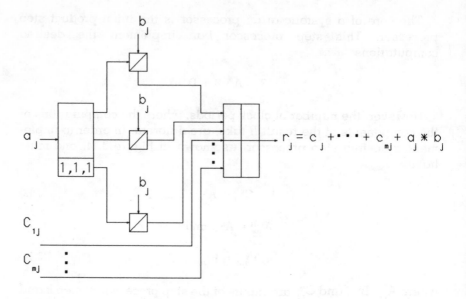

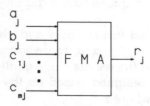

Figure 3.15.   Logic Diagram of A Full-Multiply-Add Element (FMA).

base converters and the blocks with character T_i are delay elements. The cost factors and the depths of the components and the step processor are listed in Table 3.1.

The proposed inner-product step processor can be applied to different configurations of systolic array processors. The hexagonal array architecture is used here. The step length of the proposed step processor is much shorter than the step processor developed in [34].

4.2.2. Systolic Array Processor

Using the step processor designed above, a quaternary systolic array processor is proposed. The block diagram is shown in Figure 3.17. The architecture of the systolic array processor is the same one as shown in [32]. From the design of the inner product step processor,

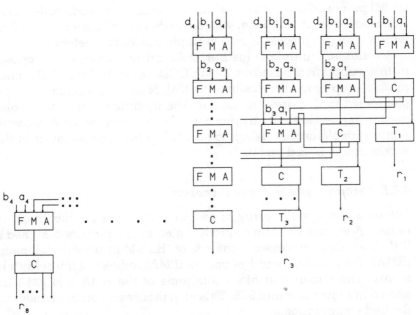

$$
\begin{array}{rrrr}
a_4 & a_3 & a_2 & a_1 \\
\text{x)} \quad b_4 & b_3 & b_2 & b_1 \\
\hline
-a_4b_1 & -a_3b_1 & -a_2b_1 & -a_1b_1 \\
-a_4b_2 & -a_3b_2 & -a_2b_2 & -a_1b_2 \\
a_4b_3 & -a_3b_3 & -a_2b_3 & -a_1b_3 \\
-a_4b_4 & -a_3b_4 & -a_2b_4 & -a_1b_4 \\
& d_4 \quad\quad d_3 \quad\quad d_2 \quad\quad d_1 \\
\text{+)} \\
\hline
r_8 \quad r_7 \quad r_6 \quad r_5 \quad r_4 \quad r_3 \quad r_2 \quad r_1
\end{array}
$$

Figure 3.16. Block Diagram of the Step Processor.

one can easily extend the designed step processor from the quaternary number system to arbitrary radix-r number system. The major drawback of CCD circuits is the low speed. In comparison with the matrix multiplication implemented in a single CCD processor, the parallel and pipeline processing in the proposed systolic array processor speeds up the matrix computation significantly.

**Table 3.1.   The Depths and the Cost Factors
of the Designed CCD Circuits.**

Circuits	Depths	Cost Factors
FMA	3	2m + 62
Fan-out facilitator	3	61m + 4
Delay elements	n	2n

4.3. Fault-tolerant CCD Systolic Array Processor

In addition to achieving high performance in VLSI technology, high reliability is also very important to ensure that the results of long computations are correct. Recently, Abraham and his colleagues [35,36] proposed a system-level fault tolerance method, called algorithm-based fault tolerance, which can detect and correct any failure within a single processor in a multiple processor system.

A reliable, multiple-valued, systolic array processor is proposed in this subsection based on basic CCD gates and the CCD inner-product step processor designed in [34]. Matrix multiplication is implemented in this array processor. The algorithm-based fault tolerance is applied to the array processor and error detection and correction are implemented using basic CCD gates. The material in this subsection is based on [4].

4.3.1. Ternary Systolic Array Processor

The core of a systolic array processor is an inner-product step processor. A ternary CCD inner-product step processor was designed in [34]. The step processor consists of Half-Multiply-Add elements (HMA), fully-multiply-add elements (FMA), adders, and delay elements. The circuit and block diagrams of the HMA and FMA are shown in Figure 3.18 and 3.19. This step processor can implement the desired computations.

$$R = A * B + D \tag{3.15}$$

To implement Eq. (3.12)–(3.14), some delay blocks are put into the block diagram as shown in Figure 3.20. Because the depth of the inner-product step processor in [34] is 52 clock periods, the step length of the systolic array processor should also be 52 clock periods too. The a_j and b_j which are components of A and B are also delayed for 52 clock periods (Figure 3.20).

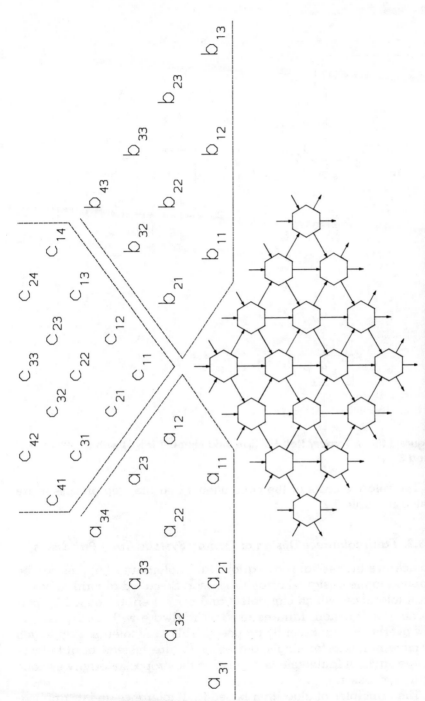

Figure 3.17. Architecture of the Multiple-Valued Array Processor.

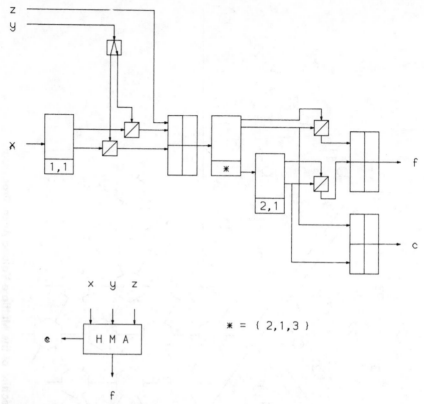

Figure 3.18.   A Ternary Half-Multiply-Add Element (HMA) with f = (x * y + z) mod 3.

The relative costs of the components and the step processor are listed in Table 3.2.

4.3.2. *Fault-tolerance Design of Ternary Systolic Array Processors*

To achieve high reliability, various fault-tolerant techniques can be applied to the designed array processor. So-called algorithm-based fault tolerance, which can detect and correct errors caused by permanent or transient failures in VLSI hardware with a surprisingly low overhead, was recently proposed. This fault tolerance approach is more suitable for single processor failure instead of gate-level single stuck-at faults and is applied to the proposed ternary systolic array processor.

The principles of algorithm-based fault tolerance and its application to matrix operation were discussed in detail [36]. Here, some

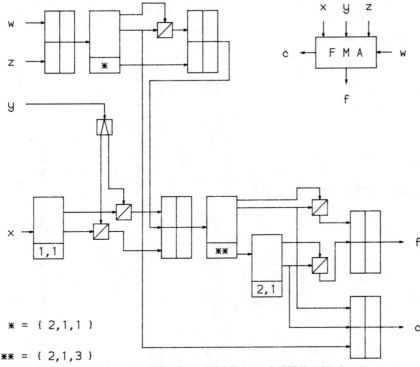

$* = \{ 2,1,1 \}$

$** = \{ 2,1,3 \}$

Figure 3.19. **A Ternary Full-Multiply-Add Element (FMA) with f = (x $*$ y + z + w) mod 3.**

basic facts and its implementation in ternary CCD circuits are addressed:

- *Checksum matrices and ternary adder.*
  The column checksum matrix A_c of an n-by-m matrix A is an (n + 1)-by-m matrix expressed by $A_c = \left[\begin{array}{c} A \\ \hline e^T A \end{array} \right]$ where e^T is a 1-by-n vector

Table 3.2. Cost Factors of Some CCD Circuits.

Circuits	Cost Factors
Adder with carry	14
Delay block of n clocks	2n
HMA	66
FMA	82
Step processor of 4 digits	1748

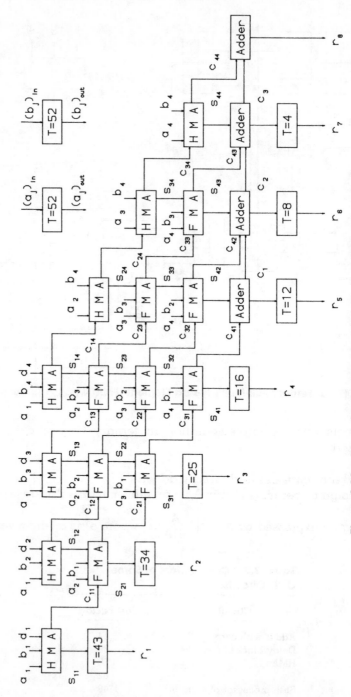

Figure 3.20. Block Diagram of An Inner Product Step Processor.

[11 . . . 1] and $e^T A$ are column checksums. The row checksum matrix A_r of an n-by-m matrix A is an n-by-(m + 1) matrix expressed by A_r = [A|Ae] where e is a m-by-1 vector [11 . . . 1]^T and Ae are row checksums. The full checksum matrix A_f of an n-by-m matrix A is an

(n + 1)-by-(m + 1) matrix expressed by $A_f = \begin{bmatrix} AB & ABe \\ e^T AB & e^T ABe \end{bmatrix}$. The

result of a column checksum matrix A_c multiplied by a row checksum matrix B_r is a full checksum matrix C_f:

$$A_c * B_r = \begin{bmatrix} A \\ e^T A \end{bmatrix} * [B \mid Be] = \begin{bmatrix} AB & ABe \\ e^T AB & e^T ABe \end{bmatrix} = C_f$$

where ABe are row checksums, $e^T AB$ are column checksums, and $e^T ABe$ is the checksum of row checksums and column checksums.

In order to compute checksums and the difference between the sum and the checksum, a CCD modulo-3 adder is designed. A four-digit ternary adder which consists of four cascaded, two-addendum full adders is shown in Figure 3.9. The depth of the adder is 10, and the cost is 56. The checksum computation can be implemented by combining inner-product step processors and modulo-3 adders, as shown in Figure 3.21.

- Error Detection, Correction, and Ternary Subtractor

Error detection, location, and correction are carried out by using column checksum and row checksum. The approaches are as follows:

Error detection: Compare the sum of each row and each column with the corresponding row checksum and column checksum, respectively. Any inconsistency in row or a column determines an error.

Error location: Any error can cause an inconsistency both in a row and in a column. The location can be determined by the intersection of that row and that column.

Error correction: The erroneous element can be corrected by adding the difference of the sum and checksum (in the inconsistent row or column) to the erroneous element.

Based on the above discussion, the comparison and subtraction of a sum and a checksum should be carried out. Instead of constructing a ternary CCD subtractor, 3's complement addition which uses complement circuits and modulo-3 adder is applied. The 3's complement addition is similar to the 2's complement addition in the binary sys-

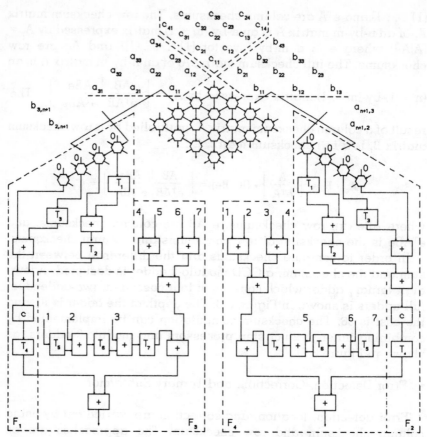

Figure 3.21. Architecture of the Fault Tolerant Systolic Array Processor.

tem. A CCD 2's complement circuit is designed and the circuit diagram is similar to Figure 3.3. This circuit can implement the following conversion: $0 \rightarrow 2$, $1 \rightarrow 1$, and $2 \rightarrow 0$. The depth of the complement circuit is 3 and the cost is 19. The comparison result can be generated by adding all the digits of the difference using an addition gate. If the output of the addition gate is zero, then no error occurs; any nonzero output indicates the inconsistency of the sum and checksum.

- Fault Tolerant Systolic Array Processor

The fault tolerant, ternary, systolic array processor proposed in this chapter is similar to the processor proposed by Huang and Abraham [36]. The whole system configuration is shown in Figure 3.21.

The ternary modulo-3 adders and the complement blocks are used in the fault tolerant block F1, F2, F3, and F4. If the band width of matrices A and B are 4, the cost of F1 and F2 (not including the 4 step processor units) is around 600 and the cost of F3 and F4 is around 700. The hardware for fault tolerance used in this design has less cost than any other fault tolerance techniques.

In principle, the design approach used here can be applied to any radix, multiple-valued CCD array processors. The fault tolerance design for floating point operations in the CCD array processor needs to be further developed.

4.4. MVL VLSI Systems for Fuzzy Inference in Expert Systems Using CCD

Artificial intelligence is a fast-growing interdisciplinary science and has found its applications in numerous fields ranging from computer science and engineering to social sciences and medical practice. Rule-based expert systems and their applications have shown great interest and rapid development. The development of hardware and software support for artificial intelligence, especially for rule-based expert systems, is an important topic in computer engineering [37,2]. In this subsection, a hardware architecture design of an MVL VLSI system for fuzzy inference in expert system is addressed and an MVL systolic array realization of the fuzzy inference is mentioned.

4.4.1. Expert Systems and Fuzzy Inference

Let us briefly review the material related to our design goal in expert systems and fuzzy inference.

Rule-based expert systems [38,39].   The inference in expert systems is based on rules supplied by human experts. A rule is a conditional statement expressed by If-Then or If-Then-Else form. Suppose that a rule is stated as "if A then B" denoted by $A => B$. If an observation is that A is true, according to the rule, we conclude that B is true. (It can be expressed as $(A => (A => B)) => B$). For example, the following rules are used in medical practice.

1. IF organism is streptococcus OR bacteroids THEN penicillin is indicated.
2. IF penicillin is indicated AND patient allergies are unknown THEN ask about allergy to penicillin.
3. IF penicillin is indicated AND NOT allergic to penicillin THEN prescribe penicillin.

This kind of rule-based inference is called *exact reasoning*. However, most of the practices one faces are described in human language and represented by imprecise knowledge. For example [39], if

1. The temperature in burning zone is OK,
2. The oxygen percentage in exhaust gas is low, and
3. The temperature at the back end of the kiln is OK

then decrease fuel rate slightly.

The terms *OK, low,* and *slightly* in the rule are not precisely defined, say, the temperature of 100°F can be thought being low, the temperature of 200°F can also be low. Of course, the degree of lowness for 100°F is different from that for 200°F. This kind of inference is called *inexact reasoning*.

Fuzzy logic and approximate reasoning.   Due to the pioneer work of Zadeh [40], fuzzy set theory and its application were widely developed. It was found that fuzzy logic and its linguistic approach are good methods for approximate reasoning. The detail discussion of fuzzy set, fuzzy logic, fuzzy linguistics, and approximate reasoning can be found in [41,38]. Only the concepts needed for a hardware design are presented here.

If A is a finite subset of a universal set U,

$$A = \{u_1, \ldots, u_n\} \subset U \tag{3.16}$$

A *finite fuzzy subset* A of U is a set of ordered pairs

$$A = \{(u_j, \mu_A(u_j))\} \qquad u_j \in U \tag{3.17}$$

where the $\mu_A(u_j)$ is the membership function and $0 \leq \mu_A(u_j) \leq 1$.

A *fuzzy relation* R from A to B is a fuzzy subset of the Cartesian product $U \times V$, where $A \subset U$ and $B \subset V$. The conditional statement, "If X is A then Y is B," is represented by the fuzzy relation R and defined as follows:

$$\mu_R(u,v) = \min(\mu_A(u), \mu_B(v)), \, u \in U \text{ and } v \in V \tag{3.18}$$

Compositional Rule: If R is a fuzzy relation from U to V, and x is a fuzzy subset of U, then the fuzzy subset y of V induced by x is denoted by:

$$y \equiv x \circ R \tag{3.19}$$

and defined as follows:

$$\mu_y(v) = \max_{u \in U} \min(\mu_x(u), \mu_R(u,v)) \tag{3.20}$$

Logic architecture of the fuzzy inference. Consider the following rule-based, fuzzy inference. Suppose that $A_j (j = 1, \ldots, N)$ is a fuzzy subset of U and B_j $(j = 1, \ldots, N)$ is a fuzzy subset of V. A fuzzy relation is defined by rules as follows:

Rule 1: If A_1 then B_1
Rule 2: ELSE if A_2 then B_2
.

.

Rule N: ELSE if A_N then B_N

The overall relation R is denoted and defined as

$$R = \underset{j}{U} R_j$$

$$= \max_j f_{\to}(\mu_{A_j}(u), \mu_{B_j}(v)) \quad \text{for } j = 1, \ldots, N \tag{3.21}$$

where $f_{\to}(\mu_{A_j}(u), \mu_{B_j}(v)) = \mu_{Aj \to B_j}(u,v)$ represents the fuzzy relation "If A_j then B_j".

Given an observation A' and a rule R_j, the action B_j' is inferred and defined as

$$B_j' = A' \circ R_j; \, A' \in U, \, B_j \in V, \text{ and } R_j \subset U \times V$$

and its membership function is expressed as

$$\mu_{B_j'}(v) = \max_{u \in U} \min(\mu_{A'}(u), \mu_{R_j}(u,v))$$

$$= \min[\max_{u \in U}(\min(\mu_{A'}(u), \mu_{A_j}(u)), \mu_{B_j}(v)] \tag{3.22}$$

The overall decision B is determined by $B_1, \ldots, B_N$; that is

$$B' = \underset{j}{U} B_j'$$

$$\mu_{B'}(v) = \max_{j}\{\min[\max_{u\epsilon U}(\min(\mu_{A'}(u),\ \mu_{A_j}(u))),\ \mu_{B_j}(v)]\} \qquad (3.23)$$

The Equation (3.23) can be decomposed into two levels with max-min operations. The functional architecture is shown in Figure 3.22.

4.4.2. Design of Unit Inference Processor

The fuzzy sets are, in fact, a kind of multiple-valued logic. Its operations can be realized by multiple-valued logic operations. The design approach is explained by CCD realizations on a four-level fuzzy subset which corresponds to four-valued logic. The design approach and architecture can be extended to more than four levels in principle.

MAX Element. The MAX element is used for composition rules. It can have either two, or more inputs. The function of a MAX element is expressed by

$$Q = \max(x_1,\ x_2,\ \ldots,\ x_n)$$

where x_j's are inputs and Q is the output. The CCD realization of the MAX element and its block diagram are shown in Figure 3.23. The depth of the realization is 4 and the cost factor is $10n + 19$. The number of inputs (n) seems to be restricted by the largest charge of an addition gate. However, if one groups the inputs to satisfy the charge restriction and slightly change the design, the MAX element can deal with any finite number of inputs. The design also can be easily extended to more logic levels by adding more series of three gates: an addition gate, a constant charge gate of 1, and an inhibit gate.

MIN Element. The MIN element is used for representing the fuzzy relation of "If X is A then Y is B" as shown in Equation (3.18). Figure 3.24 shows an n-input MIN element and its block diagram which carries out the function $Q = \min(x_1,\ \ldots,x_n)$. The MIN element has the limitation for number of inputs as the MAX element, but it can be overcome by grouping the inputs. The depth of the MIN element is 5 and its cost factor is $10n + 31$.

Single MAX-MIN Element. The CCD circuit diagram of a MAX-MIN element is shown in Figure 3.25. The function of the element is $Q = \max(\min(x,y),z)$ where the fixed overflow connected to z is separated by a dash-line box. Because each line, such as A_j (or B_j, or C_j) deals with the charge within a logic level, A_2, B_2 and C_2 can be connected to the outputs of other MIN element which are similar to

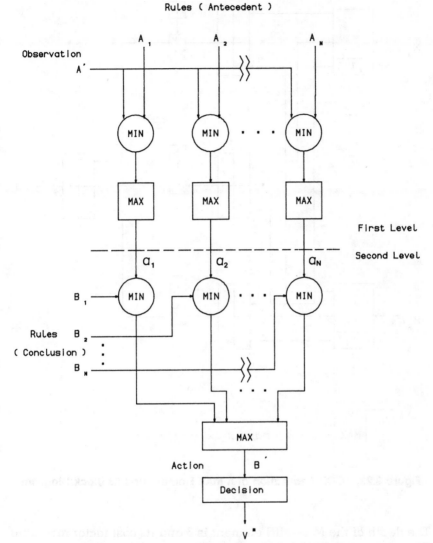

Figure 3.22.   Functional Architecture of A Fuzzy Inference.

A_1, B_1, and C_1, instead of connecting to the lines with decomposed logic level of z as shown in Figure 3.25. That is, if A_2, B_2, and C_2 are connected to the three logic levels of $\min(u,w)$, respectively, then the output of the MAX-MIN element is as follows:

$$Q = \max(\min(x,y),\ \min(u,w))$$

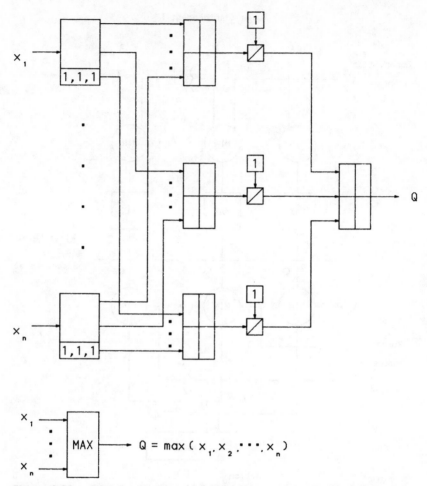

Figure 3.23.   CCD Realization of A MAX Element and Its Block Diagram.

The depth of the MAX-MIN element is 6 and its cost factor including the fixed overflow for z is 61.

4.4.3. MVL VLSI and Systolic Systems for Fuzzy Inference

To implement the fuzzy inference in Equation 3.23, an MVL VLSI inference machine is proposed. The inference machine processes the minimum and maximum operations in parallel to reduce processing time and to increase system throughput. The design of the VLSI inference machine using CCD is addressed in detail. Systolic array

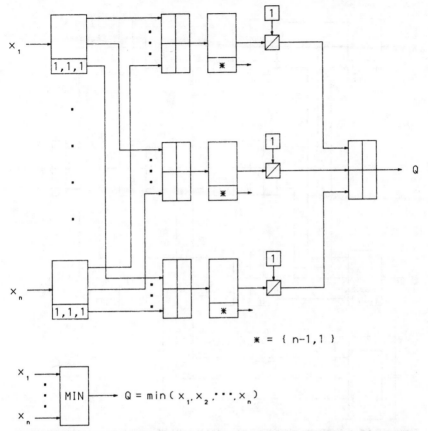

$$* = \{ n-1, 1 \}$$

Figure 3.24. CCD Realization of A MIN Element and Its Block Diagram.

realization of the fuzzy inference in expert systems will be mentioned. The material in this subsection is based on [42,43].

VLSI fuzzy inference machine.   Suppose that the universes of discourse U and V have p and q elements, respectively. A fuzzy inference based on N rules combined in the IF-THEN-ELSE form is shown in Section 4.4.1 and an observation A' is shown in Equation (3.23). For convenience, rewrite it as follows.

$$\mu_{B'}(v) = \max_{j}[\min[\max_{u \in V}(\min(\mu_{A'}(u), \mu_{A_j}(u))), \mu_{B_j}(v)]\} \qquad (3.24)$$

The architecture consists of two levels. First, the α_j is realized

$$\alpha_j = \max_{u \in V}(\min(\mu_{A'}(u), \mu_{A_j}(u,v))) \qquad (3.25)$$

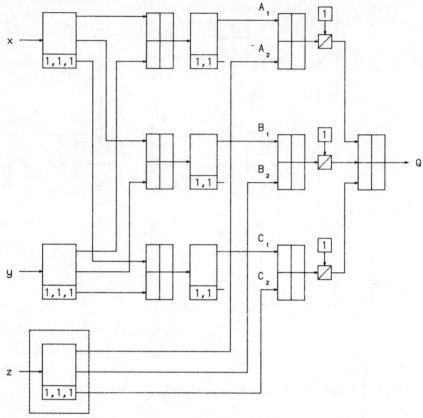

Figure 3.25. CCD Realization of a MAX-MIN Element Q = MAX(MIN(x,y),z).

Then the $\mu_{B'}(v)$ is realized as follows,

$$\mu_{B'}(v) = \max_j(\min(\alpha_j, \mu_{B_j}(v)) \qquad (3.26)$$

The main idea in the design is to manipulate the charge in each logical level individually. A MIN_j element, which is a two-input MIN element without combining all logical level together, is an elementary block in the design, as shown in Figure 3.26. The depth of the MIN_j element is 3 and its cost factor is 26. The α_j is realized by implementing the maximum among the output of the MIN_j's. The logic diagram for α_j is composed of p MIN_j-blocks, four addition gates, three inhibit gates, and three constant gates, as shown in Figure 3.27. Its block diagram is shown by a box with MAX-MIN$_p$.

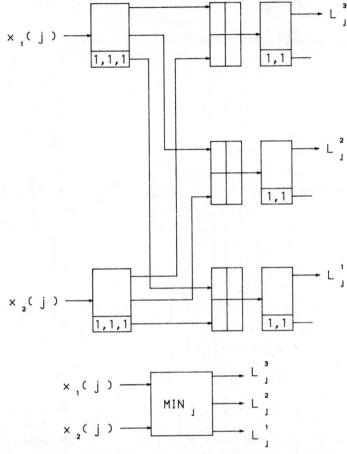

Figure 3.26.   CCD Realization of MIN$_j$ and Its Block Diagram.

The depth of the realization of α_j is 6 and the cost factor is $32p + 19$. As a matter of fact, if a max-min operation is not the final step of a fuzzy inference, a MAX-MIN$_p^1$ block can be built before combining the logical level together, as shown within the dash-line box. The inputs of the MAX-MIN$_p^1$ are two vectors A' and A_j with p components and its outputs are the three charges in each logical level, M_j^1, M_j^2, and M_j^3. The depth and the cost factor of the MAX-MIN$_p^1$ block are 5 and $32p + 15$, respectively.

Then the $\mu_{B'}(v)$ is implemented by N sets of q MIN$_j$ blocks (the k-th set from the N sets is shown in Figure 3.28a) and q maximum circuits among the output of the N sets (the k-th maximum circuit from the q maximum circuits is shown in Figure 3.28b). The final result is a

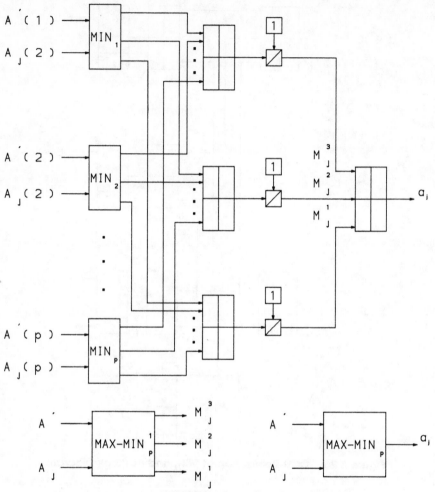

Figure 3.27.   CCD Realization of α_i and Its Block Diagram.

fuzzy subset B′ with membership function $\mu_{B'}(v)$ of q components. The architecture is shown in Figure 3.28 (a) and (b). The total depth of this part is 6 and its cost factor is $(26q + 6)N + 19$. Combining the first and the second level realization together as shown in Figures 3.26, 3.27, and 3.28, one can easily find that the total depth of the inference machine is 12 and the total cost factor is $(32p + 26q + 25)*N + 19$, where p and q are the number of the elements in U and V, respectively, and N is the number of rules. The design approach and architecture used can be extended to more than four-level logic in principle.

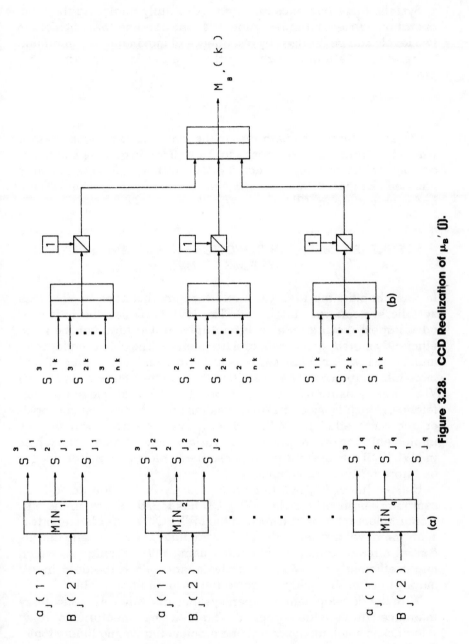

Figure 3.28. CCD Realization of $\mu_B{}'(j)$.

Systolic fuzzy inference machine. Carefully analyzing the logic operation carried out in Equation 3.24, one can find that each of the two levels can be realized by a sequence of maximum and minimum operations. The unit operation realized in Section 4.4.2 can be expressed by

$$Q = \max (\min (x, y), z),$$

which is similar to the operations in the inner-product step processor where the minimum corresponds to multiplication and the maximum corresponds to addition. In fact, the MVL systolic inference machine has been proposed and investigated. Readers can find the design and architecture in [43].

5. FURTHER RESEARCH DIRECTIONS IN VLSI AND SYSTOLIC SYSTEMS OF MVL

In this chapter, the MVL CCD and their applications in VLSI and systolic systems are introduced. The MVL CCD has the following advantages: the information in multiple-valued form can be more efficiently stored, processed, and transferred. The chip area for communication within VLSI chips can be tremendously reduced and more information can be transmitted through the limited pins of each VLSI chip by using MVL circuitry. Besides, MVL can make fuzzy inference, which is used in expert systems and other AI systems, easier and more efficient. MVL VLSI and systolic arrays will find its implementation and application in various fields. Some of the topics in MVL VLSI and systolic arrays described below may be considered as future research directions.

Huge-volume, high-performance memory is in wide demand in computer engineering. The MVL-CCD has found its way in the efficient implementation of RAM and the MVL ROM's was also reported. With the development of the MVL technology, memory cells and its control circuits could be fabricated using MVL techniques, which might efficiently use VLSI area and might reduce the data input/output lines of VLSI chips to solve the pin limitation problem.

With the development of expert systems and other AI areas, fuzzy inference can be widely applied. The MVL implementation of fuzzy inference is much more natural and efficient than using binary logic. Symbolic manipulation and other non-numerical computation are also possible implementations in MVL. MVL VLSI chips for artificial intelligence will not be far away from today's technology.

Most of computation time-intensive applications of VLSI are in signal processing, image processing, and pattern recognition. The application of systolic array and wave-front array processors to signal and image processing has attracted many researchers. The computation time could be reduced tremendously by using systolic architectures. If MVL systolic array processors or MVL wave-front array processors are used, further computation reduction can be achieved. Furthermore, the MVL could reduce the data encoding, data decoding, and transfer time in signal and image processing. For example, most of today's video cameras utilize CCD technology. The video signal must be decoded from the analog signal (if digitized, it is multiple-valued signal) to the binary signal, then input to computers. After being processed, the signal in binary form must be encoded into a multiple-valued signal for display. If multiple-valued logic would be used in the processing unit, the decoding and encoding would not be needed any more and the communication time could be reduced.

MVL can be considered as an intermediate logic between the binary logic and analog circuit. To match today's computation challenge, neural networks were proposed for more processing power and for solving some NP-complete problems, such as the travelling salesmen problem, which is nearly impossible for today's binary computers. In fact, neural networks are based on some kind of analog computation. MVL, as an intermediate logic, may play important roles in a new generation of computers.

REFERENCES

1. H.T. Kung and C.E. Leiserson, "Systolic Arrays (for VLSI), Sparse Matrix," *Proceedings 1978*, Academic Press, Orlando, FL, 1979, pp. 256–282.
2. J.A.B. Fortes and B.W. Wah, "Systolic Arrays—From Concepts to Implementation," *Computer*, July 1987, pp. 12–17.
3. C. Moraga, "Design of a Multiple-Value Systolic System for the Computation of the Chrestenson Spectrum," *IEEE Transactions on Computers*, Vol. C-35, No. 2, 1986, pp. 183–188.
4. J.Y. Han, "A Fault-Tolerant Ternary CCD Systolic Array Processor," *Proceedings of the 24th Annual Allerton Conference on Communication, Control and Computing*, University of Illinois, Urbana, IL, 1986, pp. 944–953.
5. J.Y. Han, "A Radix-r Systolic Array Processor Using CCD," *Proceedings of the 30th Midwest Symposium on Circuits and Systems*, Syracuse, NY, August 1987, pp. 1112–1115.

6. J.Y. Han and J.L. Han, "A CCD Realization of VLSI Fuzzy Inference Machine in Expert Systems," *Proceedings of the 19th Pittsburgh Conference on Modeling and Simulation*, Pittsburgh, PA, May 1988, pp. 855–859.

7. M.H. Abd-el Bar, S.G. Zaky and Z.G. Vranesic, "Synthesis of Multivalued Multithreshold Functions for CCD Implementation," *IEEE Transactions on Computers*, Vol. C-35, No. 2, February 1986, pp. 124–133.

8. M. Yamada, K. Fujishima, K. Nagasawa and Y. Gamou, "A New Multilevel Storage Structure for High Density CCD Memory," *IEEE Journal of Solid-State Circuits*, Vol. 13, October 1978, pp. 688–692.

9. H.G. Kerkhoff, M.L. Tervoert and H.A.C. Tilmans, "Design Considerations and Measurement Results of Multiple-Valued Logic CCD's," *Proceedings of the 11th International Symposium on Multiple-Valued Logic*, Oklahoma City, OK, May 1981, pp. 205–211.

10. W.S. Boyle and G.E. Smith," Charge-Coupled Semiconductor Devices," *Bell System Technical Journal*, Vol. 49, April 1970, pp. 587–593.

11. H.G. Kerkhoff, "Theory and Design of Multiple-Valued Logic in CCD," *Computer Science and Multiple-Valued Logic: Theory and Applications* (2nd edition), D.C. Rine (ed.), North Holland, Amsterdam, Holland, 1984.

12. M.J. Howes and D.V. Morgan, *Charge-Coupled Devices and Systems*, Wiley Interscience Publication, New York, 1978.

13. G.S. Hobson, *Charge-Transfer Devices*, Edward Arnold Publishers, Baltimore, MD, 1978.

14. H.G. Kerkhoff and M.L. Tervoert, "Multiple-Valued Logic CCD's," *IEEE Transactions on Computers*, Vol. C-30, September 1981, pp. 644–652.

15. H.G. Kerkhoff and H.A.J. Robroek, "The Logic Design of Multiple-Valued Logic Functions Using Charge-Coupled Devices," *Proceedings of the 12th International Symposium on Multiple-Valued Logic*, Paris, France, May 1982, pp. 35–44.

16. H.G. Kerkhoff and M.L. Tervoert, "The Implementation of Multi-Valued Functions Using CCD's," *Proceedings of the 10th International Symposium on Multiple-Valued Logic*, 1980, pp. 6–15.

17. C.M. Allen and D.D. Givone, "The Allen-Givone Implementation Oriented Algebra," *Computer Science and Multiple-Valued Logic: Theory and Applications*, D.C. Rine (ed.), North Holland and Elsevier, New York, 1984, pp. 268–288.

18. H.A.J. Robroek, "The Synthesis of MVL-CCD Circuits," Report No. 1217.3936, Twente University of Technology, January 1982.

19. F.J. Hill and G.R. Peterson, *Introduction to Switching Theory and Logic Design* (3rd ed.), John Wiley and Sons, New York, 1981.

20. M. Davio and J.P. Deschamps, "Synthesis of Discrete Functions Using I^2L Technology," *IEEE Transactions on Computers*, Vol. C-30, September 1981, pp. 653–661.

21. E.J. McCluskey, "Logic Design of Multi-Valued I^2L Logic Circuits," *IEEE Transactions on Computers*, Vol. C-28, August 1979, pp. 546–559.

22. J.K. Lee and J.T. Butler, "Tabular Methods for the Design of CCD Multi-

ple-Valued Circuits," *Proceedings of the 13th International Symposium on Multiple-Valued Logic*, 1983, pp. 162–170.

23. P. Tirumula and J.T. Butler, "On the Realization of Multi-Valued Logic Functions Using CCD PLA's," *Proceedings of the 14th International Symposium on Multiple-Valued Logic*, 1984, pp. 33–42.

24. D.C. Rine (ed.), *Computer Science and Multiple-Valued Logic: Theory and Applications*, North Holland, New York, 1984.

25. H.G. Kerkhoff and J.T. Butler, "Design of High-Radix Programmable Logic Array Using Profiled Peristalic Charge-Coupled Devices," *Proceedings of the 16th International Symposium on Multiple-Valued Logic*, Blacksberg, VA, 1986, pp. 128–1136.

26. J.L. Mangin and K.W. Current, "Characteristics of Prototype CMOS Quaternary Logic Encoder-Decoder Circuits," *IEEE Transactions on Computers*, Vol. C-35, No. 2, 1986, pp. 157–160.

27. D.A. Rich, "A Survey of Multi-valued Memories," *IEEE Transactions on Computers*, Vol. C-35, 1986, pp. 99–106.

28. R. Adlhoch, "Quaternary ROM Design Utilizing Variable Threshold Storage. Cells," *Proceedings of the 15th International Symposium on Multiple-Valued Logic*, 1985, pp. 310–316.

29. D.A. Freitas and K.W. Current, "CMOS Circuits for Quaternary Encoding and Decoding," *Proceedings of the 14th International Symposium on Multiple-Valued Logic*, 1984, pp. 164–168.

30. C.W. Current, J.L. Mangin and S.B. Haley, "Characteristics of Integrated CMOS Quaternary Logic Encoder-Decoder Interface Circuits," *Proceedings of the 1984 International Symposium on Circuit Systems*, May 1984, pp. 911–914.

31. J.Y. Han and M.A. Manzoul, "A General Radix Converter Using CCDs," unpublished manuscript.

32. K. Hwang and F.A. Briggs, *Computer Architecture and Parallel Processing*, McGraw-Hill, New York, 1984.

33. H.T. Kung and C.E. Leiserson, "Algorithms for VLSI Processor Arrays," *Introduction to VLSI Systems*, C.A. Mead and L.A. Conway (eds.), Addison-Wesley, Reading, MA, 1980, pp. 271–292.

34. M.A. Manzoul and J.Y. Han, "A Ternary CCD Inner Product Step Processor," *Proceedings of the 1987 ACM Computer Science Conference*, St. Louis, MO, February 1987.

35. P. Banergee and J.A. Abraham, "Bounds on Algorithm-Based Fault Tolerance in Multiple Processor Systems," *IEEE Transactions on Computers*, Vol. C-35, No. 4, April 1986, pp. 296–306.

36. K.H. Huang and J.A. Abraham, "Algorithm-Based Fault Tolerance for Matrix Operations," *IEEE Transactions on Computers*, Vol. C-33, June 1984, pp. 518–528.

37. B.W. Wah, "New Computers for Artificial Intelligence Processing," *Computer*, January 1987, pp. 10–15.

38. H.J. Zimmerman, *Fuzzy Set Theory and Its Applications*, Kluwer-Nijhoff, Boston, MA, 1985.

39. M. Togai and H. Watanabe, "Expert Systems on a Chip: An Engine for

Real-Time Approximate Reasoning," *IEEE Expert*, Fall 1986, pp. 55–62.

40. L.A. Zadeh, "Fuzzy Algorithms," *Information Control*, Vol. 19, 1969, pp. 94–102.

41. L.A. Zadeh, "The Concept of a Linguistic Variable and Its Application to Approximate Reasoning," Memo ERL-M4111, Berkeley, CA, October 1973.

42. J.Y. Han and J.L. Han, "Systolic Arrays for Real-Time Approximate Reasoning in Fuzzy Logic Export Systems," *International Journal of Computer Aided VLSI Design*.

43. J.Y. Han and J.L. Han, "Multiple-Valued Systolic Array for Expert Systems and Its CCD Realization," *International Symposium on Intelligent Control*, Arlington, VA, August 1988.

4
Data Path Synthesis of Pipelined Designs: Theoretical Foundations

NOHBYUNG PARK

Department of Electrical Engineering
University of California, Irvine

RAJIV JAIN
ALICE C. PARKER

Department of Electrical Engineering—Systems
University of Southern California

1. INTRODUCTION

This chapter deals with the theoretical foundations of synthesis of pipelined digital systems. Most existing industry tools perform low-level automation tasks such as layout, placement, and routing. Researchers are working towards designing tools for higher-level design automation tasks such as synthesis. In this chapter, research results which can be applied to the automatic synthesis of pipelined designs are given. First, the theory of pipelined synthesis is developed and then a mathematical model for the area-time estimation of pipelined designs is discussed.

The first section presents an introduction to pipelining and synthesis, and describes related research. Section 2 presents a detailed discussion of pipeline synthesis theory, beginning with assumptions and nomenclature. Performance estimation techniques are described, followed by the theory of scheduling and operator allocation, which uses these estimation techniques. Detection of mutually-exclusive tasks is an important topic, since operators which are mutually-exclusive in time can be shared. This topic concludes Section 2.

Section 3 presents theory and techniques for estimating the area-time tradeoff curve for pipelined designs, prior to synthesis. This theory builds on the material presented in Section 2. Determination of the optimal clock cycle is presented, followed by estimation of operators. Results using this estimation technique are given in Section 3.4. The chapter concludes with a brief statement of accomplishments to date, followed by a summary of current and future research topics.

Before presenting the chapter material, the concept of pipelining is described and the term *synthesis* defined.

1.1. Pipelining Overview

Pipelining is a desirable method for designing fast circuits. In pipelining, each unit computation task (e.g., a microinstruction) is partitioned into a sequence of subtasks and each of these subtasks is executed during a clock cycle. Every clock cycle has the same time period. Consecutive tasks are initiated at some fixed or variable intervals, called *latencies*[1], which are integer multiples of a clock cycle and are bounded by the execution time of a task. In this fashion, execution of subtasks of consecutive tasks may overlap in time on different parts of the pipeline circuits.

Several pipelined designs with the same behavior and different cost-performance values exist. A two-dimensional plane in which these designs lie, with area and time as its two axes, is known as the *design space*, and each of the designs is a *design point* in this space. Figure 4.1 shows an example design space. The design points in this design space were produced by Sehwa, a pipeline synthesis program. Figure 4.2 contains a data flow graph of a computation task partitioned into five subtasks, F1 through F5. Usually, in pipelining, each subtask is executed during a single clock cycle. Figure 4.3 shows the execution timing of a single task. An example of pipelined execution of a sequence of tasks is shown in Figure 4.4., where I1 through I5 are designated in the pipelined implementation given in Figure 4.5. The latency for this design is 1. The same data flow graph can be implemented by the cheaper and slower pipeline of Figure 4.6; the latency for this design is 2.

The pipeline strategy discussed in this chapter is actually more complex than that described above. Operators are allowed to be

---

[1] Latency means the number of clock cycles between initiations of two successive tasks, as used in [1].

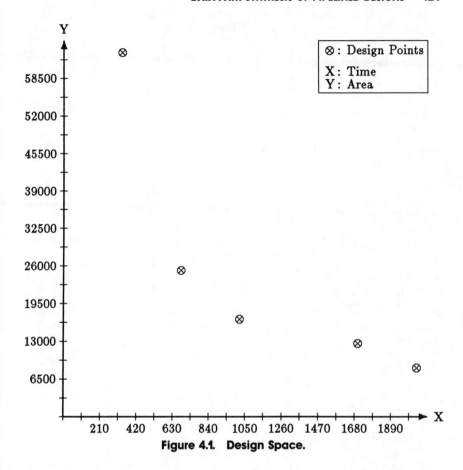

Figure 4.1. Design Space.

shared between stages of the pipe. Within a stage, some operators might be shared differently than others. Thus, an adder might be used in stages 1 and 3 of a pipe, while a multiplier is used in stages 1 and 4. Thus, there is no physical *stage* which corresponds to the logical grouping of operations in a time step. This is referred to as *functional pipelining*.

1.2. Synthesis of Digital Systems

The automatic mapping of a behavioral description of a digital system to a register-transfer level design is known as *synthesis* (Figure 4.7). The behavioral description could be represented as a data flow graph, or in a high-level hardware description language such as

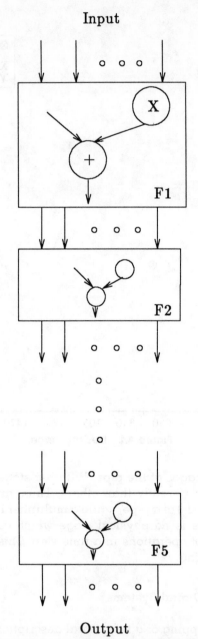

Output

Figure 4.2. A Partitioned Data Flow Graph.

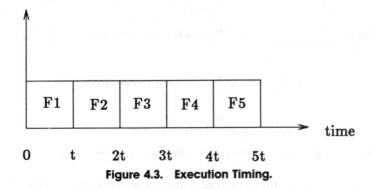

Figure 4.3.   Execution Timing.

ISPS [18]. When the controller is omitted from the design, and only operators and registers which implement the functional behavior are produced, the activity is referred to as *data-path synthesis*.

An *operation* is a node in the data flow graph. It represents a function, like addition. An *operator* is a module which computes a function. For example, a ripple-carry adder is a module which can perform addition. A *module set* is a set of module types which have been chosen for implementation of the data flow graph. Data-path synthesis will be defined more precisely now in terms of the inputs to and outputs from the synthesis process.

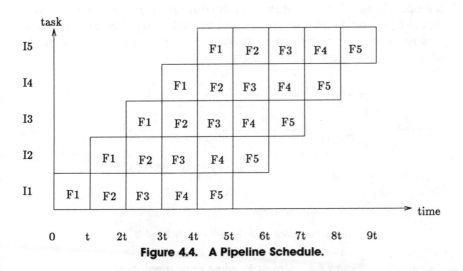

Figure 4.4.   A Pipeline Schedule.

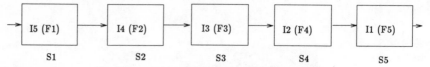

S1   S2   S3   S4   S5

Figure 4.5.   A Pipeline Implementation.

1.2.1. Input to a Data-Path Synthesis System

The input to a typical data-path synthesis system includes:

1. A data flow graph or a functional description of the hardware system in a hardware descriptive language
2. A library of modules
3. Some user-defined constraints
4. Some performance criteria for the overall design

A data flow graph is a directed acyclic graph, with operations represented by nodes and values by arcs. This graph represents an algorithm. For example, Figure 4.8 is the data flow graph of the quadratic equation solution. Algorithms can, in general, contain loops, which are indicated by subscripted values. Also, *if* conditions (conditional branches) which are represented by a pair of special *distribute* and *join* nodes in the graph, can be present in the algorithm.

A library of modules consists of operators which actually perform the operations. Every operation in the data flow graph must be realizable by at least one module present in the library. Certain parameters required by the synthesis program, such as areas of the modules, are also stored in the library.

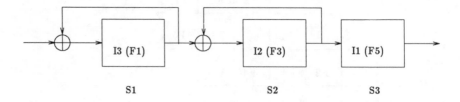

S1   S2   S3

The pipeline is currently executing I1, I2 and I3.

In the next clock cycle, S1 will execute F2 of I3

S2 will execute F4 of I2 and S3 will be idle.

Figure 4.6.   Slower Pipeline Implementation.

Data Flow Graph   Library of Modules   Design Constraint

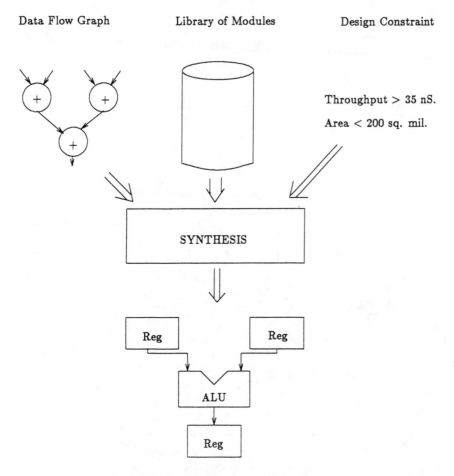

Register Transfer Level Design

Figure 4.7.   Data Path Synthesis.

For the purpose of synthesis, the synthesis programs need some measure of the relative importance of parameters to be optimized. This could be in terms of absolute values, for example, the chip area should not exceed 500 mil^2, or could be relative to other parameters, for example, give a weight of 0.75 to area and 0.25 to speed. Finally, there might be an overall performance goal which the design must achieve. This goal can be specified as an optimizing function such as *minimize delay*.

---

[2] This average is computed assuming an infinite number of tasks will be executed.

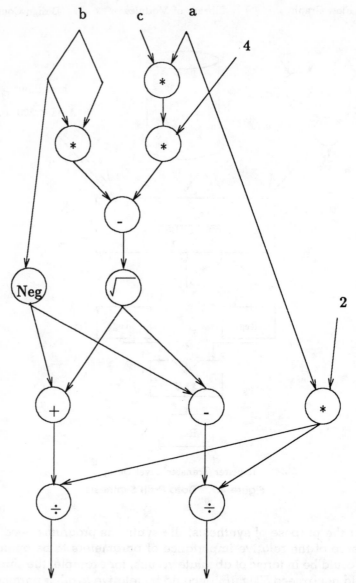

Figure 4.8. Data Flow Graph of the Quadratic Equation Solution.

1.2.2. Output of a Data-Path Synthesis System

A pipelined data-path synthesis system must be able to accept the inputs described, and perform the following functions in order to produce a *register-transfer level* design meeting the user constraints:

1. Module selection
2. Scheduling
3. Operator allocation
4. Module binding
5. Register and multiplexer allocation

The library contains one or more modules which can implement each operation. For example, a 4-bit carry look-ahead adder and a ripple carry adder can both implement the addition operation. The problem of *module selection* can be stated as follows: select modules from the library for the implementation of operations such that the constraints are satisfied and some goal is met. The goal can be, for example, minimizing the overall area of the design.

Every node in the data flow graph is assigned a time step during which it will be executed. *Scheduling* is the mapping of each data flow graph node to a particular time step for execution. The scheduling of nodes is performed during *partitioning* of the data flow graph into time steps. The partitioning of the graph is the singularly most important task in the synthesis procedure. The scheduling depends on various factors, such as user constraints, module selection, operator allocation, conditional branching, and resynchronization (rate of pipe flushing). The interaction among these various tasks makes the problem of scheduling difficult. Scheduling is known to be an NP-Complete problem [2], and several heuristics exist which perform scheduling [3,4,5]. These heuristics do not always produce optimal results, but they produce good results.

Operator allocation is the task of computing the quantity of each type of module required for a given implementation. The task of operator allocation must consider the various modules' parameters, user constraints, and scheduling in computing the number of required modules. Latency of the design is computed, and the numbers of operators of each operation type are identified.

The task of relating data flow operation nodes to modules is known as *module binding*. For example, if two addition operations are scheduled to be executed in the same time step and there are two adders available, then the decision as to which addition operation will be performed in which adder module is known as module binding. This task is complicated by the various goals which have to be met. These goals include minimizing the number of registers, minimizing the number of multiplexers, and minimizing the delay along the critical path.

The task of *register* and *multiplexer allocation* is to assign data values to registers and route them through multiplexers or busses to the operators. Also, the routing of data values from operators to the registers must be accomplished and a routing method, either multiplexers or busses, chosen.

To solve each function optimally is a difficult problem. Problems like scheduling are known to be NP-Complete. What makes the synthesis problem even more intractable is the interaction of these functions with each other. For example, while solving the module binding problem, care has to be taken that register and multiplexer cost is kept at a minimum. To increase the synthesis problem complexity even more, the overall solution should lie within the user constraints. The computational complexity of the combined five tasks is thought to be NP-hard.

For a globally optimal design, all five steps described in Section 1.2.2 must be performed concurrently. For example, the shortest schedule does not always guarantee the fastest performance since it might force operator allocation in such a way that the fastest possible initiation rate of the tasks is not feasible (due to operator conflicts between consecutive tasks). An expensive pipeline does not always guarantee better performance since the scheduling may not be able to utilize all available operators. Also, the feasibility of an operator allocation within cost constraints can be known only after the register transfer synthesis is completed.

Many current synthesis systems solve most of the functions independently of other functions. For example, module selection is performed separately from scheduling and operator allocation. This reduces the complexity of the synthesis problem and also provides an opportunity to understand these functions more easily. Some systems actually perform several tasks, like scheduling and operator allocation, concurrently. However, a system which performs all the five tasks concurrently and optimally does not exist.

1.3. Related Work

There has been considerable activity for the past 20 years on synthesis of nonpipelined data paths [6]. Of the related works on pipelined designs, there are several which deal with the use of predesigned pipelines [7,1], but few discuss the automatic generation of pipelines [3,4,5]. Even those works which automate the design of a pipeline do not attempt to solve all the issues discussed above. Most of the effort in this area has concerned scheduling and operator allocation [8,4,5].

Davio [8] discusses scheduling schemes and operator allocation techniques. Davio's schemes are restricted as all the nodes of the data flow graph are of the same type and fully pipelined designs are constructed. Furthermore, as all operations are identical, they have the same delays, which simplifies the problem of synthesis. Nevertheless, it provides an initial point for understanding scheduling and operator allocation problems.

Park [4] developed some theoretical foundations of pipelined synthesis. Sehwa [4], a part of the USC ADAM (Advanced Design Auto-Mation) system [9], is a pipeline data path synthesis program based on this theory. The input to Sehwa is a data flow graph, and a set of module types which can be used to implement the operations of the data flow graph. Sehwa gives as an output the number of each type of operator required and the scheduling of the data flow graph. Sehwa also takes into consideration conditional branches within the data flow graph and resynchronization due to operator conflicts and data dependencies. The scheduling is a static scheduling which takes into account all possible combinations of conditional branches. First, Sehwa produces the fastest and the cheapest designs to define the feasible design boundary. Sehwa then prompts the user for a speed or cost constraint and generates several solutions meeting this constraint. The user may alter the constraints and iterate to get alternate solutions. Finally, the user can request exhaustive search in a small part of the design space to tune the design. Once a design is selected, redesigning occurs using a different module set.

The HAL system [5] performs heuristic pipeline scheduling by using force-directed scheduling. Operator allocation is done concurrently. Girczyc [3] generates pipelined designs using the loop winding technique. In both these systems, latency is set by the user.

REAL is a register allocation program [10] for pipelined and non-pipelined designs. The program assigns data values to register so as to minimize the number of registers. REAL employs the *left edge algorithm* [11], which is known to be optimal for assigning wires to tracks. REAL also handles conditional branches. Also, a program which solves the module selection problem based on a mathematical model for area-time estimation (Section 3) has been developed [12].

2. THEORY OF PIPELINED SYNTHESIS

In this section of the chapter the data flow model for pipeline synthesis is developed. Before beginning the theoretical discussion, the assumptions and the nomenclature used in the remainder of the chapter are stated. After the data flow model has been developed, some theorems for scheduling and operator allocation will be given. The section concludes with an algorithm for identification of mutually exclusive operations and the effect of mutually exclusive operations on scheduling and operator allocation.

2.1. Assumptions

The following assumptions have been made to simplify the mathematical models:

1. Every operation must be completed within one clock cycle. (Slow operations can be partitioned into multiple suboperations.)
2. A fixed latency scheme is assumed. Variable latency control requires complex scheduling mechanisms [1] in order to avoid operator conflicts between consecutive tasks. In cases where the pipeline has 10 or more stages, the control mechanisms for variable latency become impractical due to the complexity of the control circuitry and its processing time, which might be comparable to the initiation interval. In fact, the maximum possible performance does not depend on the type of latency used but on the pattern of operator usage; for a fixed task, the maximum possible performance can be achieved using fixed latency [4].
3. Static scheduling of tasks onto operators is assumed. Dynamic scheduling also requires a complex scheduling mechanism and is not considered for the same reason as given above.
4. Nodes of the same operation type are mapped to the same type of module.
5. The clocking scheme consists of a single fixed-length clock. The length of the clock is determined automatically at run time.

2.2. Notation

The following notation will be used in the remainder of this chapter:

- P is the pipecycle or delay in cycles through the pipeline (the total number of stages of the pipeline).
- m is the number of different types of operations in the data flow graph.
- a_i is the area of the module used to implement operation type i ($0 \leq i \leq (m - 1)$).

- d_i is the delay of the module used to implement operation type i ($0 \leq i \leq (m - 1)$).
- c is the length of the clock cycle.
- l is the latency, that is, the number of clock cycles between initiations of two successive tasks.
- o_i is the number of modules of type i required for implementation ($0 \leq i \leq (m - 1)$).
- n_i is the number of nodes of operation type i occurring in the data flow graph ($0 \leq i \leq (m - 1)$).
- $A = \sum_{i=0}^{m-1} (a_i \times o_i)$, is the total functional area of the design.

2.3. A Data Flow Model of Digital System Behavior

Before starting the discussion of scheduling and operator allocation, some details concerning the use of the data flow graph model for the purpose of synthesis will be given. A behavioral representation of a design is essentially a data flow graph. However, since it is used for the representation of digital hardware design (both design specification and design description) it has subtle differences from computer program, or instruction data-flow descriptions [13]. The data flow graph model used in this chapter is a modified subset of the behavioral subspace representation of the *Design Data Structure* (DDS) [19] of the ADAM [9] system. The DDS data flow graph used for pipeline synthesis has the following properties:

- *Acyclic, Single Assignment Data Flow:* The data flow graph used for pipelined synthesis is a directed acyclic graph, that is, it has no inner loops except the single outer loop for the whole graph. Loops with determinate and finite iteration counts can be unrolled easily by duplicating the loop as many times as the iteration count. Inner loops with conditional or indeterminate iteration counts are hard to implement in a pipeline design. Since multiple tasks are to be executed simultaneously on a pipeline, indeterminate inner loops make task scheduling (operator sharing and initiation timing between tasks) difficult. There are two solutions. The first technique is to separate the loop and turn it into a new subgraph or a task. Another technique is to withhold initiation of a new task until the execution of the indeterminate loop completes. This can be implemented by treating such a task the same as a branch task, with the next task to be executed determined on its completion.
- *No Control or Timing Information:* A DDS data flow graph has no control or timing information such as tokens [13] or explicit control

constructs [14]. Furthermore, information influencing implementation details, such as using a carry-look-ahead adder for an addition operation, are absent giving the synthesis programs complete control in designing the pipeline.

- *Parallelism:* A data flow graph represents all potential parallelism present in the input behavior. Furthermore, a data flow graph need not be a single connected graph. Disconnected graphs automatically imply multiple, parallel data flows. With parallel pipelines, it is assumed that all the parallel data flows are synchronized and controlled by the same centralized controller.

- *Implicit Conditionals:* Conditional tests are implicit and can only be referenced explicitly through *bindings* which relate the data flow graph to the control and timing graph of the DDS. In other words, in order to check the conditions under which a certain operation is carried out, the control and timing graph must be examined.

- *Conditional Execution Paths:* To design a single pipeline which will conditionally execute more than one type of computation task the data flow of all conditional computation tasks must be represented as a single data flow graph. In such a data flow graph, the actual execution of each computation task can be represented and selected by conditional branches, depending on the type of computation task to be executed. Of the several constructs which can represent conditional execution data paths [13,14], *distribution-join* node pairs are used in this chapter. Whenever an execution path is to be selected by some condition, a *distribution* node must be used to split the values to every possible execution path. Whenever the execution path is no longer dependent upon the condition, a *join* node must be used to indicate the termination of conditional execution. A *join* node collects all the arcs which carry values that are produced by conditional paths. Only the values produced by a selected branch are passed through a join node.

Definition 4.1. *For any two operations in a data flow graph which are executed on some condition, if the condition that selects one operation always falsifies the condition selecting the other, and vice versa, then the two operations are* **mutually exclusive** *to each other.*

The distribute-join node pair can be replaced in the data flow graph with a *select* node as is done in the Value Trace [14]. With this replacement, the user can force evaluations of all mutually exclusive operations, followed by selection of the proper result values. Furthermore, the use of the *select* node can force module sharing explicitly. Two such replacements are shown in Figure 4.9.

Finally, insertion of no-operation (*NOP*) nodes in data flow graphs can serve a useful purpose. These *dummy* nodes make the data flow graph more readable to the human designers and more easily manageable for automatic procedures. In addition, they allow the insertion of arbitrary time delays which could be used for modeling interconnect delays in the circuit. For further details, see [4].

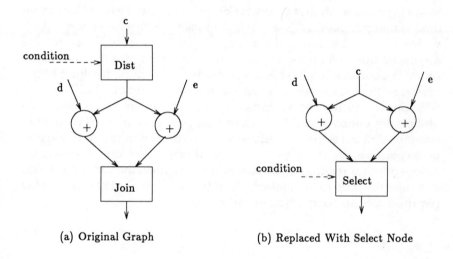

(a) Original Graph   (b) Replaced With Select Node

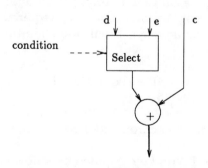

(c) Forcing Module Sharing

Figure 4.9.   Use of Select Node.

2.4. Performance Estimation

Performance estimation is useful in comparing designs. The performance measures described in this chapter are used during scheduling and operator allocation to compare designs.

The performance measures include estimation of the execution time of x tasks with resynchronization. Let P be the number of clock cycles needed for a task to complete. P is also known as the *Pipe Cycle*.

The number of clock cycles required for x tasks to complete on a P stage pipeline such that a new task can be initiated every clock cycle (i.e., latency is one) is $P + x - 1$. If the tasks are initiated every l clock cycles, the total number of clock cycles is $P + (x - 1)l$. These results are under the presumption that no flushing of the pipe (resynchronization) is caused once the tasks are started. In reality, flushing of the pipe due to some exception condition must be anticipated.

Suppose, during the execution of an instruction, some exception or data dependency problem causes the pipe to be flushed before the computation is restarted. This *resynchronization* in the pipeline can be expensive, as the pipe has to be flushed first and then set up before another result can be generated. Suppose, that, of the x tasks, x_b cause the pipe to be flushed. Then the total number of clock cycles required for the completion of the x tasks is

$$P + (x - x_b - 1)l + Px_b \qquad (4.1)$$

The first task, which fills the pipe, requires P steps. Once the pipe is full, $(x - x_b - 1)l$ clock cycles are required to compute $x - x_b - 1$ tasks. Flushing the pipe and then setting it up again x_b times requires Px_b clocks. To get the total time T_{total} required to compute x tasks, with x_b tasks causing resynchronization, multiply by the clock length c which gives

$$((x - x_b - 1)l + P(x_b + 1))c = T_{total}. \qquad (4.2)$$

If $\rho = \dfrac{x}{x_b}$ is the *average resynchronization rate*, then the average initiation time for a task T, can be computed as follows[2]:
Dividing Equation 4.2 by x yields

$$T = \left(\left(1 - \frac{x_b}{x} - \frac{1}{x} \right) l + P \left(\frac{x_b}{x} + \frac{1}{x} \right) \right) c$$

$$\lim_{x \to \infty} T = \left(\left(1 - \frac{x_b}{x} \right) l + P \left(\frac{x_b}{x} \right) \right) c$$

Substituting $\rho = \frac{x_b}{x}$,

$$\lim_{x \to \infty} T = ((1 - \rho)l + P\rho))c$$

$$\lim_{x \to \infty} T = (l + \rho(P - l))c \tag{4.3}$$

If the resynchronization rate $\rho = 0$ then $T = lc$. Also, if $P = l$, then $T = lc$, and the resynchronization rate has no effect on the performance of the pipeline.

2.5. Scheduling and Operator Allocation

Since scheduling and operator allocation are the most important functions which have to be performed for synthesis of pipelined designs, the discussion in this chapter is concentrated on these topics. Both scheduling and operator allocation (or in fact any other function mentioned in Section 1.2.2) must be performed in such a way that the result preserves the behavior of the original data flow graph as well as meets the design constraints. To ensure this, the following requirements must be satisfied:

- *Data Precedence:* The result of partitioning a data flow graph into time steps must retain the data precedence between operations in the original data flow graph. An operation can start execution only after all its input values are available.
- *Cost Constraint:* Another constraint on scheduling and operator allocation is the maximum available cost budget or the number of available modules. The sum of the operator requirements of all subtasks which are to be executed during the same clock cycle must not exceed the total available operators.
- *Stage Time Limit:* When a pipeline is being designed as a part of a larger system, the pipeline under design might be forced to use an external clock source whose timing is fixed *a priori*. Even when the pipeline is designed separately, the designer might want to optimize the speed and limit the slowest clock rate. In other words, the scheduling must be done in such a way that each

subtask can be completed within a clock cycle, inclusive of any stage latch delays.[3]

- *Minimum Required Performance:* When the minimum required performance is given as a design constraint, scheduling and operator allocation must be accomplished such that the effective execution speed of the pipeline considering resynchronization overheads, as given in Equation 4.3, meets the performance constraint.

2.5.1. Cost-Constrained Scheduling and Operator Allocation

There are two types of scheduling and operator allocation depending on the user constraint: *cost-constrained* and *performance-constrained*. When the user specifies the constraint to be cost (for example, the area of the design should not exceed 200 mil^2), the pipeline under design should not exceed the specified cost and should maximize performance (speed). For this type of scheduling, budgeting the number of modules required for implementation is done first.

With execution overlap or not, the number of modules required for any task or subtask executed during a single clock cycle cannot exceed the total number of available modules. For pipelining, all the modules allocated to a subtask are activated during the clock cycle executing that subtask. Accordingly, the first restriction on scheduling and operator allocation can be stated as follows:

Let R_i be the set of operators to be allocated to a subtask F_i, and R_{total} be the total set of available operators. Then the operator allocation must satisfy the following condition for all i:

$$R_i \subseteq R_{total} \land \bigcup_i R_i \subseteq R_{total} \tag{4.4}$$

Since subtasks of different tasks may have execution overlap, Equation 4.4 is not a sufficient condition for conflict-free operator allocation. When multiple subtasks are to be executed in a given clock cycle, the set of operators the subtasks utilize must be disjoint.

---

[3] Some researchers [5] allow subtasks to be pipelined. In this case the subtasks might be performed over multiple cycles. Since subtask partitioning into pipeline stages is known a priori, the same theory described here can be applied by treating each partition as a separate subtask.

Theorem 4.1. *For a schedule of a task partitioned into n subtasks F_1 through F_n, a fixed latency of l can be used if and only if the operator allocation satisfied the following condition for every i, $1 \leq i \leq l$, and*

for all k, $0 \leq k \leq \left\lfloor \dfrac{n-1}{l} \right\rfloor$,

$$\bigcap_k R_{i+kl} = \emptyset \qquad\qquad (4.5)$$

Proof: If a new task is initiated at every initiation interval, for every

$i, 1 \leq i \leq l$, the subtasks $F_{i+kl}, 0 \leq k \leq \left\lfloor \dfrac{n-1}{l} \right\rfloor$ of k consecutive tasks

are executed during the same clock cycle. If any initiations are skipped, a subset of subtasks in this set is executed during the same clock cycle. Therefore, the condition in Equation 4.5 is a necessary and sufficient condition for conflict-free operator allocation.

A corollary to this theorem deals with which subtasks can share the same module.

Corollary 4.1.   *For a schedule of a task partitioned into n subtasks F_1 through F_n, if a fixed latency l is used, for any i, $1 \leq i \leq l$, any two*

subtasks which are not in the same set $F_{i+kl}, 0 \leq k \leq \left\lfloor \dfrac{n-1}{l} \right\rfloor$, can

share the same module without any operator conflict.

Figure 4.10 shows examples of cost-constrained scheduling and operator allocation. Figure 10(a) shows a data flow graph with five addition operations (+1 through +5) and two multiplication operations (X1 and X2). Assuming that there are two adders A_1 and A_2, and a multiplier M_1, Figures 4.10b and 4.10c show two possible schedules and operator allocations. In case (b), any fixed latency from one to four will cause operator conflicts. Fixed latencies one, three and four will cause operator conflicts between any two consecutive initiations of tasks. In the case when the fixed latency is two, there will be operator conflicts between every other initiation of the tasks, that is, between F_5 of a task and F_1 two tasks later, for the adder A_1. In case (c), the length of the pipe is increased by one over (b). This schedule and operator allocation can be implemented with fixed latency of three. Figure 4.11 shows the average performance of each case (b and

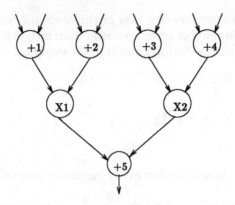

(a) A Data Flow Graph

Subtask	Operation	Resource
F1	+1, +2	A1, A2
F2	+3, +4	A1, A2
F3	X1	M1
F4	X2	M1
F5	+5	A1

(b) A Five Cycle Schedule

Subtask	Operation	Resource
F1	+1	A1
F2	+2, +3	A1, A2
F3	+4	A2
F4	X1	M1
F5	X2	M1
F6	+5	A1

(c) A Six Cycle Schedule

Figure 4.10. Example of Cost-Constrained Scheduling and Operator Allocation.

c) with varying resynchronization. The graph shows how T of each schedule varies with average resynchronization (Equation 4.3). The clock cycle is assumed to be ten units of time, and the latency of schedule (b) is five. Note that the longer pipe actually has better performance until the resynchronization rate is about 70%. Then, case (b) is superior.

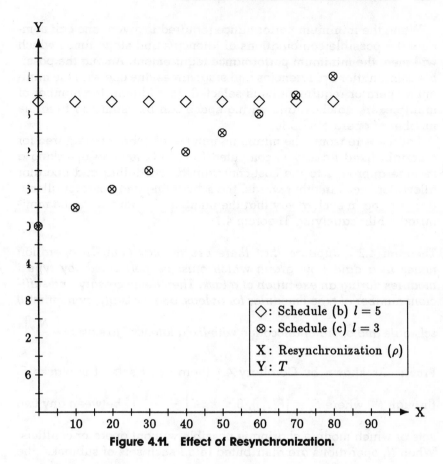

Figure 4.11.   Effect of Resynchronization.

2.5.2. Performance-Constrained Scheduling and Operator Allocation

As mentioned earlier (Section 2.5.1), this is the second of the two types of scheduling approaches. In performance-constrained scheduling, the user specifies some design constraint (for example, the pipeline should produce a result every 200 ns). The pipeline under design must be able to meet this throughput requirement and at the same time minimize the area of implementation.

As discussed in Section 2.4 the speed of the pipeline is determined by the fixed latency, the clock cycle time, the length of the pipe cycle, and the resynchronization rate. Among them, the fixed latency and the clock cycle time determine the maximum possible initiation rate.

When the minimum performance required is given, one can compute the possible combinations of latencies and stage times which will meet the minimum performance requirement. Among the possible combinations of latencies and stage times, the one with the minimum operator requirements is selected. In addition, the number of multiplexers, latches, and wiring space can be estimated from the number of operators [15,16].

For these reasons, the minimum number of operators required for a certain fixed latency is computed first. This is done by taking a reverse approach to the cost-constrained scheduling and operator allocation case. In other words, the scheduling and operator allocation is done in such a way that the number of modules can be minimized while satisfying Theorem 4.1.

Theorem 4.2. *Suppose that there are at maximum N_i operation nodes in a data flow graph which must be performed[4] by type i modules during an execution of a task. Then the necessary and sufficient number of type i modules for at least one (possibly, nonoptimal) schedule and operator allocation with fixed latency l to exist is* $\left\lceil \dfrac{N_i}{l} \right\rceil$.

Proof: As shown by Corollary 4.1 there are l sets of subtasks F_1 through F_l, where $F_i = \{F_{i+kl}\}$, $0 \leq k \leq \left\lceil \dfrac{n-1}{l} \right\rceil$, between any two sets of which module sharing is possible without operator conflicts. When N_i operations are distributed into l such sets of subtasks, the smallest possible maximum number of operations in a set is $\left\lceil \dfrac{N_i}{l} \right\rceil$ (sufficient condition). Since all the modules in each such set of subtasks must be active during the same cycle, $\left\lceil \dfrac{N_i}{l} \right\rceil$ is the minimum number of type i modules necessary (necessary condition).

A corollary states the relationships between module usages and latency.

---

[4] Any number of mutually exclusive operations which use the same module are counted as one.

Corollary 4.2. *When a fixed latency l is used, as long as a module is not used in any two clock cycles which are l cycles apart, there is no operator conflict. Accordingly, a module can be used in a maximum of l subtasks whose indices modulo-l are distinct and* (0,1,2,....,l − 1).

Thus to design a pipeline for the data flow graph given in Figure 4.10, with latency $l = 2$, $\lceil \frac{3}{2} \rceil = 3$ adders and $\lceil \frac{2}{2} \rceil = 1$ multiplier will be needed.

2.5.3. Mutually Exclusive Operations

Determining sharing of operators across conditional branches is a difficult task. In this section, the above theory of scheduling and operator allocation will be applied to data flow graphs with conditional branches. There are two kinds of operator sharing:

1. Between operations across nonoverlapping time steps.
2. Between mutually exclusive operations.

Unconditional operator sharing shares operators across non-overlapping time steps and conditional operator sharing occurs between mutually exclusive operations. The maximum unconditional operator sharing is determined by the number of modules (from Corollary 4.2) and the chosen latency. Corollary 4.2 specifies how many times a module can be used during a computation of a task.

Conditional operator sharing does not depend on either the latency or the number of available modules. Instead, it specifies how an instance of usage of a module can be shared between mutually exclusive operations. For example, suppose that a module is assigned to certain time steps according to the unconditional sharing rules. In a time step where such a module is assigned, this module can be used exactly once that time step. Conversely, since only one of the mutually exclusive operations is actually performed, all the mutually exclusive operations in a time step which can be performed by a given module can be assigned to the same module without operator conflict. Conditional operator sharing across time steps is unpredictable however, and thus not always possible. This is illustrated by an example.

In the data flow graph of Figure 4.12, there are one each of unconditional addition and subtraction nodes and two conditional additions and subtractions. Thus, at most two additions and two subtractions are performed during an execution of the data flow graph.

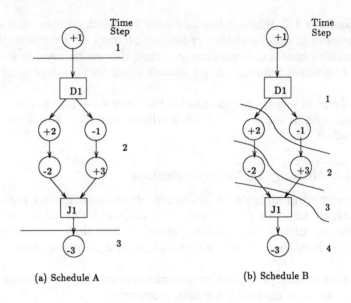

(a) Schedule A   (b) Schedule B

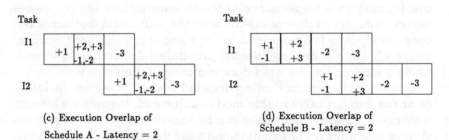

(c) Execution Overlap of
Schedule A - Latency = 2

(d) Execution Overlap of
Schedule B - Latency = 2

Figure 4.12. Operator Sharing Among Mutually Exclusive Operations.

Suppose that the design has one adder and one subtractor. Then, according to Theorem 4.2 the minimum possible latency is two. In schedule A, the two mutually exclusive subtractions, -1 and -2, are scheduled in the same time step. The two additions, +2 and +3, are assigned to the same time step also. As shown in (c), with schedule A, a fixed latency of two can be used without any operator conflict. In schedule B, two mutually exclusive subtractions, -1 and -2, are scheduled in time steps 1 and 3, respectively. With this schedule, a fixed latency of two can cause operator conflict. In the timing diagram of (d), if the -2 operation is selected in task I1, while operation -1 is selected in task I2, there will be an operator conflict as there is only one subtractor.

It is difficult to detect when operators can be shared when conditional branches are present unless exhaustive search is performed. For this reason, current algorithms based on the theory discussed in this chapter allow operator sharing across conditional branches only in the same time step. Mutually exclusive operations are determined using the *node coloring algorithm* given in Section 2.5.4.

The node coloring algorithm assigns a color code consisting of a sequence of one or more integers to each node. Testing of mutual exclusion between any two nodes can be done by simply comparing the color codes of the nodes. Whenever a task is partitioned into subtasks, it is verified that a sufficient number of modules exist. Conversely, if the task partitioning is completed, the minimum and maximum number of required modules is computed. Further, whenever an operation is assigned to a module, a check is performed to determine if the operation could be assigned to a previously used module, or a new module is required. All these design tasks require the knowledge of mutual exclusion between any two operations which can share a module. Moreover, partitioning and operator allocation tasks are repeated several times to produce a variety of pipeline designs. Thus, a fast mutual exclusion testing algorithm is necessary.

2.5.4. A Node Coloring Algorithm and Test for Mutual Exclusion

An overview of the node coloring algorithm is given here along with a working algorithm. Figure 4.13 shows the data flow graph used for the example. In this figure, the circles represent actual operation nodes and the squares represent distribution and join nodes. D_i and J_i are a matching pair of distribution join nodes forming a distribute-join block.

Definition 4.2. *A distribute-join block, $D_i - J_i$, is a subgraph of a data flow graph consisting of all edges and nodes that can be reached from the distribution node D_i and terminating at join node J_i.*

Definition 4.3. *An outermost distribute-join block is a maximal distribute-join block which is not a part of any other larger distribute-join block.*

Referring to Figure 4.13, the color code of each node is parenthesized. The length of the color code represents the number of levels of distribute-join blocks the node is nested in. A single digit color code signifies that the node is not in any conditional block. Any node

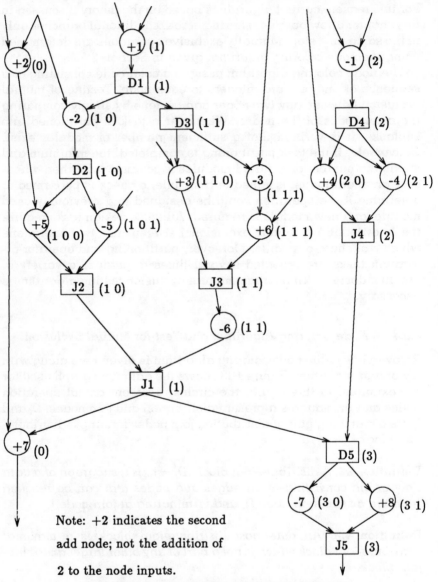

Note: +2 indicates the second

add node; not the addition of

2 to the node inputs.

Figure 4.13. A Node Colored Data Flow Graph.

within a conditional block has a color code with length two or greater. The rules for coloring are given as follows:

1. Unconditional operations, including any outermost-level distribute and join nodes, NOP nodes, and SELECT nodes have a single element code sequence. For example in Figure 4.13 the following colors are assigned: (0) for $+2$, (1) for D_1, and (3) for J_4. Any operation (or nonoperation) that is conditionally executed has a color code of length at least 2. For example, node -2 has color (1 0).

2. In an outermost distribute-join block, the first element in the code sequences of all the nodes within that block is the same. For example, D_1 is assigned (1), D_3 is assigned (1 1), and $+3$ is assigned (1 1 0).

3. The common first element of the color codes in any outermost distribute-join block is uniquely defined. Example: (1) for D_1 and (2) for D_4.

4. For any distribution node with a color code of length i, every child node except its matching join node has a color code length of at least $i + 1$, where the first i elements are the same as the distribution node's and the $i + 1^{th}$ element is a unique integer amongst its children. For example, $+3$ has a color (1 1 0) and -3 has a color (1 1 1).

5. A join node has the same color as its matching distribute node. Example: (1) for D_1 and J_1.

6. For any two connected nodes, if both are either conditional or unconditional and neither of them is a distribute or join node, they have the same color. Example: (0) for $+2$ and $+7$. Note that by this rule, the $+5$ node inherited its color from D_2 and not from $+2$.

The complete details of the node coloring algorithm are given in Figure 4.14. The runtime complexity of this algorithm for a data flow graph with n nodes is $O(n^2)$. Each node can be in the wavefront, WF, only once. For each node in WF there can be at most n children, and thus the inner loop iterates at most n times for each node in WF. One iteration of the loop (the CASE statement) takes a constant number of steps. Therefore, the time complexity is $O(n^2)$. However, if the fanout of each node is limited to some value m, then the inner loop will be executed at maximum m times for every node, which makes the complexity of the algorithm $O(mn)$. If m is a constant, then the complexity reduces to linear.

Mutual exclusion testing between two operations in different par-

```
BEGIN  /* coloring */
/* Phase 1: Initialization */
1. color-code = 0.  /* initialize color palette */
2. {roots} = set of all root nodes.
3. FOR EVERY node in {root} DO
color[node] = color-code.
color-code = color-code +1.
4. WF = all root nodes.  /* initializing the coloring wavefront */
/* Phase 2: Color Wave Propagation */
5. FOR EVERY node in WF DO
FOR EVERY child of node DO
   CASE node OF BEGIN  /* case */
   DISTRIBUTE: IF (child is join) THEN color[child] = color[node]
ELSE color[child] = APPEND(color[node], child#).
/* append child# to node's color */
   JOIN: IF (node has a single digit color) THEN
color[node] = color-code. color-code = color-code +1.
  IF (child is a join) and (previous color of child has less
      # of digits than node) THEN
color[child] = REMOVE(color[node], child#).
/* delete last digit from node's color */
  ELSE
IF (previous color of child has less # of digits than node's)
color[child] = color[node].
   OTHERS: IF (child is a join) and (previous color of child has
       less # of digits than nodes) THEN
   color[child] = REMOVE(color[node], child#)
   ELSE IF(previous color of child has less # of digits
than node's) THEN
   color[child] = APPEND(color[node], child#).
   END /* case */
END  /* child */
      END /* node */
6. WF = All new children of the nodes in WF all of whose parents are
  already colored.  /* Choose New Wavefront */
7. IF (WF NOT EMPTY) GO TO 5.
END
```

Figure 4.14. Node Coloring Algorithm.

allel distribute-join blocks is a debatable case. For example, in Figure 4.13, are the nodes -4 and -3 mutually exclusive or not? The answer to such a question varies. If the condition selecting the -3 operation in $D_3 - J_3$ block always falsifies the condition selecting the -4 operation in $D_4 - J_4$ block and vice versa, then the two operations are mutually exclusive. However, such a case is exceptional and seldom expected to occur. Even if there is such a case, such parallel conditional blocks with very tight control dependency would tend to be merged together. For the sake of completeness and safety, -3 and -4 will be treated as nonmutually exclusive operations.

The outline of the mutual exclusion testing procedure for any two nodes in a data flow graph is as follows:

1. IF either of the two nodes have single element color code sequence, THEN the nodes are not mutually exclusive. By Rule 1 of the color assignment algorithm, at least one node is not a conditional node.
2. IF the first elements of the color codes are different, THEN the nodes are not mutually exclusive. By Rule 2, these nodes are in different outermost distribute-join blocks.
3. IF two color codes are identical, THEN the nodes are not mutually exclusive and STOP. By Rule 6, there is a data dependency between these two nodes, and if one is executed, then the other must be executed.
4. IF two color codes are not identical but of same length THEN the nodes are mutually exclusive. By Rule 4, these nodes have a distribution node as their closest common ancestor, thus, they are mutually exclusive.
5. IF none of the conditions in Steps 1 through 4 is true (i.e., both color codes have more than one digit with the same first digit but their lengths are different), THEN delete the last element from the longer color code until both the color codes have the same length (i.e., trace back from the more deeply nested node, say n_l, to its closest ancestor that is in the same level as the other node under comparison). If the closest ancestor of n_l is mutually exclusive with the other node, then n_l is also mutually exclusive with the other node.
6. IF the two color codes resulting from Step 5 are identical, THEN the nodes are not mutually exclusive. There is a data dependency between the two nodes as per Rule 6.
7. ELSE the nodes are mutually exclusive.

All sets of mutually exclusive nodes of the same function type in the data flow graph of Figure 4.13 are listed below:

- -2 (1 0) and -3 (1 1 1),
- -2 (1 0) and -6 (1 1),
- -3 (1 1 1) and -5 (1 0 1),
- -5 (1 0 1) and -6 (1 1), and
- +5 (1 0 0), +3 (1 1 0) and +6 (1 1 1).

As mentioned earlier, in order to compute the minimum necessary set of modules, the maximum number of operations which are actually performed during an execution of a task is necessary. Usage of modules of type M can be computed as the sum of (a) the number of unconditional operations assigned to module type M, and (b) for every outermost distribute-join block, the maximum number of conditional operations using type M modules on a directed path in it.

The first item sums all the unconditional operation nodes (using type M modules) which must always be performed. The second item sums the maximum possible number of actual usages of type M modules in each outermost distribute-join block. Since no operations across the outermost distribute-join blocks are mutually exclusive, this is the minimum necessary number of uses of module type M.

An example showing the computation of the number of subtraction nodes in Figure 4.13 is described. There is only one unconditional subtraction node, -1. In the $D_1 - J_1$ block, the maximum number of subtraction operations is 2 (either -2 and -5, or -3 and -6). Both the $D_4 - J_4$ and $D_5 - J_5$ blocks have one subtraction operation. Thus the total number of subtraction uses in Figure 4.13 is $1 + 2 + 1 + 1 = 5$. The number of addition uses can be computed as follows. There are three unconditional addition nodes, +1, +2 and +7. Nodes +4 and +8 do not have any addition operations to which they are mutually exclusive. In $D_1 - J_1$, +5, +3, and +6 are all mutually exclusive to each other. Thus the total use of add modules is $3 + 2 + 1 = 6$.

If the total number of operations actually performed using a certain type of module is known, then the minimum number of modules required for a design with fixed latency can be computed easily using Theorem 4.2. Conversely, if there are M_i modules of type i, then the minimum latency of the design can be fixed.

3. AREA-TIME ESTIMATION

Synthesizing data paths automatically is computationally expensive for production designs. Many trial synthesis passes or computations have to be made before a final design is arrived at. Experimentation with different module sets, operator allocation, and scheduling have to be made during this process. Thus, if one could predict where optimal design points lie in the design space, search for a satisfactory design could be narrowed considerably. In this section, a prediction tool—developed as a part of the University of Southern California's ADAM system—is presented. This technique works in conjunction with Sehwa. However, the technique is general and is applicable to any pipeline synthesis system.

Given a data flow graph which specifies the required behavior of the hardware to be synthesized, and a set of possible module types which implement the operations, the technique to be presented here is able to predict an area-time curve in the design space which forms a lower bound for all possible designs; all the design points lie either on the curve, or above it. Design points which lie on the curve itself represent optimal designs.

The area-time estimation model predicts the design points in the design space for operator optimal designs. The area-time tradeoff curve is estimated to have the shape $AT = k$ where k is a constant, and is a *lower bound estimate* on the cost-speed curve of the resulting design. Theoretical results obtained from these lower bound estimates have been verified through designs generated by Sehwa using exhaustive search. (Sehwa produces near-optimal designs and hence such a comparison is possible.)

Before presenting the formal approach, an intuitive feeling for the area-time estimation model using an example is given. Suppose there is a data flow graph with six addition operations. If the latency of the design (that is, the number of clock cycles between two successive inputs) is three, the design will require at least $6/3 = 2$ add modules. Similarly, if the latency of the design is two, then the design will require at least $6/2 = 3$ add modules. This concept leads to the more formal area-time estimation procedure.

Definition 4.4. *An operator-optimal design is one in which every module produces a useful result every clock cycle.*

3.1. Basic Assumptions

In developing an area-delay estimation model for pipelined designs, it is assumed that the module set is predetermined and fixed. The estimation procedure assumes that resynchronization does not occur. As the estimation technique gives a lower bound, this assumption is valid. The following definition will be starting point for the estimation technique.

Definition 4.5. *The utilization of each module $0 \leq i \leq m - 1$ is defined as*

$$u_i = \frac{n_i}{l \times o_i} \tag{4.6}$$

n_i is the effective number of nodes of operation type i. For a data flow graph with no conditional branches, this is the same n_i defined in

Section 2.2. For a data flow graph with conditional branches, computation of n_i is described in Section 2.5.4.

A utilization of one is *operator-optimal*. Of course, in practical pipeline designs, it is often not possible to utilize all the operators in every cycle, yielding suboptimal designs.

3.2. Determining the Clock Cycle For Optimal Design

Prior to estimating the AT curve itself, the value of clock cycle which is used for the lower bound estimates is derived. This value is dependent on the delays (d_i) of the modules which implement the various operations of the data flow graph and is computed as follows.

Theorem 4.3. *For a operator-optimal design, c = maximum(d_i), where the maximum is taken over all modules used in the final implementation.*

Proof: For an optimal design, $u_i = 1$ and Equation 6 reduces to

$$o_i = \frac{n_i}{1}$$

From the definition of total functional area A (Section 2.2),

$$A = \sum_{i=0}^{m-1} (a_i \times o_i) = \sum_{i=0}^{m-1} \left(a_i \times \frac{n_i}{1} \right)$$

For a given module set, a_i is constant. Likewise, for the given data flow graph n_i is a constant. Hence *for a fixed value of latency*, the total area of the operator-optimal design becomes a constant. Consider two pipeline designs of the same data flow graph with the same latency, and hence same area, but different clock cycles. The design with lower clock cycle will have a lower[5] AT (as the latency and area of the two designs is the same).[6] Under the above assumptions, the minimum value c can take is maximum(d_i).

As this argument holds good for every value of latency, and for every value of latency the minimum value of c = maximum(d_i), we conclude that for lower bound estimates, c = maximum(d_i).

---

[5] With zero resynchronization, $T = lc$ (from Equation 4.3).

[6] The reason for comparing $A \times T$ of two designs will become apparent after the next section.

3.3. Operator Estimation

Having estimated the optimal value of the clock cycle, the optimal number of operators required for each latency will be determined, and used in predicting the area-time tradeoff curve for pipelined designs. Using Definition 4.5, the estimation technique is based on the following theorem.

Theorem 4.4. *Given a data flow graph, for operator-optimal pipeline design* $\forall_i u_i = 1$, $(AT)_{min} = constant$, *where* $(AT)_{min}$ *is the lower bound of all possible ATs for that graph.*

Proof: For any operator, $l \geq n_i / o_i$ (Theorem 4.2). For the particular case where the operator i is utilized every clock cycle, which is the best case,

$$l \times o_i = n_i \qquad (4.7)$$

and therefore,

$$l \times a_i \times o_i = a_i \times n_i$$

Summing this over m operations and multiplying by the clock cycle,

$$c \times l \sum_{i=0}^{m-1} (a_i \times o_i) = c \sum_{i=0}^{m-1} (a_i \times n_i)$$

$$A \times T = c \sum_{i=0}^{m-1} (a_i \times n_i) \qquad (4.8)$$

For a given data flow graph and a module set, the right hand side is a constant, and hence

$$(AT)_{min} = constant \qquad (4.9)$$

Theorem 4.4 predicts a curve $(AT)_{min} = constant$ for optimal designs. This means that for every possible latency and for all operators i, $u_i = 1$. For many data flow graphs, $u_i \neq 1$, and hence $(AT)_{min} = constant$ is not possible for every latency and every operator. In this case, a lower bound curve $(AT)_{lb}$ can be computed. The estimation technique given in Figure 4.15 calculates $(AT)_{lb}$. Algorithm AT is executed n_i times with latency l varying from 1 to n_i to get n_i design points. A

procedure *estimate_lower_bound(l)*
begin

for $0 \leq i < m$ calculate $o_i = \lceil n_i/l \rceil$;
for $0 \leq i < m$ calculate $A = A + o_i \times a_i$;
$c = maximum(d_i)$;
$T = c \times l$;
print $A \times T$;

end;

Figure 4.15.   Algorithm 1—Procedure to Estimate $(AT)_{lb}$.

lower-bound curve is composed of all the design points generated by Algorithm AT and may be different from an operator-optimal curve. This difference is illustrated by an example: Consider a data flow graph with three add operations. If latency is one, then three adders will be necessary for the design, and every adder will be kept busy every clock cycle. This design is operator-optimal and is also a lower-bound design point. However, if the latency is two, we shall need two adders. In this case there will be one adder which will lie idle for one clock cycle. This design point is not operator-optimal, however it is the lower-bound because for latency equal to two we cannot achieve a better design. In Algorithm AT, whenever the equality $[n_i/l] = n_i/l$ holds we have the case where an operator-optimal design is the same as the lower-bound design. Thus, if the design points generated by Algorithm AT for all values of latency are operator-optimal, the $(AT)_{min}$ curve is identical to the lower bound $(AT)_{lb}$ curve.

A design with the above computed minimum $(AT)_{min}$ or $(AT)_{lb}$ may not exist. In fact, the best possible actual design might not be one with a minimum clock cycle. However, there can be no design which will have an AT curve lower than the one computed by Algorithm AT under the above assumptions.

3.4. Experiments and Results

Several experiments using the pipeline synthesis program Sehwa [4] and the estimation technique presented in Section 3 were conducted. The experiments were conducted using the module parameters given in Table 4.1. These parameters were obtained from an area estimation program, PLEST [16].

Of the several experiments which were conducted, results of three

Table 4.1. Module Parameters.

Module	Area mil^2	Delay nS
adder	4200	340
subtractor	4200	340
multiplier	49000	375

data flow graphs [12] are presented in Tables 4.2 through 4.4. These data flow graphs are representative of three different types of computing: (i) a signal processing algorithm (SR Graph) which is very structured and has no conditional branches; (ii) a data flow graph with several conditional branches (C Graph) (Figure 4.13); and (iii) a data flow graph generated using a random number generater (R Graph).

Table 4.2. Results for SR Graph.

	Sehwa		Estimation Algorithm	
Latency	Clock Cycle	Area	Clock Cycle	Area
1	375	834400	375	834400
2	375	417200	375	417200
3	375	310800	375	310800
4	375	208600	375	208600
5	375	208600	375	208600
6	375	155400	375	155400
7	375	155400	375	155400
8	375	106400	375	106400
9	375	106400	375	106400
10	375	106400	375	106400
11	375	106400	375	106400
12	375	102200	375	102200
13	375	102200	375	102200
14	no result		375	102200
15	no result		375	102200
16	375	53200	375	53200

Table 4.3.   Results for C Graph.

Latency	Sehwa		Estimation Algorithm	
	Clock Cycle	Area	Clock Cycle	Area
1	340	46200	340	46200
2	340	25200	340	25200
3	340	16800	340	16800
4	340	16800	340	16800
5	340	12600	340	12600
6	340	8400	340	8400

Table 4.4.   Results for R Graph.

Latency	Sehwa		Estimation Algorithm	
	Clock Cycle	Area	Clock Cycle	Area
1	375	207200	375	207200
2	375	107800	375	107800
3	375	86800	375	86800
4	375	82600	375	82600
5	375	74200	375	74200
6	375	70000	375	70000
7	375	70000	375	70000
8	no result		375	70000
9	375	61600	375	61600
10	375	61600	375	61600
11	no result		375	61600
12	no result		375	61600
13	no result		375	61600
14	no result		375	61600
15	no result		375	61600
16	no result		375	61600
17	375	57400	375	57400

Sehwa produces the best result given a design constraint. As such it misses several *bad* designs. For example, in Table 4.2 Sehwa does not produce a result for latencies 14 and 15. This is because, a design with latencies 14 or 15 is inferior to a design with latency 13. Furthermore, the design with latency 13 meets all the design constraints (area and speed) of the designs with latencies 14 and 15.

As seen from Tables 4.2 through 4.4, the results produced by Sehwa are identical to the estimation technique. The experiments show that Sehwa produces optimal results in several cases and that the estimation tool is accurate. The results of the remaining experiments using other data flow graphs were identical.

4. CONCLUSION

The theory presented in this chapter has provided the basis for the Sehwa pipeline synthesis program. Sehwa is operational, and has been tested with a number of signal processing problems, along with other examples.

This theory has been used to predict the area-time tradeoff curve for designs which are too large for the current version of Sehwa [4] to handle, and for designs where the design space is too large to search with Sehwa. The theory has also been used for a module selection program which is a preprocessor to Sehwa [17].

Future plans include the use of the theory to predict the quality of manual designs and partially completed designs, along with extensions to Sehwa to handle partially completed designs.

REFERENCES

1. P.M. Kogge, *The Architecture of Pipelined Computers*, McGraw-Hill, New York, 1981.
2. M.R. Garey and D.S. Johnson, *Computers and Intractability: A Guide to the Theory of NP-Completeness*, W.H. Freeman, New York, 1979.
3. E. Girczyc, "Loop Winding—A Data Flow Approach to Functional Programming," *IEEE International Symposium on Circuits and Systems*, Philadelphia, PA, May 1987.
4. N. Park, "Synthesis of High-Speed Digital Systems," Ph.D. Thesis, University of Southern California, Los Angeles, CA, 1985.
5. P.G. Paulin and J.P. Knight, "Force-Directed Automatic Datapath Synthesis," *Proceedings of the 24th Design Automation Conference*, June 1987.
6. A.C. Parker and S. Hayati, "Automating the VLSI Design Process Using

Expert and Silicon Compilation," *Proceedings of the IEEE*, Vol. 75, No. 6, June 1987.

7. K. Hwang and F.A. Briggs, *Computer Architecture and Parallel Processing*, McGraw-Hill, New York, 1984.

8. M. Davio, J.P. Deschamps and A. Thayse, *Digital Systems With Algorithm Implementation*, John Wiley, New York, 1983.

9. J. Granacki, D. Knapp and A.C. Parker, "The ADAM Advanced Design Automation System: Overview, Planner and Natural Language Interface," *Proceedings of the 22nd Design Automation Conference*, Las Vegas, NV, June 1985.

10. F.J. Kurdahi and A.C. Parker, "REAL: A Program for Register Allocation," *Proceedings of the 24th Design Automation Conference*, Miami, FL, June 1987.

11. A. Hashimoto and J. Stevens, "Wire Routing by Optimizing Channel Assignment Within Large Apertures," *Proceedings of the 8th DA Workshop*, Atlantic City, NJ, 1971.

12. R. Jain, A.C. Parker and N. Park, "Predicting Area-Time Tradeoffs for Pipelined Designs," *Proceedings of the 24th Design Automation Conference*, Miami, FL, June 1987.

13. J.B. Dennis, "First Version of Data Flow Procedure Language," *Lecture Notes in Computer Science*, Springer-Verlag, New York, 1974.

14. E.A. Snow, "Automation of Module Set Independent Register-Transfer Level Design," Ph.D. Thesis, Carnegie-Mellon University, Pittsburgh, PA, 1978.

15. S. Sastry, "Wiring Space Estimation of Master Slice IC's," Technical Report, Digital Integrated Systems Center, University of Southern California, Los Angeles, CA, 1983.

16. F.J. Kurdahi and A. Parker, "PLEST: A Program for Area Estimation of VLSI Integrated Circuits," *Proceedings of the 23rd Design Automation Conference*, Las Vegas, NV, June 1986.

17. R. Jain, A.C. Parker and N. Park, "Module Section for Pipelined Designs," Technical Report CRI-87-59, University of Southern California, Los Angeles, CA, 1987.

18. M. Barbacci, "Instruction Set Processor Specification (ISIP): The Notation and its Applications," *IEEE Transactions on Computers*, Vol. C-30, January 1981.

19. D. Knapp and A.C. Parker, "A Data Structure for VLSI Synthesis and Verification," Technical Report, Digital Integrated Systems Center, University of Southern California, Los Angeles, CA, 1983.

5

VLSI Design Using Caesar and MOSIS: A Detailed Tutorial*

E. J. CHARLSON
E. M. CHARLSON
H. L. GRAHAM

Department of Electrical and Computer Engineering
University of Missouri-Columbia

1. INTRODUCTION

Automation in the design, layout, and simulation of electronic circuits is becoming increasingly important to circuit manufacturers in meeting todays market demand for fast turnaround time. The time between concept and parts delivery is currently being measured in months instead of years as was the case only five years ago. Indeed, one company was able to clone the essential features of the IBM PC AT in only six months [1]. The short turnaround times needed to remain competitive have also put severe restrictions on testing. In some cases the time required for accelerated life tests is not practical and, as a result, technology changes requiring verification are being avoided in many application-specific designs. The only alternative for providing known reliability is to use standard proven technologies designed for a variety of applications. Today most companies making electronic components are moving towards standardized procedures for the whole gamut of manufacturing activity, from design to fabrication.

To participate in this technology, today's engineers and scientists

---

* The authors would like to acknowledge the assistance of Mr. Lynn Diel, system manager of the Engineering Computer Network, for installation and maintenance of the Berkeley tools. G. Ramakrishnan is responsible for the "C" code in Listing II, and Linda Valentine handled all the BITNET transmissions to ISI. The W87 class ECE442 designed the ROM and did the initial simulation.

must assimilate, in a short period of time, the techniques and software associated with computer-aided design and manufacture. While most large companies initially created their own systems for automating this function, recently there has been a trend toward standardization. The use of the Berkeley VLSI design tools [5] and fast turnaround mask generation and silicon foundry services such as MOSIS supports have played a significant role in setting the standards. This chapter will present a detailed look at these two very important facilities for the production of VLSI integrated circuits. While not intended as an instruction manual, the presentation will use specific code and options from the Berkeley Tools and MOSIS. It is the intention of this chapter to provide a brief tutorial for the total process of designing and fabricating a VLSI circuit. Two common digital circuits will be used to illustrate the process, namely, a read-only memory (ROM) and a small random-access memory (RAM). The ROM circuit provides a good example for the design of an array-type combinational logic integrated circuit which is amenable to reprogramming by changing only one mask. The RAM will show the use of standardized cells in both design and simulation.

This chapter is intended for people who have access to both the Berkeley VLSI Design Tools and MOSIS, and who are just beginning the process of learning the capability of these facilities. It is also the intention of this chapter to present this material in such a manner that those who have a general interest in this area may "read through" the code and pick up the general philosophy of automated design of VLSI circuits.

2. FUNDAMENTALS

2.1. Silicon Gate Technology

The fundamental element (individual device) used in this implementation of VLSI is the n-channel silicon gate MOS transistor. This structure is a variation of the basic metal gate MOS which uses polycrystalline silicon (poly) for the gate metal. A principal feature of this device is that the highly doped poly silicon, which acts as a moderate conductivity interconnect line, can be oxidized and crossed-over by aluminum metal lines. This provides a two-level interconnect capability with the minor difficulty that some restrictions must be placed on the current density in the poly silicon.

The process of fabricating a silicon gate MOS is shown in cross-section in Figure 5.1 and in a top view in Figure 5.2. In process (a),

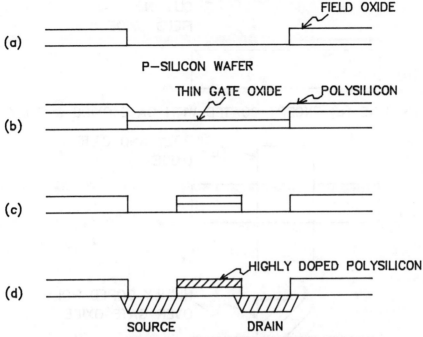

Figure 5.1.   Cross-section of silicon gate MOS process.

the thick field oxide (usually about 10,000 Å thick) is patterned by etching a well (or hole) in the oxide defining the area of the transistor. The field oxide is thick because it supports the metal and poly interconnect lines, which must be more than some minimum distance from the silicon surface to prevent significant inversion. Inversion, which refers to the field-induced conversion of p-type material to n-type material, can cause leakage from adjacent devices under or near the interconnects. A thin oxide is then thermally grown over the entire wafer, followed by chemical vapor deposition of a layer of poly silicon as shown in (b). The poly silicon and underlying gate oxide are next etched, as in (c), to define the gate area. The diffusion which follows is used to dope the regions of the wafer which are not coated with field oxide, as shown in (d). This procedure forms the source and drain regions of the transistor and converts the poly region to a conducting interconnection layer. In the area under the gate, the gate oxide prevents doping of the underlying silicon and thus allows a channel to be formed between source and drain. This process is called self-aligned because the source-drain and gate regions are automatically formed and delineated by physical processes and not by mask alignment. The only overlap between gate

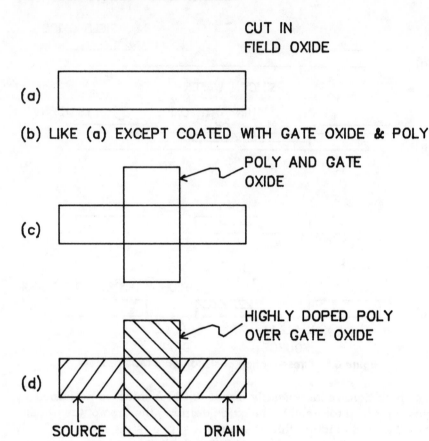

Figure 5.2.   Top view of silicon gate MOS process.

and source-drain is from the lateral component of diffusion that takes place during the formation of the source-drain.

The silicon gate transistor with a load resistor provides us with the basic inverter from which other more complex logic functions can be built. The resistor function can be provided by a transistor connected as a depletion load as shown in Figure 5.3. When connected in this manner, the depletion load transistor approximates a constant current source, as can be seen by observing the mostly flat load line on the current-voltage characteristic curves shown for the inverter. This translates into a steep vertical section on the transfer curve as seen in (c). Using an MOS transistor as the load is preferred to using a planar resistor because of the relatively smaller size. Several references including [3] and [4] describe the design of a depletion load inverter and should be consulted for detail. It is common practice to use a minimum size standard inverter cell and let the compu-

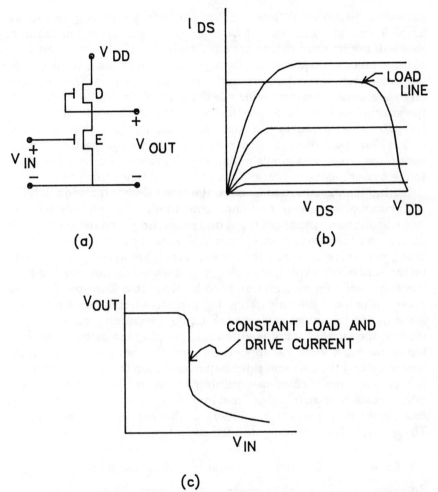

Figure 5.3.   (a) Depletion load inverter (b) current-voltage characteristic with load line and (c) transfer characteristic.

ter do the detailed analysis. A standard inverter cell called shift-cell.ca is included in the Caesar package and can be used as a starting point in the layout. A variation of this basic inverter is shown later in the layout section.

2.2. Circuit Layout

Circuit layout with the Berkeley Tools uses a graphics software package called Caesar, or more recently the upgraded version called Magic. We will refer to this package by the original name since Magic is a superset of Caesar with some advanced features that will not be used in this project. The layout work station consists of three pieces of equipment, the high-resolution color graphics monitor, a monochrome input terminal, and a digitizer pad. The user logs on to the input terminal, which is the primary controller, to call up the various tools and execute the total package. The graphics monitor, which is slaved to the input terminal using a shell program called "sleeper," displays in real time, using the pertinent color codes, the boxes and labels making up the layout. Designs are input to the system using a four-button puck on the digitizer pad.

During the execution of Caesar, the input terminal screen is filled with summaries of long and short commands, leaving only the bottom line to show command input and prompting from the program. It also shows the coordinates of both the locator box and screen cursor, along with information on the files currently being edited. Locations on the screen are visualized using a grid whose modulus is lambda, the universal dimensional unit used by Mead and Conway [6]. Filled boxes, which are the only geometric primitive implemented, are entered by the following sequence. First the lower left corner is set by moving the cursor to that position and pushing the extreme left button on the puck. Next the upper right corner is positioned in a similar fashion using the extreme right button and then the inside of the box is painted with a color designating its layer. The resulting box, whose corners snap to the nearest lambda position, represents areas associated with the various layers of the silicon gate technology. These layers are currently defined as follows.

Layer	Symbol	Color	Monochrome
diffusion	d	green	narrow line
polysilicon	p	red	dashed line
metal	m	blue	wide line
cut	c	black X	black X
implant	i	yellow	dotted line
buried contact	b	brown hash	hash

A simple transistor shown in Figure 5.4 will be used to illustrate the method. First the lower left corner of the diffusion box is placed by positioning the cursor at (0,0) and pushing the extreme left button of the puck. The upper right corner is placed in a similar fashion using the extreme right button on the puck. The resulting box will be outlined in white on the color monitor. To assign this box to layer d,

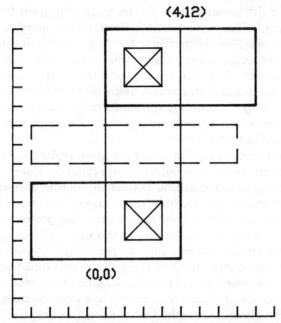

Figure 5.4. Caesar layout of simple silicon gate MOS transistor.

one uses the command :*paint d ENTER* issued on the input terminal. *Enter* is the normal carriage return which terminates each command. Since an *Enter* is usually implied for unprompted entries, it will not be included in subsequent commands given here. After execution of the paint command the area included within the box will appear green on the color monitor and this area will be treated as a diffusion region when a :*save* command has been executed. The polysilicon area is created as explained above with a box at $(-4,5)$ and $(7,7)$ and the command :*paint p*. It should be observed that during diffusion, the polysilicon that covers the diffusion area will prevent dopants from entering the area directly underneath. Thus the union of red and green will define a channel area of p-type material between n-type diffused regions on either side (the source and drain). During this process the poly above the channel becomes doped and serves as a conducting field plate or gate. Therefore everywhere that red crosses green a silicon gate MOS transistor is formed. To complete the structure a contact box is formed at $(1,1)$ and $(3,3)$ with :*paint c* and replicated at $(1,9)$ and $(3,11)$. The cut areas allow an opening to be etched into the field oxide above the diffusion so that contact can be made to the silicon below by the aluminum metal interconnect layer. Finally the metal is placed at $(-4,0)$ and $(4,4)$ and at $(0,8)$ and $(8,12)$.

The use of the lower button on the puck is a great time saver in complex layouts. Its purpose is to eliminate the need to type in the :*paint* command. The button has the capacity to duplicate in the locator box the colored area under the cursor at the time the lower button is pressed. Thus one can place the locator box, move the cursor to an area identical in color to the desired paint, and push the lower button to paint the box automatically. Most users find it advantageous to set up a permanent palette file, containing all of the colors, for use in this manner.

The top button on the puck is used to identify an area of the layout which has been stored as a separate file for subsequent processing. For example to make multiple copies of such a pattern using an array command, the pattern to be duplicated must be identified. This is done by placing the locator box around the pattern to be duplicated and pressing the top button on the puck. This makes the pattern enclosed within the box the "current cell." There are some restrictions on the assignment of the current cell and trial and error seems to be the best way to learn these. One major restriction is that the pattern enclosed within the locator box must be fully expanded. Expansion involves the method of storing the graphic information and will be explained in detail in the Graphics Format section. Use of a file expansion program ciff.l described in that section will eliminate any of the most common restrictions and allow for versatile editing.

2.3. Standard Cells

Because of the highly repetitious nature of VLSI circuits, it is usually possible to identify some circuit primitives, the repeat of which will build the entire circuit. As will be explained later in this chapter the use of these primitives, which will be called standard cells, greatly simplifies simulation and results in very efficient storage in certain graphics protocols. Once these standard cells have been designed and rule-checked, they can be duplicated in the proper locations with :*array* commands. Assuming connections are made properly, if the standard cell works alone, the total array has a high probability of working as designed. The basic philosophy of SPICE, the circuit analysis program, is consistent with standard cells since fundamental circuit elements are modeled with a limited number of model cards. These cards, or blocks of code, contain the detailed information for modeling a limited number of generic devices which make up the overall circuit. Thus the circuit at the highest level is made up of a limited number of identical devices, which are distinguishable only by calls to specific model cards. Since accessing different subroutine calls is time consuming in simulation, it is beneficial to minimize the variety of models. This philosophy will be used in the two design examples that follow.

Several very general ground rules can be stated with regard to the use of the three possible layers for interconnects. These rules ensure small voltage drops across the interconnect for signal level current. Signal paths should be as short as possible and not exceed the following:

Layer	Maximum Length of Path
metal	20,000 lambda
polysilicon	2,000 lambda
diffusion	20 lambda

For greatest accuracy, a rule of thumb is to increase interconnection "area" capacitance by a factor of 0.15 to allow for fringe fields. The following factors should influence the choice of layer for interconnection.

Layer	Relative R	Relative C	Comment
metal	low	low	Good current capacity without large voltage drop. Best for buses.
poly	high	moderate	Moderate RC product. High IR drop.
diffusion	moderate	high	Moderate IR drop but high C, therefore difficult to drive.

The read-only memory (ROM) to be designed will be implemented with conventional combinational OR logic. As a result, the variety of standard cells needed is minimal, since only a standard inverter is required. The general philosophy will be that input lines and their complements will proceed left to right across a decoding plane and enable one and only one intermediate line. This intermediate line will be vertical and selectively enable a group of output lines running horizontally in the lower encoder matrix. Since inputs and their complements will only connect to MOS gates, high sheet resistance poly silicon can be used. With the higher current "output" intermediate lines, metal will be used and these can cross over the poly input lines. The same philosophy will be used for the encoder, with the standard inverters in this case rotated 90° counterclockwise. This will require a changeover from metal to poly in the intermediate lines.

This topology is shown in the stick diagram of Figure 5.5. Stick diagrams, an intermediate design step between circuit diagram and layout, are minimal sketches of layouts using lines to represent layers. Normally these diagrams are in color but they can be used effectively with different line types. Conventions on line types used here follow the layer definitions previously stated. The circuit theory corresponding to this layout will be explained in detail in the ROM design section. At this point, Figure 5.5 should be interpreted as defining the placement and interconnections of the standard cells.

The decoder part of the layout corresponding to the stick diagram of Figure 5.5 is shown in Figure 5.6. Where possible, known transistor shapes for both depletion mode and enhancement mode transistors were used to avoid having to refer repeatedly to design rules. These design rules, used by Mead and Conway [6], define how close layers can be to one another in terms of a single length unit called

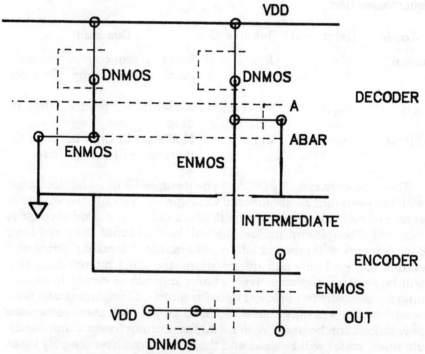

Figure 5.5. Stick pattern for basic ROM pattern.

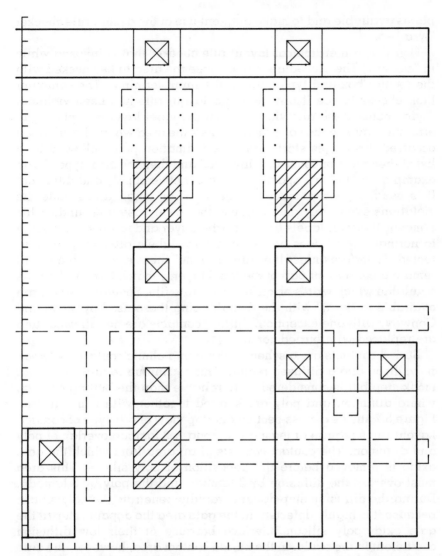

Figure 5.6.   Caesar layout of standard cells showing complementing inverter and intermediate line driver.

lambda. For example diffusion and poly lines, not constituting a transistor,can be no closer than 1 lambda unit. Two parallel poly lines must be separated by at least 2 lambda. These design rules were formulated to ensure that normal technology variations, such as side etching or lateral diffusion, would not cause the circuit to fail. The best approach to using these rules is to have summary color plates available and to make frequent use of the design rule checker "lyra."

"Lyra" is a hierarchical layout rule checker that is invoked while in "caesar." The procedure is to enclose the area to be checked with the locator box and type :lyra on the input terminal. The computer then checks to see if any standard layout rule has been violated. "Lyra" notes these rule violations on the label layer and places an error message on the color monitor near the area where the violation occurred. Messages start with an exclamation point followed by a list of the layers or constructs involved and then the error type. As an example "!P/D_s" is a spacing violation between poly and diffusion. It is usually good practice to run "lyra" on small areas, note the violations separately and then use the lower case u for undo. This removes the error labels from the label layer and returns the display to normal. "lyra" does not remove error labels after they are corrected. Therefore unless they are "undone" these error notations will remain a permanent part of the label layer. A batch form of "Lyra" is available which writes errors to a separate file. Several rule sets are available to "lyra," with the default being those used by Mead and Conway, with one exception. Butting contacts are not allowed, and are replaced with buried contacts [4].

Buried contacts are a scheme for making ohmic contacts between polysilicon and a diffused region. This technique requires an extra mask step but is considered more reliable than the butting contact, where diffusion and poly are shorted together with a metal line. Figure 5.7 shows a cross-section and top view of this type of contact. Layout rules require at least a 2 lambda × 2 lambda overlap of poly and diffusion. The contact consists of an area from which the gate oxide is removed before the deposition of poly silicon. This area must overlap the diffusion by 2 lambda and the poly by 3 lambda. During the diffusion step dopants rapidly penetrate the poly silicon because it is highly defected. In the gate area the dopants stop at the gate oxide/poly silicon interface because of their low diffusion coefficient in the oxide. In the buried contact area, however, the gate oxide has been removed and dopants move down into the diffusion area creating the contact. Buried contacts are used in this layout wherever diffusion and poly must contact each other, including the shorting of the gate and drain in the depletion mode transistors.

A transfer curve showing output voltage versus input voltage for the standard cell inverter is shown in Figure 5.8. The SPICE model for this cell was automatically generated using a circuit extractor, "mextra," and the "sim2spice" file converter as will be explained in the simulation section. A key factor in the shape of the transfer curve

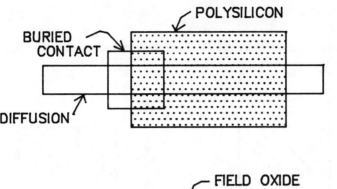

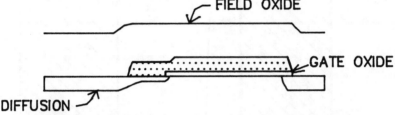

Figure 5.7.   Cross-section and top view of buried contact.

is the location of two defined operating points. Operating points refer to the two points on the transfer curve corresponding to the inverter being off "1" and being on "0," assuming inverters are infinitely cascaded. Thus the state of a given inverter is determined for the case of its input connected to the output of the previous inverter and its output connected to the input of the succeeding inverter.

To determine the two operating points, consider two adjacent inverters in an infinitely cascaded chain. Let va be the input to the first inverter and vc be the output of the second inverter. Then clearly for a stable infinite chain, $va=vc$, either high or low. If one constructs a transfer curve for the inverter *pair* as shown in Figure 5.9, the locus of points representing $va=vc$ will intersect the curve at three points, the lower point being the "0" operating point, and the higher point being the "1" operating point. Note that the center intersection point V_{TH} is not a stable point. That is, if an input in an infinitely cascaded chain of inverters were near this point, subsequent outputs in the chain would not be predictable. It is possible to have a transfer curve for the inverter pair that does not intersect the locus at three points. This would result in a degradation of the high and low signal levels and limit the amount of cascading that would be possible in a given design.

Another important aspect of inverters when used in logic circuits is the degree to which an input or output can be perturbed by a short

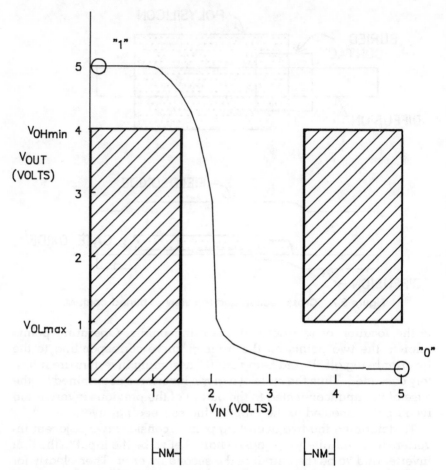

Figure 5.8. Transfer characteristic for standard inverter simulated on SPICE.

duration noise pulse and not cause the inverter to change logic levels. This figure of merit is called the noise margin and is defined as the amount of voltage on the input superimposed on a stable operating point that causes an inverter to switch to the other logic level. In reference to the above two-stage transfer curve, noise margin is the voltage difference between each operating point and the middle intersection point. Since there are two such values, the lesser of the two is considered to be the defined noise margin (NM).

A central issue in the design of a logic circuit is the ability of the inverter to be indefinitely cascaded without responding to the maximum noise expected to be encountered in its application. To design for these criteria, one needs to define the following four voltage levels in relation to the transfer curve.

V_{OHmin} minimum output voltage at logic level "1"
V_{OLmax} maximum output voltage at logic level "0"
V_{IH} minimum gate voltage considered a "1"$<V_{OHmin}-NM$
V_{IL} maximum gate voltage considered a "0"$>V_{OLmax}+NM$

The best way to determine V_{OHmin} and V_{OLmax} is to use experimental data with gates of a fixed design and driven with V_{IL} and V_{IH}, respectively. However, lacking that information, one can estimate these two constants using worst case conditions for transistor parameters and power supplies [7]. For example the worst case conditions for V_{OLmax} would be for

Input voltage V_{IH}
Highest driver transistor threshold voltage
Largest load constant current value
Highest power supply VDD.
Lowest driver transistor gain constant (k_p).

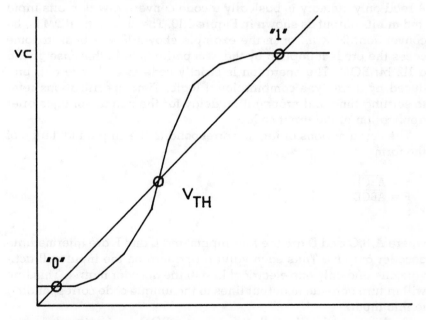

Figure 5.9. Transfer curve for an inverter pair showing the two operating points and threshold point.

By generating a transfer curve in SPICE using the last four conditions and using the first condition for an input voltage, the corresponding output voltage would be a model-determined V_{OLmax}. Parameter V_{OHmin} can be determined in a similar fashion.

Having determined V_{OHmin} and V_{OLmax} and given a noise margin NM_{min}, a convenient way of setting limits on an acceptable transfer curve is to use a graphical approach [8]. First a shaded box is drawn with the lower left corner (0,0) and upper right corner (V_{OLmax}+ NM_{min}, V_{OHmin}), as shown in Figure 5.8. Another box is drawn with lower left corner at ($V_{OHmin}-NM_{min}$, V_{OLmax}) and extended to the limit of the graph up and to the right. If a transfer curve does not cross into the shaded area, one can be assured that the inverter can be indefinitely cascaded and will not change logic levels when noise less than the noise margin is encountered.

3. DESIGN AND LAYOUT

3.1. Read Only Memory

A read only memory is basically a code converter, with n bits input and m bits output as shown in Figure 5.10. The size of the ROM is, by convention, $2^n \times m$, or in the example shown 16 × 7 bits. In some cases the product implied by the × is performed, in this case giving a 112 bit ROM. The operation is strictly code in and code out, produced by array-type combinational logic. Time specifications refer to settling time and propagation delay for the output voltages after application of the input code.

The combinations of inputs correspond to the 2n product terms of the form

$$E = \overline{ABCD}$$
$$F = \overline{ABCD}$$
$$\vdots \quad \vdots$$

where A,B,C and D are the four inputs and E and F are intermediate decoder outputs. Thus each valid bit pattern on the input will activate one and only one electrical line in the decoder matrix. This line will in turn activate m output lines to the unique code corresponding to this input.

To illustrate details of the design of a ROM, a circuit was implemented that takes an input code in hexadecimal format and drives a 7-segment alphanumeric display which has the capability of dis-

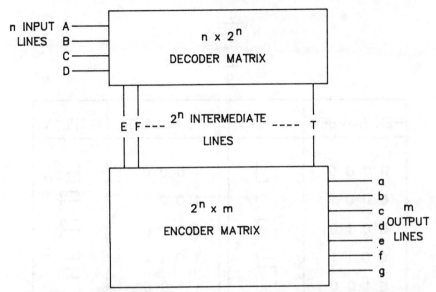

Figure 5.10. ROM block diagram showing general layout scheme for decoder and encoder matrix.

playing the characters 0-9,A-F. This circuit is called a 7-segment decode drive, and standard versions are commercially available. The 7-segment format is shown in Figure 5.11 along with the lower-case segment identification convention for a standard display. Thus for an input of zero, or hexadecimal code 0000, segment d would be unlit, while the remaining segments, a-g, would be lit. This design also involves the use of a set of intermediate lines, labeled E thru T, which correspond to the 16 alphanumeric characters which can be displayed. The appropriate truth table is shown in Figure 5.12. Designations of intermediate state decoder lines corresponding to all possible inputs are shown in Figure 5.13 in what is termed the symbolic decoder matrix. Each column corresponds to a <u>unique</u> product of input combinations, for example E=0000 represents ABCD, F=0001 represents ABCD, and so on. Also shown in Figure 5.13 is the symbolic encoder matrix involving intermediate states E thru T and seven segment outputs a thru g. This matrix is read as follows: With E high, which occurs for a 0 input, column E is 1110111 meaning a,b,c,e,f,g are high and d is low. In the 7-segment display all peripheral segments are lit (high) while the crossbar d is unlit. This forms the required 0 figure on the output.

A standard method of implementing this coding is shown in Figure 5.14. Here the complements of all inputs are formed. Consider the

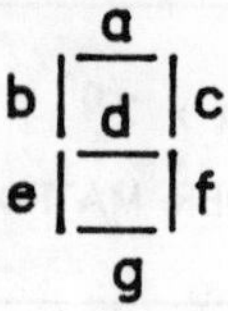

HEX NUMBER	DISPLAY	HEX NUMBER	DISPLAY
0 0 0 0		1 0 0 0	
0 0 0 1		1 0 0 1	
0 0 1 0		1 0 1 0	
0 0 1 1		1 0 1 1	
0 1 0 0		1 1 0 0	
0 1 0 1		1 1 0 1	
0 1 1 0		1 1 1 0	
0 1 1 1		1 1 1 1	

Figure 5.11. Seven segment display format and hexadecimal conversion code to lower case alpha-numeric representation.

E column on the decoder matrix. Every input line (A through D) is connected to the gate of an enhancement mode MOS transistor in this column. The drain of each of these MOS transistors is connected to VDD through a resistor and the sources are connected to ground. Thus when the input is 0000, all four MOS transistors have zero gate voltage and consequently are turned off. Since there is no conducting path between column E and ground, that intermediate line will remain high. A similar connection scheme exists between the complements of the input lines and the gates of MOS transistors which results in a high gate voltage where there is a 1 in the matrix of Figure 5.13. The principle behind this scheme is that there will be only one unique combination of bits on the input that will allow the intermediate line to remain high. In the case of input code 0000, gates of all transistors tying line E to ground will be low, allowing the line to remain high. Any of the other 15 combinations will have at

ABCD	abcdefg
0000	1110111
0001	0010010
0010	1011101
0011	1011011
0100	0111010
0101	1101011
0110	1101111
0111	1010010
1000	1111111
1001	1111011
1010	1111110
1011	0101111
1100	1100101
1101	0011111
1110	1101101
1111	1101100

Figure 5.12. Truth table for the hexadecimal to seven segment display format.

least one of the input lines A, B, C, D high, which will drive E to ground. Therefore, in general, if the low level of each unique input, either the input line or its complement, is connected via an MOS transistor to the intermediate line corresponding to that state, it will allow that line to remain high. For any other combination of inputs, one or more of these transistors will drive the line low. A high level on the intermediate line is then a unique indicator of a particular input code.

The encoding pattern depends on the output state pattern, as previously explained but also on how the output is matched to the display. Displays usually require large amounts of current and for this reason, an inverting buffer is placed between the ROM and the dis-

	E	F	G	H	I	J	K	L	M	N	O	P	Q	R	S	T
A	0	0	0	0	0	0	0	0	1	1	1	1	1	1	1	1
B	0	0	0	0	1	1	1	1	0	0	0	0	1	1	1	1
C	0	0	1	1	0	0	1	1	0	0	1	1	0	0	1	1
D	0	1	0	1	0	1	0	1	0	1	0	1	0	1	0	1

SYMBOLIC   DECODER   MATRIX

E	F	G	H	I	J	K	L	M	N	O	P	Q	R	S	T	
1	0	1	1	0	1	1	1	1	1	1	0	1	0	1	1	a
1	0	0	0	1	1	1	0	1	1	1	1	1	0	1	1	b
1	1	1	1	1	0	0	1	1	1	1	0	0	1	0	0	c
0	0	1	1	1	1	1	0	1	1	1	1	0	1	1	1	d
1	0	1	0	0	0	1	0	1	0	1	1	1	1	1	1	e
1	1	0	1	1	1	1	1	1	1	1	1	0	1	0	0	f
1	0	1	1	0	1	1	0	1	1	0	1	1	1	1	0	g

SYMBOLIC   ENCODER   MATRIX

Figure 5.13.   (a) Symbolic decoder matrix and (b) encoder matrix.

play. Furthermore most buffers require about 4mA per segment, which means ROM output transistors will have to be scaled up in size to be able to supply this amount of current. Assuming the actual encoding is to be done with normal signal level transistors, scaled up output inverters will be required along with inverting buffers to the display. Because of this double inversion, at the last signal level, encoding will follow the truth table of Figure 5.12. Following the example for numeric zero as was done previously, with E high, only segment d should be low. This can be implemented by placing a transistor to ground from the intermediate line wherever there is a zero in the encoder matrix. The intermediate line is the input to the gate, the drain is connected through a resistor to VDD, while the source is connected to ground. This is represented in Figure 5.14, where only one transistor is shown with line E as input. Line d is forced low, when line E is high.

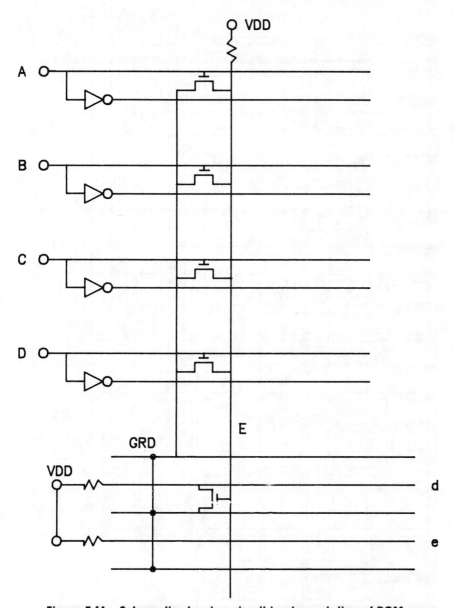

Figure 5.14.   Schematic showing circuit implementation of ROM.

A partial layout for the implementation of the truth table of Figure 5.12 is shown in Figure 5.15. Input and output pads as well as output driver transistors have been eliminated to show more overall detail in the coding matrices. Two additional changes have been incorpo-

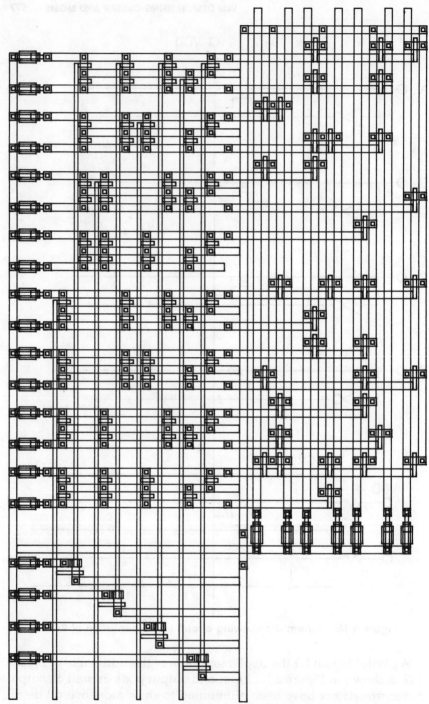

Figure 5.15.   ROM Caesar layout without output drivers and pads.

rated into this design. First, resistors in Figure 5.14 have been replaced with depletion mode transistors. As mentioned in a previous section, this substitution is consistent with the current technology of MOSIS and cuts down markedly on the amount of chip area devoted to this function. On the other hand, more chip area was included per transistor in the set of output transistors (not shown). Using a design parameter of 4 mA per output line and the results of a SPICE simulation, a W/L of 39.5/1 was determined to be appropriate. Typical SPICE parameters supplied by MOSIS were used for all constants.

3.2. Systematic Approach to ROM Design

Summarizing the approach used in the example given above, a general purpose systematic approach to ROM design can be devised. To visualize the approach one should refer to Figure 5.15.

1. Construct a truth table showing all valid inputs and corresponding outputs. "Don't cares" can be ignored since this general method will eliminate their effect.
2. Construct a symbolic decoder matrix consisting of rows of inputs and columns of intermediate lines. There should be one column for each valid input combination. Each horizontal input code in the truth table is replicated vertically (left goes to top).
3. Construct a symbolic encoder matrix consisting of rows of output lines and columns of the same intermediate lines as in 2 above. Each horizontal output code in the truth table is then replicated vertically.
4. Poly lines are then laid out horizontally for each input. Each input is inverted using depletion loads and that output is laid out horizontally. Thus one should have alternating lines of A, Ā, B, B̄, and so on.
5. Vertical metal lines are then tied to VDD through depletion loads located at the top of the decoder. These constitute the intermediate lines.
6. Vertical metal ground lines should alternate between the intermediate state lines.
7. Using the decoder matrix for every 0 entry, connect a transistor between the input poly line and ground. That is, a green diffusion box will bridge the intermediate line and the ground line. A poly line from the input will cross the green diffusion box. For every 1 in the decoder matrix, connect a transistor between the complement of that input and ground.

8. All of the intermediate metal lines will then be converted to vertical poly lines going down into the encoder matrix.
9. Construct horizontal depletion loads for each output, along with horizontal metal lines. Horizontal ground lines should alternate between these lines.
10. Using the encoder matrix, everywhere there is a 0 connect a transistor to ground from that intermediate line to the respective output line.
11. Layout output inverter drivers according to required interfacing specifications.

3.3. Random Access Memory

Registers for temporary storage of input or output data as well as other variables are a necessary component of any computer. For this reason, a 4 × 4 addressable register was chosen as the example for demonstration of a design technique which is based on the use of a library of standard cells. This library consists of a collection of elementary cells, previously designed and tested, which are subsequently available for incorporation into larger designs. A list of the typical set of standard cells which will be used for this example is given below.

STANDARD CELL LIBRARY

load
inverter
NOR gate
TTL driver
master/slave flip-flop
1 of 2 multiplexer

Although the circuit which was chosen for this example is relatively simple compared to most VLSI design projects, it is sufficiently complex to demonstrate the philosophy behind the design approach which will be used. A detailed description of this approach will be given.

The RAM consisting of a 4 × 4 addressable file register to be designed is shown in Figure 5.16. When the LOAD line is HIGH, one file register, specified by the address input, is selected and the four-bit data word is input to that register. As is the case in all design projects, a decision was made at the outset concerning the charac-

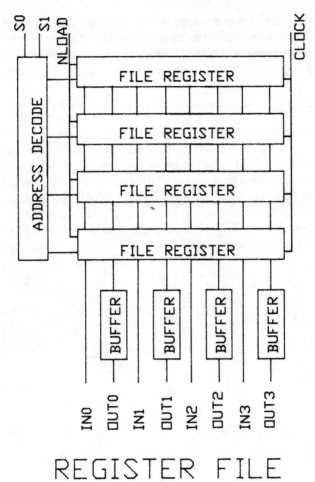

REGISTER FILE

Figure 5.16.   Block diagram of RAM register file.

teristics of the finished register. It will be designed for high noise margin and will have static memory, use a single synchronizing clock, low-power transistor-transistor logic (TTL) compatible inputs and outputs, and a single five-volt power supply.

The design sequence will involve extension of the idea of standard cells into a modular approach, which will be effective for even the most complex designs. The circuit shown in Figure 5.16 can easily be broken down into simpler modules. For the present example, this top-level decomposition of the circuit involves breaking it into an address decode module, four 4-bit file registers and four output buffers.

Comparison of the components of the circuit with the list of available standard cells indicates that none of the intermediate modules required are standard cells. Consequently, it is necessary to do a bottom-up layout of these cells using the library of standard cells.

3.3.1. Operation

When it is necessary to access a particular register for the purpose of reading or writing data, the two bit address of the register which will be accessed is input to the address decoder, Figure 5.17. The select line to the proper register is set HIGH by the address decoder. If the necessary operation is to input data, the NLOAD (LOAD complement) line is set LOW, as shown in Figure 5.17b. For the single register whose select line is HIGH, the combination of SEL and NLOAD each being HIGH will cause the select input to the one-of-two multiplexer

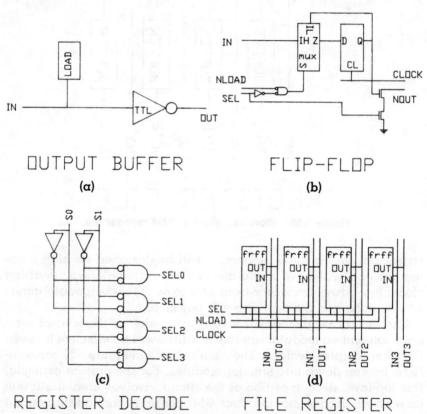

OUTPUT BUFFER
(a)

FLIP-FLOP
(b)

(c)
REGISTER DECODE

(d)
FILE REGISTER

Figure 5.17. Four subcircuits used in register file.

to go HIGH. The bit available at the input then appears at the output of the multiplexer. At the next clock pulse, the bit just read in becomes available at the output of the master-slave flip-flop, which means that it is available to be output by the register.

The output process can be understood by visualizing the signals associated with the AND output of Figure 5.17b. It is apparent that NOUT is LOW for a particular file register bit only when the SEL line to that cell is HIGH and Q, the output from that cell is also HIGH. Thus, NOUT from the 4 × 4 bit file register goes LOW (which means the output bit is HIGH) only when the output from the register being addressed is HIGH.

4. GRAPHICS FORMAT AND PLOTTING

Three different formats are used by the graphics layout software for storing data. All three formats use ASCII files and can easily be altered using standard word processors and transferred to other computers using communications protocols such as Kermit and Pro-Com. The primary storage, executed by a :save command while in Caesar, is called the Manhattan format. This method of graphic storage is multileveled with nested calls to other files and is very efficient in use of memory space. However, the multiple calls to standard cells, which are very common in VLSI layout, cause complicated nesting and as a result make breakdown of the file to plottable units difficult. Another disadvantage inherent to this multilevel structure is the difficulty in editing. For example, suppose one would like to develop an n by m array of dynamic n-channel storage gates to provide the memory plane for a RAM. To do this one would first position a locator box on the graphic screen with the lower left corner at the start position of the array and use a :getcell command to place the first pattern. The array command could then be used to multiply the pattern n by m. As will be shown later, this would involve only three lines of code in the Manhattan format, regardless of the array size. Thus a very complicated, highly repetitive pattern can be very efficiently represented. The disadvantage comes into play when one attempts to edit graphically within the array area. Since only the total array is represented, individual units of the array are not available to be changed. The standard cell can be changed with a :subedit command but this change will be reflected in all instances of that cell in the array. Clearly careful planning is required at the standard cell level to make this graphics protocol work effectively.

The most versatile and standardized format used in Caesar is the CalTech intermediate form (CIF) [6]. This form is used to transmit the overall VLSI design to MOSIS for fabrication. All graphic information is included in the single file and is arranged in defined symbols containing box descriptions. The compact array commands in the Manhattan format are removed and are replaced by multiple calls to a defined symbol representing the repeated definition. Calls both include other symbols and translates them and can be nested. In addition a scale factor can be specified for each defined symbol.

The CIF format is a universally used standard which is efficient in memory use. However, it is not easy to parse the CIF format into plottable units, such as boxes with either absolute or relative addresses. For example, in going through a file sequentially, it is not uncommon to find a call of a symbol which has not yet been defined. Therefore multiple passes are required. To eliminate this difficulty, an easy-to-parse format is available within Caesar. This format is called Structured CIF and is formed using the "cifplot" command. Using appropriate options, a highly structured output file is generated (along with a plot if you have the required plotter) which serves as the primary source for graphical output.

Two features of this format make it easy to parse. First, the CIF scaling factor is included in each box definition and secondly, the symbols are arranged hierarchically so that calls are made only to symbols already defined. Thus one can go through the file sequentially, expanding each symbol only to box definitions with absolute coordinates.

A very simple graphics layout will be used to explain in detail the format for each of the forms described above. This is shown in Figure 5.18 and includes:

1. An explicitly defined group of two boxes which were input separately using the bit pad
2. A call to a group of three boxes defined in a separate file which was subsequently arrayed to a 2 by 1 matrix
3. A rotation of the group of three to show the translation protocol.

4.1. Manhattan Format

Table 5.1 contains the three files generated within Caesar to represent the layout of Figure 5.18. In the Manhattan format, the first line defines the particular technology to be used, for example *nmos* as

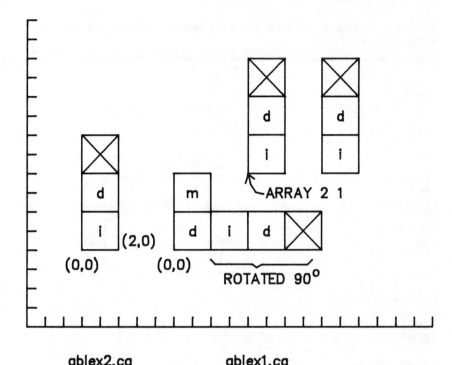

ablex2.ca   ablex1.ca

Figure 5.18.   Color monitor layout of two files used as example in text.

shown or *cmos* which is currently supported. Following this line are eight groups of explicitly defined rectangles (*rect*) representing the following layers:

    <<polysilicon>>
    <<diffusion>>
    <<metal>>
    <<implant>>
    <<cut>>
    <<overglass>>
    <<errors>>
    <<buried_contact>>.

Rectangles are specified in the form *rect num1 num2 num3 num4*, where *num* represents an integer number. The first two integers following *rect*, *num1* and *num2*, define the lower left coordinates of the box, while the last two, *num3* and *num4*, define the upper right coordinates. Coordinates in this case are weighted 2 for 1 lambda

Table 5.1. Listings of the Three Graphics Formats in Caesar for the Layout of Figure 5.18.

```
tech nmos                        DS 1 200 4;
<< diffusion >>                  9 ablex2.ca
rect 0 0 4 4                     L ND; B 8 8 4 12;
<< metal >>                      L NI; B 8 8 4 4;
rect 0 4 4 8                     L NC; B 8 8 4 20;
use ablex2.ca                    DF;
transform 0 1 4 -1 0 4           DS 2 200 4;
box 0 0 4 12                     9 ablex1.ca
use ablex2.ca                    L ND; B 8 8 4 4;
transform 1 0 8 0 1 8            L NM; B 8 8 4 12;
box 0 0 4 12                     C 1 R 0 -1 T 8 8;
use ablex2.ca                    C 1 R 1 0 T 16 16;
array 0 1 8 0 0 12               C 1 R 1 0 T 16 16;
transform 1 0 8 0 1 8            C 1 R 1 0 T 32 16;
box 0 0 4 12                     DF;
<< end >>                        C 2
                                 End
```

```
(UCB Structured CIF 2.0)
(joechar: Tue Oct 30 11:02:26 1987);
DS 1; 9 ablex2.ca
L ND; B 400 400 200 600 1 0;
L NI; B 400 400 200 200 1 0;
L NC; B 400 400 200 1000 1 0;
DF;
DS 2; 9 ablex1.ca;
L ND; B 400 400 200 200 1 0;
L NM; B 400 400 200 600 1 0;
C 1 R 0 -50 T 400 400;
C 1 R 50 0 T 800 800;
C 1 R 50 0 T 800 800;
C 1 R 50 0 T 1600 800;
DF;
DS 3;
C 2;
DF;
C 3;
E
```

unit, which is the default grid size, reproduced in Figure 5.18. The format for the extreme lower left box of *ablexl.ca* in Figure 5.18, box d, is

rect 0 0 4 4

and is listed under <<diffusion>> in Table 5.1. This box appears green on the color monitor. In a complex layout all eight layers listed above would be included with rectangles specified in absolute units. In this form, editing is unlimited and boxes may be resized and moved at will.

The lines beginning with "use ablex2.ca" show how an external graphics file is included in the Manhattan format. The syntax is as follows:

```
use <filename>
transform intl int2 numl int3 int4 num2
box numl num2 num3 num4
```

where <filename> is the Caesar file to be included with a .ca extension, and *int* refers to a single digit integer. The four successive numbers after the word box refer the lower left and upper right coordinates in Manhattan units of the smallest box enclosing the layout to be included. The transform line describes how the the layout to be included is placed in the source file, which is called the edit file. *Numl* and *num2* are, respectively, the coordinates of the lower left of the box from the included file translated to the edit file. The remaining entries in the transform line are defined by the following matrix equation:

$$\begin{bmatrix} \text{intl} & \text{int2} \\ \text{int3} & \text{int4} \end{bmatrix} = \begin{bmatrix} \cos\Theta & \sin\Theta \\ -\sin\Theta & \cos\Theta \end{bmatrix} \qquad 5.1$$

where Θ is a clockwise rotation angle thru which the included box is rotated. The matrix on the right of Equation 5.1 is the standard two-dimensional transformation matrix in Cartesian coordinates. For example, the rotated combination *i d x* in Figure 5.18 was a box 0 0 4 12 in *ablex2.ca* and is now located with lower left coordinates (4,4) in the edit file and subject to a rotation of

$$\begin{bmatrix} 0 & 1 \\ -1 & 0 \end{bmatrix}$$

which corresponds to 90° clockwise.

The two array cells shown in Figure 5.18 correspond to the last four lines of the edit file and use the same format as the include described above with an additional line

array 0 numl num2 0 num3 num4.

To describe the format it is necessary to describe the method of generating the array. First the lower left corner of the box on the color monitor is placed at the start position of the array. A *:getcell* <*filename*> is used to make the form to be repeated into the current cell. The current cell will be placed with its lower left corner at the start position. A box is then formed around this cell defining the form to be repeated. This allows extra blank space to be included in the repeated unit. A command *:array num1 num2* will then repeat this boxed cell *num1* times in the *x* direction and *num2* in the *y* direction. In the above array form in the edit file, *num2* and *num4* give the *x* units and *y* units box size of the repeated unit, respectively. *Num1* and *num3* are 1 minus the number of *x* repeat units and 1 minus the number of *y* repeat units, respectively.

4.2. CalTech Intermediate Form

The CIF file corresponding to a *.ca* file is generated within Caesar using the *:cif* <*filename*> command. A separate file is generated with the .cif extension. Table 5.1 shows the CIF file for the layout of Figure 5.18. Notice the general form is

> DS num1 a b;
> 9 filename;
> L ND; B num2 num3 num4 num5;
>   :
>
>   :
> C num6 trans
> DF;

which defines a callable block of definitions called a symbol. The symbol starts with DS, definition start, and ends with DF, definition finish. Included within the symbol are lines which are either comments, beginning with 9, layer box definitions, beginning with L, or calls preceded by C.

In the first line of the symbol, *num1* is the symbol's label and is used in calls as in *num6* of the general form listed above. Any references to the total symbol uses *num1* as the defining label. Numbers *a* and *b* are scale factors for values of box numbers such as *num2-5* above. In other words, any program reading this file will multiply *num2-5* by the factor *a/b*. After multiplication, box sizes and coordinates are scaled by a factor of 200 in relation to Caesar units by default. However any factor can be specified as an option in the *:cif* string. For example the first box specified in the Manhattan form, rect 0 0 4 4, had a length of 2 and a width of 2 in Caesar units on the color monitor. This will translate to a width of 400 and length of 400 after being scaled in the CIF form.

The second line of the symbol is a comment, having been preceded by a 9. This line gives the name of the file used for the explicit definitions of boxes in the symbol. Each line beginning with an L defines a box in a specific layer defined as follows:

ND	Diffusion
NP	Polysilicon
NC	Contact cut
NM	Metal
NI	Implant
NB	Buried contact
NG	Overglass

The B in the layer line denotes the box geometric primitive, followed by two numbers, *num2* and *num3* which are the length and width, respectively. *Num4* and *num5* are the box center location. For example, for the first box in symbol 1, the length is 8, the width is 8 at location *x,y* of (4,12). Since $a/b=50$, the scaled length is 400, width is 400 and location *x,y* is (200,600).

Call lines start with C followed by the number of the symbol being called. The remainder of the line is devoted to translation according to the following definitions:

T Point	Translate called symbol to this point
MX	Mirror in x; multiply all x's by -1
MY	Mirror in y; multiply all y's by -1
R Point	Rotate symbols x-axis to this direction

Order is important in the translation and operations are done sequentially left to right. These operations are most conveniently done by matrix multiplication, which will be explained in the parsing program which follows. As an example, the first call in symbol 2 rotates symbol 1 along the vector 0 *ax* $-1ay$, with *ax* a unit vector in the *x* direction and *ay* a unit vector in the *y* direction. Thus the rotation of the positive *x* axis (1 0) to this direction is a clockwise rotation of 90 degrees. The rotated three box combination in Figure 5.18, *i d x*, is the result of this call. Initially the lower left corner of the bounding box of this pattern was at 0,0. The pattern was then rotated 90 degrees clockwise about the lower left corner and then translated 8,8 or 200,200 scaled. In Caesar units the lower left translates to 2,2.

A salient feature of the CIF representation is that array commands in the Manhattan form are transformed into call commands. The 2×1 array of *ablex2.ca* corresponds to the last two calls in symbol 2.

4.3. Structured CalTech Intermediate Form

The form of structured CIF is similar to standard CIF as can be seen in Table 5.1. One difference is the application of the scaling factor a/b to all nums within the box definitions. This can be seen in the first box line where, for example, length and width are 400 and 400, respectively. This corresponds to the default scaling of 200 per Caesar unit. Also added to the box definition line are two integers following the box center coordinates. In the case of the first named box, these integers are 1 0, implying a rotation in the direction of line 1 ax + 0 ay (0 degrees) of the box length vector centered at the lower left corner.

The primary difference between structured and standard CIF is the method and order of symbol definition. Structured CIF starts with a symbol containing only box geometric primitives without calls to other symbols. The next symbol may have calls but only to symbols above it, and so on. Therefore to break the file down into plottable units, namely a single symbol with no calls, one can start at the top of the file and expand each symbol sequentially knowing each call will be to a completely expanded symbol. This will require only a single pass and transformations will not be nested.

4.4. Plotting Caesar Output

Most graphics languages used by pen plotters require data input in the most primitive form. Specifically, boxes are formed by *move absolute* or *move relative* commands with arguments of x and y coordinates in absolute plotter units. This protocol is compatible with the rectangle and B primitives described in the last section, with the following qualifications. Any transformation of the box must be complete with no rotation allowed in the command line. Of course a 1 0 rotation of 0 degrees can be ignored. Secondly all calls (or *use* commands) and the concomitant transformations must be performed so that the resultant file is totally expanded. The resultant expanded file will look as though each box were individually placed with the bit pad, for example the first symbols of the CIF forms of Table 5.1. A CIF file converted in this manner will consist of simply one large symbol, requiring a large amount of memory for a typical

VLSI layout. The size of the expanded file and the temporary storage space required during the expansion does put some restrictions on the method of parsing. As an example, the expanded CIF file for the chip designed in this project (ROAM) consisted of 477,078 characters. A totally recursive LISP program for expanding the CIF file for this chip rapidly used up the 2 megabytes of available memory.

4.4.1. Transformations

The most involved part of the expansion procedure for CIF files is the removal of the calls. Since Caesar has conveniently provided a hierarchically structured form in the structured CIF, it will be assumed that this version provides the starting data base. Therefore starting sequentially from the first symbol, any calls to other symbols will encounter a completely expanded symbol with only unrotated geometric primitives. Transformations will only operate on box center locations in the matrix form

$$[x'\ y'\ 1] = [x\ y\ 1]\ T\ ,$$

where x', y' are the transformed coordinates corresponding to starting coordinates x, y, and T is a 3x3 transformation matrix. The T matrix can be any one of four basic forms as follows.

Translate a,b   Tab $\begin{bmatrix} 1 & 0 & 0 \\ 0 & 1 & 0 \\ a & b & 1 \end{bmatrix}$

Mirror in x   MX $\begin{bmatrix} -1 & 0 & 0 \\ 0 & 1 & 0 \\ 0 & 0 & 1 \end{bmatrix}$

Mirror in y   MY $\begin{bmatrix} 1 & 0 & 0 \\ 0 & -1 & 0 \\ 0 & 0 & 1 \end{bmatrix}$

Rotate by a,b   Rab $\begin{bmatrix} a/c & b/c & 0 \\ -b/c & a/c & 0 \\ 0 & 0 & 1 \end{bmatrix}$

$$\text{where } c^2 = a^2 + b^2$$

For compound transformations the T matrices are ordered time sequentially, left to right, as

$$T1\ T2\ T3,$$

where Tl is the first operation and T3 the last. These matrices are then premultiplied by the starting row vector as

$$[x'\ y'\ 1] = [x\ y\ 1]\ T1\ T2\ T3$$

As an example of the algorithm required to eliminate a call, the processing of the first call to another symbol in the structured CIF of Table 5.1 will be detailed below.

Process	Result
1. Find symbol, identify first box definition	L ND B 400 400 200 600 1 0 ;
2. Extract box center	[200, 600, 1]
3. Find first transformation, left to right	R 0 −50
4. Transform	$a=0,\ b=-50;\ c=50$

$$T1 = \begin{bmatrix} 0 & -1 & 0 \\ 1 & 0 & 0 \\ 0 & 0 & 1 \end{bmatrix}$$

$$[x',\ y',\ 1]=[200,\ 600,\ 1]\ T1=[600,\ -200,\ 1]$$

| 5. Find next transform | T 400 400 |
| 6. Transform | |

$$T2 = \begin{bmatrix} 1 & 0 & 0 \\ 0 & 1 & 0 \\ 400 & 400 & 1 \end{bmatrix}$$

$$[x',\ y',\ 1]=[600,\ -200,\ 1]\ T2=[1000,200,1]$$

| 7. Write to current symbol | L ND B 400 400 1000 200 1 0 ; |

Table 5.2 shows the result of applying this procedure to all calls in the structured CIF of Table 5.1. The LISP program used to perform this task, "ciff.1," will be described below. A listing of this program can be found in the Appendix, Listing I.

Table 5.2.   Listing of a Single Symbol Graphics Format for the Layout of Figure 5.18.

```
( UCB Structured CIF 2.0 ) ;
( joechar: Tue Oct 20 11:02:26 1987 ) ;
L ND ; B 400 400 200 200 1 0 ;
L NM ; B 400 400 200 600 1 0 ;
L ND ; B 400 400 1000 200 1 0 ;
L NI ; B 400 400 600 200 1 0 ;
L NC ; B 400 400 1400 200 1 0 ;
L ND ; B 400 400 1000 1400 1 0 ;
L NI ; B 400 400 1000 1000 1 0 ;
L NC ; B 400 400 1000 1800 1 0 ;
L ND ; B 400 400 1000 1400 1 0 ;
L NI ; B 400 400 1000 1000 1 0 ;
L NC ; B 400 400 1000 1800 1 0 ;
L ND ; B 400 400 1800 1400 1 0 ;
L NI ; B 400 400 1800 1000 1 0 ;
L NC ; B 400 400 1800 1800 1 0 ;
E
```

4.4.2. File Expansion

Expansion of the structured CIF file by removing calls is straightforward but laborious. Several versions of software to do this were written and tested, including implementation in BASIC, C, and LISP. Because Franz Lisp is included with the operating system used to run Caesar, namely, Berkeley BSD 4.2 or DEC Ultrix, the LISP version would appear more universal, if not the simplest to decipher. The source code for this version is included in Listing I in the Appendix along with a block diagram describing the algorithm. A brief explanation of each of the most important defined functions will be given to aid in the interpretation.

The first two defined functions, fst-line and tot-lst, are input utilities which read the CIF file, line by line, put parentheses around each line and make a single list (tot-lst) comprised of these lines. The format is

((L ND ::: B 400 400 200 600 1 0 :::) (L ND -------) ()) .

The last two defined functions, *ppage* and *pline*, take the above format after expansion and disassemble it from a list to a series of lines and store it in the output file.

The main defined function is *fixit*. This function prompts for an input file (the structured CIF), for an output file <filename>, and then opens input and output ports. *Tot-lst* is called to read and reformat the input file as lst, a list of lines. *Mk-lib* uses *scan-def* and *find-def* (see below) to create, from *lst*, a library of definitions free of definition calls. At the same level *rem-def* extracts the top level (non-definition portion) from lst. Finally *iscan* fills all top-level definition calls from the library and *ppage* reformats to structured CIF and writes the output file.

Other internal definitions are:

find-def: identifies each distinct definition in lst, formats the definition as a separate list tagged with a definition number, and returns the resulting list of tagged definitions.

scan-def: translates a single definition, with calls, into an equivalent definition without calls.

calc-mod: creates the modification matrix discussed in the last section.

def-mod: performs the transformation described by the modification matrix. Ip, first_row and mmul: performs matrix multiply.

4.4.3. Plotter Driver

Because the output of *ciff.l* is a single symbol CIF file, it is easily parsed into command codes for a pen plotter. Another option is to use the *cif2ca* command and generate a Manhattan version of the single symbol CIF file. In either case, the parsing software would go through the file sequentially, find each box definition, record the layer, box dimensions, and center. This information, which is usually written to a temporary file, can be scanned and grouped by layer. Absolute box coordinates can then be output, layer by layer, requiring a single command to prepare the plotter for the particular format for that layer. Generally each layer is plotted in a different color using the same scheme as Caesar uses on the color monitor. A "C" version of a plotter driver for an HP DraftPro 8 color pen plotter is given in Appendix, Listing II. The graphics commands are in Hewlett-Packard graphics language (HPGL). This version uses the .ca form derived from the single symbol CIF file. The plotter is driven serially from a /tty port.

The output from the *cif2ca* command using the single symbol CIF file, is in the proper .ca format and can be edited within Caesar. Since the file is totally expanded, all boxes can be edited without the necessity of resorting to a subedit. This provides maximum flexibility, but has the disadvantage of being the maximum possible size. Another advantage to the single symbol form is that it is relatively easy to move rectangular areas of the chip to provide space for additions. In the simplest form this would involve locating box definitions within a certain area and translating them in the desired shift direction. Of course this would be strictly a cut-and-translate move, and interconnections would have to be re-established to the main chip. The main advantage of working with this form is the simplicity of the box definitions, which should require minimum time for editing procedures.

5. SIMULATION

Two general approaches to simulation are used and each will be described here. The first approach is direct simulation, using the capability of the CAD software to generate models for all elements (individual devices) in the layout. In some cases the models and their topological placement are generated directly from the geometrical layout, as can be done within the Berkeley tools. In other cases each element can be placed in a large circuit representing the layout by using circuit symbols and then using schematic capture to write the circuit description. NETED and SYMED running on the Apollo work station has this capability. In both of the above cases, the circuit simulation package SPICE is used to analyze electrically the overall chip.

The second approach to simulation is to use standard cells made into subcircuits which are then callable as a total package. To use this approach, it is necessary to start with predefined cells which are arrayed to provide the primary circuit functions. Typically the only explicitly defined elements in the layout are the interconnect lines and bonding pads. Such a scheme lends itself to very efficient representation, as in the case of the previously described RAM, however, at the analysis point in SPICE all elements must be represented individually. Therefore this approach to simulation is unique only in the method of circuit representation, which becomes transparent to SPICE during nodal analysis. If however, subcircuits are first simulated and modeled separately in a simpler fashion, considerable savings in computation time and expense can result. For example, in certain simulation packages inverters are modeled as dependent voltage source which inverts the signal. Then the entire timing effect is represented by a constant propagation delay. This can speed up simulation considerably, sometimes by a factor of 10 to 100, but the output lacks precise waveshapes and shows only linear pulse edges.

The straightforward approach to direct simulation using the Berkeley tools is to use a circuit extractor on the CIF file to form a simulation file. This file is then reformatted to a SPICE file, to which can be added the necessary additional code representing power supplies, inputs, and the desired output. Direct simulation will be explained in detail for the ROM layout.

Before beginning graphics file conversion to SPICE code, it is useful to place labels into the file to identify critical nodes where extra connections must be made. Without these labels conversion of the overall layout to lines of SPICE code will result in nodes whose numbers have no explicit relation to inputs or outputs. If node names, such as VDD or A, are placed on or near boxes in the layout, the circuit extractor will use these names to identify the node. Furthermore, when converting the .sim file that results from the circuit extraction to SPICE, a ".names" file is generated that shows the equivalence of node names and node numbers in the final SPICE code. This is very useful when writing SPICE code for such ancillary connections as inputs, outputs, and power supplies. It is also possible to create a ".defs" file where explicit assignment of a node number is made to a node name. This is done using the [-d defs] option in the "sim2spice" command.

5.1 Conversion of Caesar Files to SPICE Files

The procedure for converting a ".cif" file to a usable simulation SPICE file will be outlined below.

1. Write short alphanumeric labels for each important node point on the layout. All inputs, outputs, and power points should be included, along with those points inside the circuit where either current or voltage output data is required. Within Caesar do a :save to backup the latest changes and :cif -lp to generate a CIF file that includes labels and a point for each label.

2. Exit Caesar and invoke the circuit extractor with the command mextra <filename.cif>. Output from this operation follows the general format below.

```
d   g   g   VDD num1 num2 num3 num4
e   4   g   GRD num1 num2 num3 num4
C   4       GRD 218
```

The first symbol identifies the element and uses d for depletion mode transistor, e for enhancement mode transistor, and C for capacitance. The convention on transistor terminals is listing in the order gate, drain, and source. The four numbers following the transistor nodes refer to locations in Caesar units. For this application since the software automatically "connects" the transistors these are only internally important. The two nodes after C are the connections for the capacitor with the following number giving the value in femtofarads.

3.   Convert the ".sim" file to a spice file using *sim2spice [-d defs] filename.sim*. As mentioned previously the option -d refers to a file named "defs" which contains forced equivalence of node labels to node numbers in the SPICE file. If for example a file named "defs" contains the line

    set GND 0,

node 0 in the SPICE code generated will correspond to node GND on the layout. In any case a "filename.names" will be generated defining this equivalence, either forced or automatically assigned. A typical "filename.spice" generated with this command will have the general form below.

    M1 5 5 4 3 DNMOS   L=12.0U W=4.0U
    C32 13 0 764.0F

The first term defines the element. For example M1 is MOS 1 and C32 is capacitor 32. After M1, the nodes are defined in the order, drain, gate, source and bulk. The label DNMOS refers to depletion mode MOS and must be detailed in a *.MODEL* card. L and W are channel length and width respectively and are given in absolute units or L=12 microns. Scale factors can be internally set. The convention for capacitance is the same as in 2. above with F referring to femtofarads.

4. Using the "vi editor" write SPICE code for power supply and inputs. The "filename.names" file will now refer you to specific node numbers for these connections.

5. After the "filename.spice" is complete run the simulation. Direct simulation is time consuming. The ROM in the ROAM chip required several hours to simulate.

5.2. ROM Direct Simulation

The first step in this process is to obtain the SPICE code for the circuit description using the procedure explained above. For the ROM example, the resulting file consists of 143 lines of MOS transistors and 39 small values of capacitance in the range of 50 to 250 femtofarads. The capacitors represent parasitics generated within the Manhattan circuit extractor, "mextra," and correspond to actual areas at each node. These capacitors should not be removed, as their absence would cause "internal time step too small" errors in SPICE. The "filename.names" file appeared as follows.

GND 0		D	16
BULK 2		α	17
DNMOS 3		b	18
VDD 4		c	19
ENMOS 11		d	20
A 12		e	21
GRD 13		f	22
B 14		g	23
C 15			

Nodes shown after DNMOS and ENMOS refer to a common bulk connection for each type of transistor. The two apparent ground connections 13 and 0 come from the choice of labels. Referring to the layout, one can note a crossunder for the VDD line which routes the power for the decoder loads to the encoder. Even though the poly line connecting the two sides of circuit ground has only a few ohms impedance, "mextra" will treat each side of the crossunder as a separate node. Therefore they were labeled with two different names to locate the crossunder. Using the "names" file, the following additional code was written to test the logic functionality of the overall chip.

R1 4 17 2.2K	; 2.2K output load	
R2 4 18 2.2K	;	
R3 4 19 2.2K	;	
R4 4 20 2.2K	;	
R5 4 21 2.2K	;	
R6 4 22 2.2K	;	
R7 4 23 2.2K	;	
R8 0 13 0.001	; connect layout	
	ground to 0	

```
R9 11 0 0.001                               ; connect etrans
                                              bulk to 0
R10 3 0 0.001                               ; connect dtrans
                                              bulk to 0
VA 12 0 PULSE(0 5 4MS 1MS 1MS 6MS 10MS);
VB 14 0 PULSE(0 5 9MS 1MS 1MS 11MS 20MS);
VC 15 0 PULSE(0 5 19MS 1MS 1MS 21MS 40MS)   ; } see Fig. 5.19
VD 16 0 PULSE(0 5 39MS 1MS 1MS 41MS 80MS)   ;
.TRAN 1MS 80MS                              ; 80MS transient analy
                                              1MS interval
.PLOT TRAN V(17) V(18) V(19) V(20)          ; output points
+V(21) V(22) V(23)
.END
```

Resistors R1 through R7 are loads connected to the output transistors. Connection points were determined from the "names" file where, for example, output point a is connected to 17. R8, R9, and R10 are 1 milliohm resistors connecting transistor bulk points to ground and GND to GRD as previously discussed. The voltage inputs VA-VD follow the waveshapes shown in Figure 5.19. Since this is a logic function test, moderate time transitions were specified. With this choice of inputs all combinations of inputs shown in the truth table of Figure 5.12 are present at different times. For example at 42 ms the input pattern is (A B C D)=1000 or decimal 8. The outputs at the gates of the output transistors should be (a b c d e f g)= 1111111 to turn on all segments in order to display the Figure 5.8. For outputs defined as the collectors of the output transistors, (a b c d e f g)= 0000000 because of the intermediate inversion.

The logic functionality test is very useful in determining whether or not the overall chip will function as designed. At this point missing connections and inadvertent shorts will show up and can be corrected. Intermediate signal point testing is usually advisable. For example with the SPICE inputs above, intermediate lines E through T should toggle up and down one at a time. As with the testing of actual circuits, normal troubleshooting methods can be used to look for and eliminate connection problems. The only difference is that with this type of simulation and with this size VLSI, the turnaround time between a new application of inputs and the plotted outputs is usually around two hours. As a result, people writing simulation code become clever in choosing input pulse shapes that exercise the circuit a maximum number of permutations in a given computer run.

Another important aspect of any digital circuit is its transient

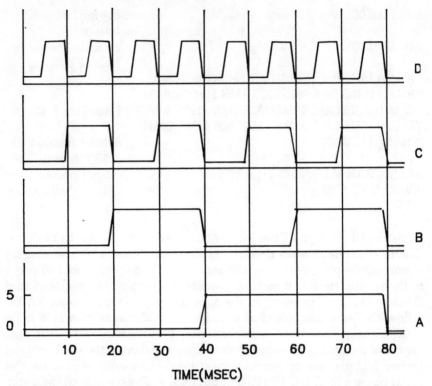

Figure 5.19. Four input waveshapes to fully exercise the Hex-7 ROM.

pulse response. Therefore, output rise and fall times in response to sharp input pulse edges are of interest and can be determined by simulation. Since, in general, one can identify worst case conditions that are a subset of the overall logic conditions, the circuit can be simplified for this type of analysis. For example with the ROM of Figure 5.15, the worst case of propagation delay would be that for which the input and intermediate lines are driving the maximum number of gates. Since all input lines drive 8 gates with this scheme, the encoding determines the worst case. This would involve the second intermediate line from the left (F) since it drives 5 gates corresponding to a hexadecimal output of 0001 and a 1 on the display.

Since it is advantageous to simplify the circuit as much as possible in order to minimize turnaround time on the analysis, we chose to partition the ROM into its critical areas for this analysis. With the totally expanded symbol representation, the circuit can be separated into pieces and *yanked* into the temporary "yank buffer." The segments can then be *:ysaved* into a new file and a partial circuit constructed for simulation. For the worst case transient analysis outlines above, the ROM layout can be separated on a vertical line just to the left of the third poly line in the encoder (G). This would include intermediate line F and the five transistors it drives when at logic level 1. To see the effect of a transition, the conversion from hexadecimal code 0000 to 0001 was chosen. This drives segment a of the output from high for the case of number zero displayed to low for number 1 displayed. Once the left third of the ROM is in a separate Caesar file, one can add any additional elements that would affect the transient response. If the input is a zero impedance voltage pulse source, then any additional gates on D removed by the circuit split would not affect the transient response. However, the critical transition is when $\overline{D}$ goes from 1, holding F to ground, to 0 when the eight transistors on $\overline{D}$ must discharge to ground through the D inverter. Therefore the seven transistors on the D line removed by the partition must be reconnected. Also since the output drivers were removed, a single output transistor must be replaced in the partial circuit.

Primary considerations in simulation are the selection of models for MOS transistors and capacitive loading from interconnections. If one follows the guidelines given in the layout section, parasitic resistances associated with interconnections will generally be negligible compared to other impedances in the overall circuit. However parasitic capacitance associated with interconnection areas usually is the determining factor in the circuit's transient response [2]. "Mextra" determines these capacitances and reports them from two different sources, one, from node to substrate and two, from poly overlapping diffusion but not forming a transistor. Capacitance is calculated for each layer by taking the area of a node on the layer and multiplying it by a constant. This is then added to a product of the perimeter and a constant, which accounts for sidewall contribution. The following are default constants used by "mextra," with area values in femtofarads per square micron and perimeter values in femtofarads per micron.

Layer	Area constant	Perimeter constant
metal	0.03	0.0
poly	0.05	0.0
diff	0.1	0.1
poly/diff	0.4	0.0

"Mextra" extracts what appear to be small values of capacitance. However, these are realistic values for this size circuit and should not be removed when converting to a SPICE file. Typically removal of only one of these capacitors will cause time step errors within SPICE and no convergence in the solution.

Significant circuit delays are also added to the SPICE simulation by reference to device areas and resistive and capacitive parameters specified in the *.model card*. There are three levels of sophistication in the models, with level 1 usually used in the design phase and level 2 or 3 used in the latter phase of simulation which occurs after devices are made and actual SPICE parameters from test structures on the chip are determined. Table 5.3 gives the usual device parameters for level 1 simulation along with defining equations and SPICE names. The following model cards give good simulation for normal layouts with current MOSIS fabrication parameters.

+NSUB=6.6E15 TOX=603E-10
+XJ=0.4U LD=0.54U
+CJ=0.00011 CJSW=5E-10 CGSO=3.17E-10 CGDO=3.17E-10

+NSUB=1.46E16 TOX=603E-10
+XJ=0.4U LD=0.311U
+CJ=0.00011 CJSW=5E-10 CGSO=1.82E-10 CGDO=1.82E-10

The fully implemented level 2 model cards will be given by MOSIS along with the fabricated chips. One should be aware that using level 2 versus level 1 significantly increases the simulation time in SPICE.

Results from the transient simulation on the partial circuit described above are shown in Figure 5.20. This response shows a propagation delay of approximately 40 ns pull-up and 80 ns pull-down.

5.3. RAM Modular Simulation

Logical simulation with propagation delay for the RAM was performed on an Apollo DN660. The 4 × 4 register file was first entered into the Apollo system for logical design verification. This system permits circuit modules to be constructed from standard cells. These modules may then be assigned circuit symbols and used in more complex circuits. The intermediate modules and final circuit are logically simulated by the system's "Quicksim" package which will display output waveforms and lists in response to any desired forcing functions.

Table 5.3. Definition of SPICE Parameters for an MOS Model Card.

Parameter	Symbol/Equation	Value	Unit	SPICE Name
Threshold voltage	$V_{Ta} = 0.2V_{DD}$ $V_{Td} = -0.6V_{DD}$	0.815 -2.705	V	VTO
Trans-conductance	$K' = \mu_n C_{ox}$	19.3E-6 20.35E-6	$\dfrac{A}{V^2}$	KP
Body factor	$r = \dfrac{\sqrt{(2q\epsilon_{si}N_A)}}{\left(\dfrac{\epsilon_{ox}}{t_{ox}}\right)}$	0.271 0.281	–	Gamma
Body doping	N_A	6.6E15 1.46E16	cm^{-3}	NSUB
Source/Drain doping	N_D	7E18	cm^{-3}	NSUB
Gate oxide thickness	t_{ox}	590E-10 603E-10	m	TOX
Junction depth	x_j	0.4E-6	m	XJ
Lateral diffusion	L_D	0.541E-6 0.311E-6	m	LD
Bulk junction potential	$\phi_o = V_t \ln\left(\dfrac{N_A N_D}{n_i^2}\right)$	0.70	V	PB
Zero-bias bulk junction bottom capacitance	$C_{jo} = \sqrt{\dfrac{q\epsilon_{si}N_A}{2\phi_o}}$	1.1E-4	$\dfrac{F}{m^2}$	CJ
Sidewall capacitance	$C_{jsw} = X_j\sqrt{10C_{jo}}$	5E-10 5E-10	$\dfrac{F}{m}$	CJSW
Gate-source (drain) overlay capacitance	$C_{gso} = C_{gdo} = \left(\dfrac{\epsilon_{ox}}{t_{ox}}\right)*LD$	3.17E-10 1.82E-10	$\dfrac{F}{m}$	CGSO CGDO
Dielectric constant oxide/silicon	$\dfrac{\epsilon_{ox}}{\epsilon_{si}}$	3.45E-11 1.05E-12	$\dfrac{F}{cm^2}$ $\dfrac{F}{cm^2}$	
Mobility	μ_n	692.4 847.8	$\dfrac{cm^2}{V\,sec}$	UO

*When two values are given, they refer to enhancement, depletion, top to bottom.

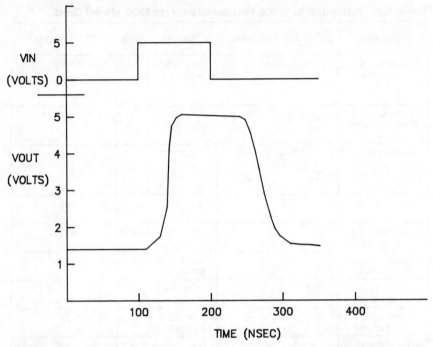

Figure 5.20. Simulated pulse response of 'a' segment for worst case conditions, 2.2 kohm load.

For our design, the intermediate modules, consisting of (a) address decode, (b) file register, and (c) output buffer were built from the generic library of logical elements using the "Neted" package. The standard cells may then be assigned "rise and fall times" as the modules are constructed. These times are translated to delay times by the simulator. Since propagation delay in nMOS circuits is primarily a function of capacitance loading, these simulated delays have little validity. However, to insure a correct logical simulation, rise time of 10 ns and fall times of 5 ns were assigned to each standard cell as the modules were constructed.

The system's "Symed" package was used to define a circuit with name, connection points, and signal names for each intermediate module. The final circuit was then constructed and prepared for use by "Quicksim" using the "Expand" package. The modular test circuit's schematic is shown in Figure 5.21.

Two simulations were run on the register file. First, a single path from decode inputs to buffer output was simulated, with intermediate points monitored. The second simulation was performed on the

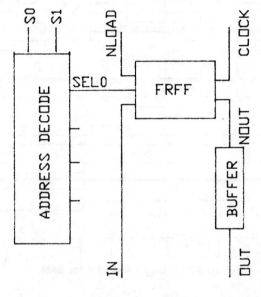

DELAY TEST CIRCUIT

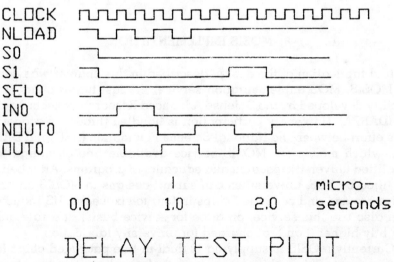

DELAY TEST PLOT

Figure 5.21. Modular test circuit and test voltages for RAM simulation.

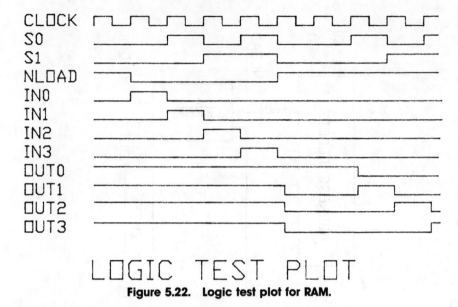

LOGIC TEST PLOT

Figure 5.22.   Logic test plot for RAM.

total network with patterns loaded and read from each of the four registers. Results of this simulation are shown in Figures 5.21 and 5.22 and followed design predictions.

6. MOSIS IMPLEMENTATION

Actual fabrication of the design described in this chapter was done at MOSIS, MOS implementation service, the fast turn-around VLSI facility developed by the Defense Advanced Research Projects Agency (DARPA). University participation is handled through a cooperative effort between the National Science Foundation (NSF) and DARPA, which makes the MOSIS service available free of charge for qualified university research and educational programs. After being certified by NSF, universities can submit designs to MOSIS and receive bonded and packaged chips in four to six weeks. US industry can also use this service, on a fee-for-service basis, at a rate only slightly higher than that charged for university fabrication.

Currently MOSIS is supplying 12 dual-in-line packaged chips for each project. These chips come from wafers whose test structures perform within certain specification ranges required by MOSIS and guaranteed by the fabricator. Thus, in using the facility, one is assured that an established technology will be used and that predictable results have been obtained on the chips returned for testing. This is a major reason for the high success rate of working chips from this service. As described in the simulation section, MOSIS also supplies detailed SPICE parameters which make possible accurate post fabrication verification of the effectiveness of the chip design.

Access to MOSIS is by means of digital transmission using either BITNET, ARPANET, or TELENET. The method of transmission for this design was EDU of ARPANET, routed through WISCVM.EDU and ending at the Information Sciences Institute at the University of Southern California. This Institute handles the scheduling and administrative details of the fabrication and is the primary source of information on the use of MOSIS. Once the user is certified for MOSIS, a password is issued and budgetary and scheduling information is provided. The password along with a network address allows one to communicate directly with ISI. Details for communication and information concerning design rules and technology are contained in a Users Manual supplied by MOSIS. A few examples will be given here to illustrate the protocol and show how design features are input to the system.

The general format for transmission follows the normal ARPANET message system. For example the intent to submit a new project follows the format listed below.

```
To:   MOSIS@MOSIS.ARPA
From:   CHARLSONE
Subject:   Intent to submit new project

REQUEST: NEW-PROJECT
        D-NAME:              CHARLSONE
        AFFILIATION:         UMO-COL-ECE
        D-PASSWORD:          Popeye
            :
            :
        P-NAME:              ROAM
        TECHNOLOGY:          NMOS
        LAMBDA:              2.0
        MIN-LAMBDA           1.5
        MAX-LAMBDA           2.5
        PADS:                40
REQUEST:   END
```

A key issue here is the selection of the technology (nmos) and the value of lambda in microns. A range is usually specified to allow for timely inclusion of the project in the schedule, since each run has a fixed lambda. Thus any nmos fabrication with lambda of between 1.5 and 2.5 microns could include the ROAM project. As implied, typically several projects are bundled together in a given run to lower overall production costs. MOSIS will respond back with an OK New-Project and an ID number. At this point one must decide whether or not to use a "standard frame," which refers to a particular placement of bonding pads. If this is desired, a message similar to the one above is sent with the REQUEST being STANDARD FRAME. MOSIS will respond with a CIF file describing the pad placement. All references to WIRES will have to be deleted from this file as the Berkeley Tools do not support this primitive. The CIF file can then be converted to a .ca file using the "cif2ca" utility. The actual circuit without pads can then be pulled into the .ca file using a :getcell <filename> and metal lines placed from pads to appropriate circuit points. A CIF description of the composite file then represents the total project file.

Before fabricating any project, MOSIS performs an in-house CIF check. At the present time since several different sets of design rules are used, the in-house check is mostly syntactical. An additional verification feature is a standard checksum which is run on the file before submission and is included in the request for CIF check. Rules regarding the checksum are provided in the users' manual. The format for sending the CIF file is shown below.

```
To:  MOSIS@MOSIS.ARPA
From:  CHARLSONE
Subject:  SUBMIT FOR CIF CHECK

   REQUEST: SUBMIT
      ID:                  12345
      P-PASSWORD:          KAZIBOO
      SIZE:                4600 X6800
      CIF-CHECKSUM:        931160 18320
      CIF:
         (----- ROAM.CIF);
         DS 1 200 4 ;
         9 ablex2.ca;
         L ND ; B 8 8 4 12;
         L NI ; B 8 8 4 4;

                 :
                 :
         DF;
                 :
      End
   REQUEST: END
```

Once MOSIS has obtained the correct checksum from the file, it will run the CIF check. If the CIF check is valid, the user may then issue a REQUEST: FABRICATE, and the chip will be made in the next appropriate run. Figure 5.23 shows the completed ROAM chip. A bonding pad assignment is included with the 12 packages.

6.1. Testing

The ROM part of the ROAM chip, which is the smaller of the two distinct areas of the chip, was tested using a digitester. Pullup resistors of 11 kohm were inserted between a-g outputs and power supply. Inputs A-D were driven with low impedance voltage sources and outputs connected to LED lamp monitors. The logical operation was then verified by going through the truth table of Figure 5.12.

The circuit transient response was tested by pulsing one input, fixing the other three, and observing the response of a segment that changed states for that particular transition. For example for A=0, B=0, C=1 and D pulsed from 0 to 1, the e segment would switch from a 0 to 1. Figure 5.24 shows oscilloscope traces for a pull-up, low to high transition (b), and pull-down, the opposite transition (a). As can be seen the longest time constant is for pull-up, as would be expected. In this case the output transistor is turned off after a delay of approximately 45 nsec and then shows the classical RC time constant shape in moving toward a 5 volt pulse height. Pull-down has approximately the same delay time, estimated at 60 nsec and then a sharp drop of fall time of nearly the same value. In pull-down, the output capacitance is discharging through the high W/L output transistor and hence the small time constant. However, in pull-up after the delay time with the output transistor off, the output capacitance must charge through the 11 kohm output load. In this case with the capacitance consisting of the oscilloscope probe capacitance (13pF) plus the capacitance of the digitester connector bus (4.2pF), the RC time constant is approximately 190 nsec. This matches reasonably well with the experimental values shown.

A simulation of the ROM driving the e segment, similar to that done previously for worst case conditions (Figure 5.18), and using the load conditions described above was done and results are shown in Figure 5.25. Also shown in the figure are the experimental values taken from Figure 5.24. Two transient time constant definitions appropriate for analyzing this type of data are as follows. Delay time is the time after an input transition for appreciable output change. This is estimated by the intersection point of tangents to the curve on

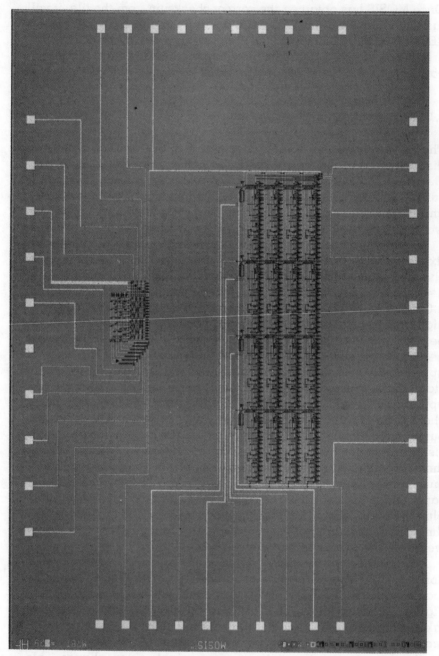

Figure 5.23. Photograph for the complete ROAM chip built by MOSIS.

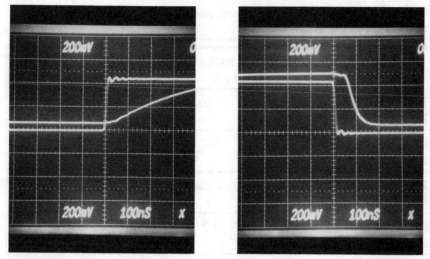

Figure 5.24. Pulse waveshapes for driving D input and monitoring e segment.

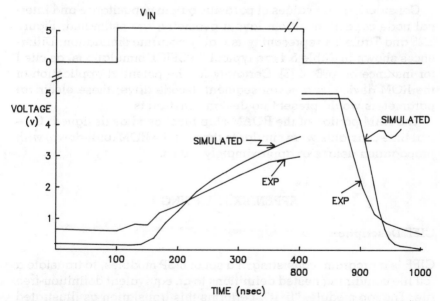

Figure 5.25. Comparison of simulated and experimental pulse response for (a) pull-up and (b) pull-down for Hex-7 ROM.

Table 5.4.   Comparison of Actual and Simulated Transient Parameters for the ROM in the ROAM Chip.

	Simulated (nsec)	Experimental (nsec)
Propagation Delay Pull-up	180	210
Delay Time Pull-up	50	45
Propagation Delay Pull-down	115	90
Delay Time Pull-down	80	60

either side of the transition. Propagation delay is defined as the time between the start of the input pulse and the midpoint of the output transition. Table 5.4 is a comparison of these two time constants for simulated and actual pulse response.

Considering that values of parasitic output capacitance and internal node capacitance from layout geometry, are estimated, Figure 5.25 and Table 5.4 represent reasonably accurate simulation. Differences shown in Table 5.4 are typical for SPICE simulations, as cited for instance on p96 of [3]. Certainly for the potential application of the ROM device as a seven segment decode drive, these electrical parameters would present no design constraints.

The RAM portion of the ROAM chip functioned as designed. Critical time constants were similar to those of the ROM (pull-down) with propagation delays of approximately 100 ns.

APPENDIX 1: LISTING I

CIFF Description

CIFF is a program, consisting of a set of LISP modules, to translate a .cif file containing nested definitions to an equivalent definition-free file. The top module, "fixit", performs this translation as illustrated in the figure.

FIXIT:

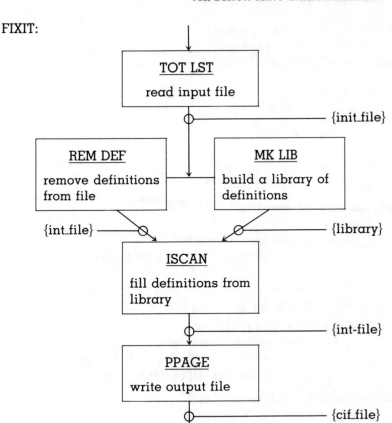

Data formats, indicated with brackets { }, are defined:

{init_file} ::= ({line})
    a list of lines
{line}   ::= (atom)
    a list of atoms
{library ::= ({def})
    a list of definitions
{def}   ::= (CONS name {init_file})

Ciff.1

By H. L. Graham

```
(defun fst-line (port)   (let
        ((fst (tyipeek port)))
        (cond
```

```
                    ((eq fst 10)   (progn
                             (tyi port) nil))
                    (t (cons (ratom port) (fst-line port))))))))

(defun tot-lst (port) (let
        ((fst (tyipeek port)))
        (cond
                ((eq fst -1) nil)
                (t (cons
                        (fst-line port)
                        (tot-lst port))))))))

(defun find-defs (lst) (cond
        ((eq (caar lst) 'DS)
                (let ((x (sep-def nil (cdr lst))))
                (cons (cons (cadar lst) (car x)) (find-defs
                                                (cdr x)))))
        ((null lst) nil)
        (t (find-defs (cdr lst))))))

        (defun sep-def (def lst) (cond
                ((eq (caar lst) 'DF) (cons (reverse def)
                                                (cdr lst)))
                (t (sep-def (cons (car lst) def) (cdr lst))))))

(defun mk-lib (defs) (imk-lib nil defs))
        (defun imk-lib (lib defs) (cond
                ((null defs) (reverse lib))
                (t (imk-lib
                        (cons (scan-def lib (car defs)) lib)
                        (cdr defs))))))
        (defun scan-def (lib def) (iscan lib (list (car def))
                                                (cdr def)))

(defun iscan (lib ndef def) (cond
        ((null def) (reverse ndef))
        ((eq (caar def) 'C) (iscan lib
                (def-fill (def-fetch (cadar def) lib)
                        (calc-mod (cddar def)) ndef)
                (cdr def)))
        (t (iscan lib (cons (car def) ndef) (cdr def))))))

(defun calc-mod (tlst) (cond
        ((null (cdr tlst)) (ident 3))
        ((eq (car tlst) 'T) (mmul
                (list '(1 0 0) '(0 1 0) (list (cadr tlst)
                                                (caddr tlst)1))
```

```
                  (calc-mod (cddr tlst))))
        ((eq (car tlst) 'MX) (mmul
              '((-1 0 0) (0 1 0) (0 0 1))
              (calc-mod (cdr tlst))))
        (eq (car tlst) 'MY) (mmul
              '((1 0 0) (0 -1 0) (0 0 1))
              (calc-mod (cdr tlst))))
        ((eq (car tlst) 'R) (let*
              ((aa (float (cadr tlst)))
               (bb (float (caddr tlst)))
               (cc (sqrt (add
                          (times aa aa)
                          (times bb bb)))))
              (mmul
                    (list
                          (list
                                (quotient aa cc)
                                (quotient bb cc) 0)
                          (list
                                (quotient (minus bb) cc)
                                (quotient aa cc)
                                0)
                          '(0 0 1))
                    (calc-mod (cdddr tlst)))))
        (t (calc-mod (cdr tlst))))))

(defun def-fetch (id lib) (cond
        ((eq id (caar lib)) (cdar lib))
        (t (def-fetch id (cdr lib)))))

(defun def-fill (def mod ndef) (cond
        ((null def) ndef)
        (t (def-fill
              (cdr def)
              mod
              (cons (def-mod (car def) mod) ndef)))))
        (defun def-mod (def mod) (let*
              ((xx (nth 6 def))
               (yy (nth 7 def))
               (new (mmul (list (list xx yy 1)) mod)))
              (list
              (nth 0 def)
              (nth 1 def)
              (nth 2 def)
```

```
            (nth 3 def)
        (cond
            ((eq 0 (fix (cadar mod)))(nth 4 def))
            (t(nth 5 def)))
        (cond
            ((eq 0 (fix (cadar mod)))(nth 5 def))
            (t(nth 4 def)))
        (fix (caar new))
        (fix (cadar new))
        (nth 8 def)
        (nth 9 def)
        (nth\10 def))))
(defun rem-def (lst) (irem-def 0 nil lst))
        (defun irem-def (flg nlst lst) (cond
            ((null lst) (reverse nlst))
            ((null (car lst)) (irem-def flg nlst
                                            (cdr lst)))
    ((eq flg 0) (cond
                ((eq (caar lst) 'DS) (irem-def 1 nlst
                                            (cdr lst)))
                (t (irem-def 0 (cons (car lst) nlst)
                                            (cdr lst)))))
            ((eq flg 1) (cond
                ((eq (caar lst) 'DF) (irem-def 0 nlst
                                            (cdr lst)))
                (t (irem-def 1 nlst (cdr lst)))))))

(defun fixit () (let*
        ((file (progn (pp 'TYPE_INPUT_FILE) (ratom))
         (ofile (progn (pp 'TYPE_OUTPUT_FILE) (ratom)))
         (iport (infole ifile))
         (oport (outfile ofile))
         (dum (load 'matrix))
         (lst (tot-lst iport))
         (lib (mk-lib (find-defs lst)))
         (result (iscan lib nil (rem-def lst))))
        (ppage result oport)
        (close iport)
        (close oport)))

(defun ppage (lst port) (cond
        ((null lst) nil)
        (t (progn
                (pline (car lst) port)
                (ppage (cdr lst) port)))))
```

```
(defun pline (lst port) (cond
        ((null lst) (patom (ascii 10) port))
        (t (progn
                (patom (car lst) port)
                (patom (ascii 32) port)
                (pline (cdr last) port)))))

(defun ip (x y) (cond
        ((null x) 0.0)
        (t (add
                (times (car x) (car y))
                (ip (cdr x) (cdr y))))))

(defun first_row (x y) (cond
        ((null y) nil)
        (t (cons
                (ip (car x) (car y))
                (first_row x (cdr y))))))

(defun mmul (x y) (mm x (trans y)))
(defun mm (x y) (cond
        ((null x) nil)
        (t (cons
                (first_row x y)
                (mm (cdr x) y)))))

(defun first (x) (cond
        ((null x) nil)
        (t (cons (car (car x)) (first (cdr x))))))

(defun rest (x) (cond
        ((null x) nil)
        (t (cons (cdr (car x)) (rest (cdr x))))))

(defun trans (x) (cond
        ((null (car x)) nil)
        (t (cons (first x) (trans (rest x))))))
```

APPENDIX 2.   LISTING II

```
#   ------------------------------------------------------------------------------------------
#
    PROGRAM NAME: VLPLOT
#
#   AUTHOR:         G. RAMAKRISHNAN,
```

```
#                              ENGINEERING COMPUTER NETWORK,
#                              UNIVERSITY OF MISSOURI-COLUMBIA.
#
#    DATE:             9 - 14 - 87
#
#    DESCRIPTION:
#
#    The following command procedure is for plotting VLSI
#    design circuits on HP plotters which support HP-GL
#    software. The input is a .ca file which contains only
#    'rect' commands and layer identifications. Some pre-
#    processing is necessary to convert .ca files with
#    commands like transform, etc.
#
#    -------------------------------------------------------------------------------------------
# First run the vlsiplot program to create a file for each
    layer
vlsiplot
# Set the baud rate of the serial port (to which
# the plotter is connected) to 600 if handshaking
# is not available on that port.
# In the following list   '/dev/ttyhl' should
# be replaced with the serial port to which the
# plotter is connected
# Make sure that plotter baud rate is same as that
# of the serial port.
echo "insert various(color) pens as given below:"
echo "   slot number            pen color"
echo " "
echo "         1                 Red"
echo "         2                 Yellow (or) Orange"
echo "         3                 Blue"
echo "         4                 Black"
echo "         5                 Brown"
echo "         6                 Green"
echo "   "
echo "Hit any key when you are ready: "
read RESPONSE
echo "plotting started"
cat ecnini.dat > /dev/ttyhl
echo "plotting polysilicon layer"
cat ecnpol.dat > /dev/ttyhl
echo "plotting implantation layer"
cat ecnimp.dat > /dev/ttyhl
echo "plotting metal layer"
cat ecnmet.dat > /dev/ttyhl
echo "plotting cut"
cat ecncut.dat > /dev/ttyhl
```

```
echo "plotting diffusion layer"
cat ecndif.dat > /dev/ttyh1
echo "plotting buried-contact layer"
cat ecnbur.dat > /dev/ttyh1
cat ecnclo.dat > /dev/ttyh1
rm ecnini.dat ecnclo.dat ecnbur.dat ecncut.dat
rm ecndif.dat ecnmet.dat ecnpol.dat ecnimp.dat
echo "plotting over"
exit


/*    ---------------------------------------------------------------------------

      PROGRAM NAME: VLSIPLOT.C

      AUTHOR:        G. RAMAKRISHNAN
                     ENGINEERING COMPUTER NETWORK,
                     UNIVERSITY OF MISSOURI-COLUMBIA.

      DATE:          9 - 14 - 87

      DESCRIPTION:

          This program accepts an input file name and then does the
      following:
          (1)  Determines the co-ordinates of the lower-leftmost and
               top-rightmost points in the plot during the first
               scan of the input file
          (2)  Creates a file (for each layer) which contains the
               appropriate plotter commands

      Compile this program and then run the shell procedure 'vlplot.'
      To understand this program, one should be familiar with the
      structure of a '.ca' file

      ---------------------------------------------------------------------------   */
#include <stdio.h>
#define   CR   0x0a                     /*       Carriage Return        */
FILE *fopen(), *fclose(), *outf, *inf, *freopen();
static char in[25];
/*
      File  'ecnini.dat' contains the commands for initializing the
      plotter and drawing the border of the plotting area.
                                                                        */
static char ou[] = {"ecnini.dat"};
static char met[]={"<< m"};
static char bur[]={"<< b"};
static char cut[]={"<< c"};
static char dif[]={"<< d"};
```

```
static char imp[]={"<< i"};
static char pol[]={"<< p"};
static char rect[]={"rect"};
char data[48];
char *fid3,c;
int xmin,xmax,ymin,ymax,stat;
int de1,de2,de3,de4;
float fxmin,fxmax,fymin,fymax;
main()
{
 printf("enter the input file name\n"j);
 scanf ("%24s",in);
 inf = fopen(in,"r");
 if (inf == NULL)
   {
     printf("input file error \n");
     exit();
   }
 find_min_max();
/*
```

fxmin,fymin & fxmax,fymax are the left lowermost and right uppermost
points of border of the plot.

```
     fxmin=xmin-(xmax-xmin)*0.02;
     fymin=ymin-(ymax-ymin)*0.02;
     fxmax=xmax+(xmax-xmin)*0.02;
     fymax=ymax+(ymax-ymin)*0.02;
     inf = freopen(in,"r",inf);
     if (inf == NULL)
       {
         printf("input file reopen error \n");
         exit();
       }
     outf = fopen(ou,"w");
     if (outf == NULL)
       {
         printf("output file error \n");
         fclose(inf);
         exit();
       }
     fprintf(outf,"vs;sc%f,%f,%f,%f;",fxmin,fxmax,fymin,fymax);
     fprintf(outf,"sp1;pu;pa%f,%f;pd;pa%f,%f;",fxmin,fymin,fxmax,fymin);
     fprintf(outf,"pa%f,%f,%f,%f;",fxmax,fymax,fxmin,fymax);
     fprintf(outf,"pa%f,%f;pu;sp0;",fxmin,fymin);
     make_diff_files();
     outf=freopen("ecnclo.dat","w",outf);
     if (outf == NULL)
       {
```

```
            printf("close file error\n");
            exit();
            }
        fprintf(outf,"sp 0;df;");
         fclose(outf);
        }
/*
    The following function goes through the input file and creates one
    file for each layer in the integrated circuit (like metal,
    diffusion, polysilicon etc.)
                                                                    */
    make_diff_files()
        {
            fid3 = fgets(data,48,inf);
/* first line has no info. for plotting
        while ((fid3 = fgets(data,48,inf)) != NULL)
            {
            if ((stat = strncmp(data,rect,4)) == NULL)
                {
                get_coords();
                fprintf(outf,"pa %d,%d;pd;pa %d,%d;",del,de2,de3,de2);
                fprintf(outf,"pa %d,%d,%d,%d;",de3,de4,del,de4);
                fprintf(outf,"pa %d,%d,",del,de2);
                fprintf(outf,"pu;");
                continue;
                }
            if ((stat = strncmp(data,pol,4)) == NULL)
                {
                outf=freopen("ecnpol.dat","w",outf);
                test();
                fprintf(outf,"spl;");
                continue;
                }
            if ((stat = strncmp(data,imp,4)) == NULL)
                {
                outf=freopen("ecnimp.dat","w",outf);
                test();
                fprintf(outf,"sp2;");
                continue;
                }
            if ((stat = strncmp(data,met,4)) == NULL)
                {
                outf=freopen("ecnmet.dat","w",outf);
                test();
                fprintf(outf,"sp3;");
                continue;
                }
```

```
        if ((stat = strncmp(data,cut,4)) == NULL)
          {
          outf=freopen("ecncut.dat","w",outf);
          test( );
          fprintf(outf,"sp4;");
          continue;
          }
        if ((stat = strncmp(data,bur,4)) == NULL)
          {
          outf=freopen("ecnbur.dat","w",outf);
          test( );
          fprintf(outf,"sp5;");
          continue;
          }
        if ((stat = strncmp(data,dif,4)) == NULL)
          {
          outf=freopen("ecndif.dat","w",outf);
          test( );
          fprintf(outf,"sp6;");
          continue;
          }
        }
    }
/*
```

Function 'test' checks for error condition while opening
a file

```
                                                          */

test( )
  {
  if (outf == NULL)
    {
    prinf("file open error\n");
    exit( );
    }
  }
/*
```

The following function goes through the input file (.ca type)
and determines the xmin,ymin,xmax & ymmax

```
                                                          */

find_min_max( )
  {
  int lcnt,stat,min1,min2,max1,max2;
  lcnt=0;
  fid3 = fgets(data,48,inf);
  while (( fid3 = fgets(data,48,inf)) != NULL)
    {
/*
```

worry only about those lines which start with 'rect'

```
                                                                    */
     if ((stat = strncmp(data,rect,4)) == NULL)
       {
       get_coords():
       min1=min(de1,de3);
       max1=max(de1,de3);
       min2=min(de2,de4);
       max2=max(de2,de4);
       if (lcnt == 0)
         {
         xmin=min1;
         xmax=max1;
         ymin=min2;
         ymax=max2;
         lcnt=1;
         }
       else
         {
         if (min1 < xmin)
          xmin = min1;
         if (min2 < ymin)
          ymin = min2;
         if (max1 > xmax)
          xmax = max1;
         if (max2 > ymax)
          ymax = max2;
         }
       }
   }
}
/*    This function finds out the minimum of two numbers        */
   min(d1,d2)
   int d1,d2;
    {
     int min;
     min=d1;
     if (d2 < min)
      min=d2;
     return(min);
    }
/*    This function finds out the maximum of two numbers        */
   max(d1,d2)
   int d1,d2;
    {
     int max;
    max=d1;
```

```
    if (d2 > max)
     max=d2;
    return(max);
   }
/*
```

This function takes a line of data from the input file as a string and returns the co-ordinates of left-lowermost and right-topmost points of each rectangle (in intger format) in the plot.

                                                                    */

```
get_coords( )
  {
   int k,l,j;
   char str1[8],str2[8],str3[8],str4[8];
   for (l=0; l<8; l++)
    {
      str1[l]=' ';
      str2[l]=' ';
      str3[l]=' ';
      str4[l]=' ';
    }
   l=0;
   k=5;
   j=0;
   while (data[k] != CR)
    {
     if (data[k] == ' ')
       {
        l++;
        j = -1;
       }
     else
       {
        if (l == 0) str1[j]=data[k];
        if (l == 1) str2[j]=data[k];
        if (l == 2) str3[j]=data[k];
        if (l == 3) str4[j]=data[k];
       }
     j++;
     k++;
    }
   de1=atoi(str1);
   de2=atoi(str2);
   de3=atoi(str3);
   de4=atoi(str4);
  }
```

REFERENCES

1. B.C. Cole, "Competition Soars in PC AT Clone Chips," *Electronics*, Vol. 60, No. 20, 1987, p. 33.
2. L.A. Glassner and D.W. Dobberpuhl, *The Design and Analysis of VLSI Circuits*, Addison-Wesley, Reading, MA, 1985.
3. D.A. Hodges and H.G. Jackson, *Analysis and Design of Digital Integrated Circuits*, McGraw-Hill, New York, 1983.
4. J. Mavor, M.A. Jack and P.B. Deneyer, *Introduction to MOS LSI Design*, Addison-Wesley, London, UK, 1983.
5. R.N. Mayo, J.K. Ousterhout and W.S. Scott, "1983 VLSI Tools: Selected Works by the Original Artists," Technical Report No. UCB/CSD 83/15, University of California, Berkeley, CA, 1983.
6. C. Mead and L. Conway, *Introduction to VLSI Systems*, Addison-Wesley, Reading, MA, 1980.
7. W.M. Penney and L. Lau, *MOS Integrated Circuits*, McGraw-Hill, New York, 1972.
8. D.L. Schilling and C. Belove, *Electronic Circuits, Discrete and Integrated*, McGraw-Hill, New York, 1979.

6

New Directions in Semicustom Arrays

MICHIEL A. BEUNDER

Institute for Microelectronics
Stuttgart, West-Germany

1. INTRODUCTION

After the emergence of the semiconductor era in the 1960s, development of applications was concentrated on the fabrication of standard components. Only mass production could bring down the costs of integrating circuits on silicon.

With the maturing of semiconductor technology, the environment became more customized. The end of the 1970s and the start of the 1980s can be marked as the start of the ASIC era. Still, costs of producing an application-specific circuit were a major handicap for widespread application and opening of the market. Cost factors were mainly made up of engineering costs (design time) and fabrication costs (masks). Two developments caused a major opening of the ASIC market:

1. The introduction of the gate array
2. The introduction of computer-aided design tools

The gate array became a widespread implementation medium. The main advantages of the gate array are the reduction in mask fabrication costs and the reduction in *design time*. As a third advantage, resulting from the reduction in process steps, *fabrication time* is reduced from around six weeks down to two weeks. Figure 6.1 shows the different turnaround times for full custom and semicustom design.

1.1. Terminology

Throughout the literature there is no general consensus on the terminology used to designate the different semicustom and full-custom

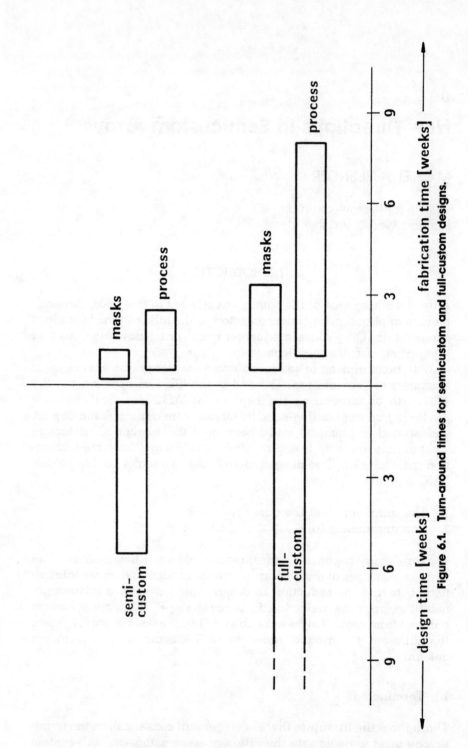

Figure 6.1. Turn-around times for semicustom and full-custom designs.

concepts. This section will therefore define a number of terms which are used in this chapter. Five concepts will be explained: *full-custom, semicustom, gate array, master slice,* and *master image.*

A *full-custom* implementation within a certain technology, uses *all* available layers of the process to personalize the design. All degrees of freedom, available within the specific process, are used by the designer to layout the circuit.

A *semicustom* implementation uses only a limited number of the available process layers to personalize the design. Usually the personalization layers are the last layers to be processed. The personalization layers use the underlying, predefined features to implement the circuit.

The term *gate array* defines an approach within the semicustom concept. A gate array implementation is based on a preprocessed master on which arrays of identical transistors have been placed. Personalization of the master is done on the metal and contact layer(s).

The term *master slice* describes an approach similar to that of the gate array. However, instead of identical transistors, identical groups of transistors are used. Within such a group (or slice), transistor sizes are varied to provide different characteristics for different functions. Personalization of the master slice is done on the metal and contact layer(s).

The term *master image* describes a full-custom implementation of the previous two concepts. The master image is based on a fixed transistor grid for implementation of logic. Slices are used for density reasons; they usually implement memory or other high-density functions with a high regularity degree.

The previous three approaches can be classified according to their implementation concept:

Full-Custom	Semicustom
Master Image	Gate Array
	Master Slice

Within this chapter, the terms semicustom and gate array will be used as much as possible. In section 2, a formal description of an array architecture will be presented, which will enable a much more precise classification of the array than a general classification possible with terms such as master slice and gate array.

1.2. Technology

The first gate arrays were produced in nMOS technology. However, after the appearance of CMOS technology with its advantages over nMOS technology, the majority of gate array designs shifted to CMOS. Currently semicustom arrays are available for FET-, bipolar- and gallium arsenide technologies. This chapter will concentrate on the CMOS gate arrays, since these arrays make up the major part of the semicustom market.

One of the main advantages of semicustom arrays is the quick introduction of new technologies. Because of the significant lower overhead in the support of the design environment (e.g., standard cell libraries) and the simple customer interface, new technologies can be introduced much faster than would be possible in a full-custom environment. This makes it possible to keep semicustom arrays at the leading edge of technology.

Section 2 will describe important characteristics of the technology used to implement semicustom arrays.

1.3. Semicustom Principles

This section describes the principles of semicustom arrays, using the gate array approach as an example.

The gate array approach consists of the individualization of logic networks by simply routing the connections between cells and between devices inside a cell on the so-called masters. The devices on the master chip are placed in a simple arrangement, without any device interconnections. The personalization of the master is done on the metal and contact levels. A standard semicustom design interface is shown in Figure 6.2. This standard interface consists of the following components:

1. Schematic entry tool
2. Cell libraries
3. Logic simulation tool
4. Place and route tool
5. Back-annotation tool
6. Detailed timing simulator

Usually a customer will only use the first three tools. Subsequent steps are done by the foundry, which will process the design.

The schematic entry together with the (standard) cell libraries enables the designer to enter his or her circuit description. Designers are bound to the cell libraries since there is usually no (schematic) interface with the transistor layout of the image which would allow the implementation of "customized" standard cells or macros. After

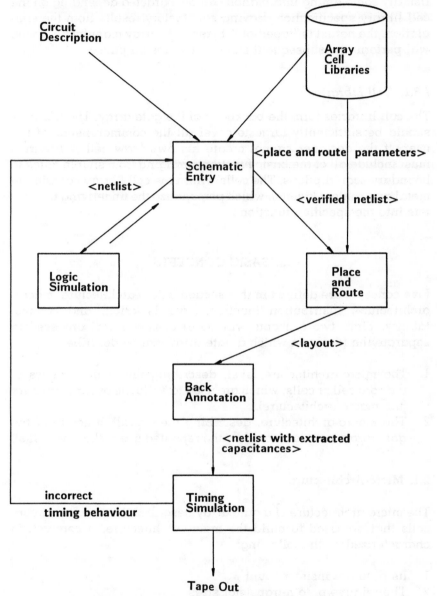

Figure 6.2.   A semicustom design interface.

schematic entry, the circuit can be simulated with a logic simulator. Usually some timing information can be extracted depending on the cell library specification. Having satisfactory results from the simulation, the netlist is "taped-out" to the gate array manufacturer who will perform the subsequent steps in the design phase.

1.3.1. Cell Libraries

The cell libraries form the backbone of the gate array. The libraries should be sufficiently large to cover all the common needs of the user. If the designer cannot create his own "raw cells," libraries must include all of the basic functions, ranging from simple gates to boundary-scan flipflops. The cells within the cell library contain the metal and contact layer(s), which personalize the underlying transistors into the specified function.

2. BASIC CONCEPTS

Five concepts are defined in this section: micro-architecture, macro-architecture, distribution function, gate isolation, and connectability. First, two concepts will be discussed which are used to separate the levels on which a gate array can be described:

1. The micro-architecture level, describing the characteristics of the core cell or cells, which are used to build the overall structure (the macro-architecture).
2. The macro-architecture, describing the overall structure of the gate array, as it is created by the repeated use of the core cell(s).

2.1. Micro-Architecture

The micro-architecture of a gate array describes the core cell or core cells that are used to build the macro-architecture. A core cell is characterized by the following:

1. Its p- to n-transistor count
2. The relative p- to n-transistor sizes
3. The isolation technique(s) used
4. Its connectability characteristics:
   diffusion geometries (diffusion to diffusion, diffusion to poly)
   poly geometries (poly to poly, poly to diffusion)

5. The degree of cell specialization
6. Its grid
7. The design rules (technology)

The concepts of isolation technique and cell specialization are discussed separately.

2.1.1. Gate Isolation

The isolation technique refers to the technique(s) used to isolate neighbouring transistors from each other. Two techniques are currently available: gate isolation [1], or isolation by means of the field oxide (geometrical isolation). The use of geometrical isolation does not require any additional wiring. Gate isolation requires that, if two neighboring transistors must be isolated, a third transistor must be located between the two transistors and that it must be switched into "off" mode. This requires the wiring of either a V_{dd} or a V_{ss} connection to the gate of the isolation transistor. Each of the techniques has its advantages and disadvantages. The major advantages of the gate isolation technique are as follows:

1. Significant increase in transistor packing density
2. Less wiring when creating complex functions
3. Easy control of the data flow (active bound).

The advantages of gate isolation become clear when reviewing the two examples, shown in Figure 6.3. A 4-input NOR is used to demonstrate the difference in area between both implementations. The advantage of gate isolation becomes even more obvious when longer strings of series and parallel transistors are needed. The separation of p- and n-transistor poly gates is necessary for the use of gate isolation.

2.1.2. Cell Specialization

Specialization refers to the use of layout features in the core cell, which support specific functions, for example, a core cell could contain a specific structure for PLA implementation support or a dedicated RAM structure. Usually the design of a core cell will be directed towards a general applicable architecture. When developed in conjunction with other core cells, each of the core cells will cover an area of commonly needed functions within an architecture. If not, the application area of the master will be significantly reduced. This

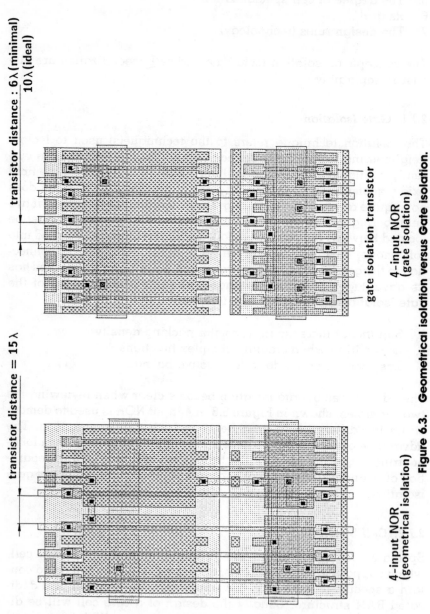

transistor distance : 6 λ (minimal)
10 λ (ideal)

transistor distance = 15 λ

gate isolation transistor

4-input NOR
(gate isolation)

4-input NOR
(geometrical isolation)

Figure 6.3.   Geometrical isolation versus Gate isolation.

will reduce the cost-effectiveness of the semicustom approach since a number of different masters must be kept in storage, combined with the effect of extra overhead on design support. However, it will allow the manufacturer to address a larger portion of the application market.

Figure 6.4 shows a number of cells with a specialized architecture.

2.1.3. Connectability

The concept of connectability actually covers two characteristics of the core cell:

1. The accessability of the different "connectors" in the cell, both horizontally and vertically (horizontal and vertical access factor). Connections can either be poly gates or source-drain areas.
2. The transparency of the cell to its environment. The number of signals that can be routed through the cell (horizontally and vertically) without inhibiting the use of one or more transistors. When for instance, a signal is routed over a polysilicon gate, thereby covering all contacts, the transistor is no longer available for use.

In conjunction with the description of the connectability characteristics, three other terms need some clarification:

- *Route-through track*. A track which can be used to wire through a cell without disabling the use of one or more transistors. A route-through track is a feature which has to be designed into the micro-architecture of the core cell.
- *Feed-through track*. A track contained by a so-called feed-through cell, which is *inserted* between two cells to enable the wiring from one cell row to the next cell row. Feed-through cells are used in the circuit design phase, when the semi-custom array is being personalized.
- *Track switch*. A geometry which allows a personalization wire to change from one track to another without blocking intermediate track(s). A track switch is part of the micro-architecture of the core cell.

Figure 6.5 shows the difference between a route-through and a feed-through track, and the use of a track switch.

The connectability characteristics of a cell should be seen in con-

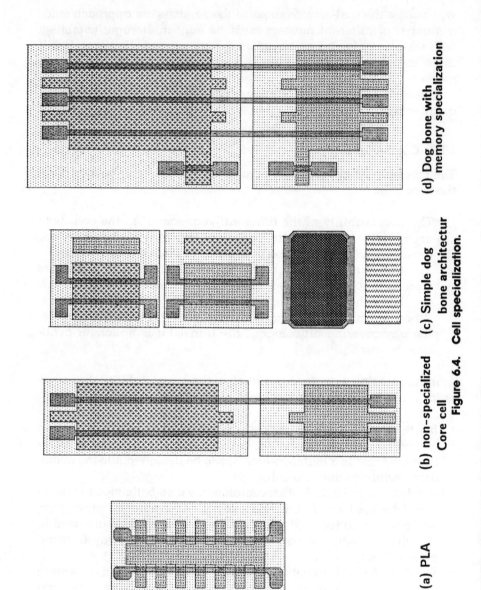

(a) PLA

(b) non-specialized Core cell

(c) Simple dog bone architectur Cell specialization.

(d) Dog bone with memory specialization

Figure 6.4. Cell specialization.

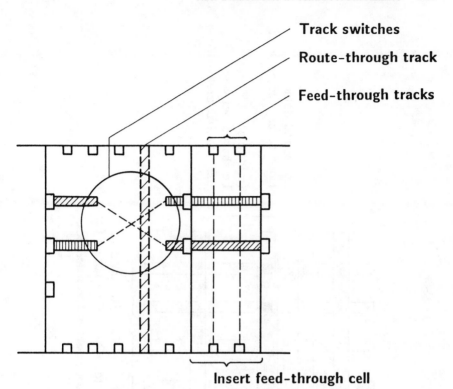

Track switches

Route-through track

Feed-through tracks

Insert feed-through cell

Figure 6.5.   The Concepts of Route-through, Feed-through, and Track-switch.

nection with both its environment and its internal contacts. The connectors of the cell are the poly gate contacts and the drain/source
contacts (passive elements like resistors and capacitors are ignored
here). The poly gate is usually associated with the control flow,
whereas the diffusion regions are associated with the data flow of
the core cell. The vertical and horizontal contact aspects of both
flows are reviewed independently. An example is shown in Figure
6.6. In the example, the control flow has an access factor of 2, for
both horizontal and vertical direction. The data flow has horizontally
an access factor of 1.5, and vertically a value of 2.

The transparency of the cell is evaluated using the following conditions: available gates and source/drain areas are contacted once.
Remaining tracks can be used for route-through purposes. In the
previous example, the cell can accommodate both horizontally and
vertically 2 route-through tracks.

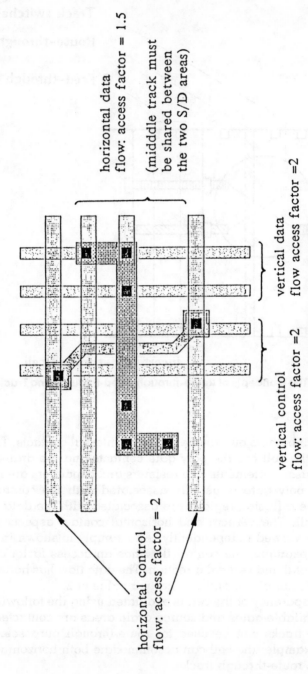

horizontal data
flow: access factor = 1.5

(middle track must
be shared between
the two S/D areas)

vertical data
flow access factor =2

vertical control
flow: access factor =2

horizontal control
flow: access factor = 2

Figure 6.6. Connectability Characteristics.

2.2. Macro-Architecture

The macro-architecture of the gate array is basically characterized by two items:

1. The number of core cells used to build the macro-architecture
2. The global routing policy.

If, for instance, the macro-architecture contains a dedicated (macro) RAM block, one can identify two core cells, one to build the regular gate forest structure, and one to build the dense RAM block.

The global routing policy determines if global routing channels—areas not covered by the core cell(s)—are available to the designer. The global routing policy will also determine the size of these channels and their organization. The absence of any routing channels is usually described with the term *channelless architecture*. The global routing policy is expressed in the distribution function. For each of the core cells used, a separate distribution function is used, which determines the grid in which the core cells will be placed. Apart from just the global routing policy, the distribution function(s) will also determine the granularity of the array. A distribution function which binds identical core cells into macro blocks will generate a coarse grid. A distribution function which will distribute the different types of core cells evenly over one (channelless) block creates a master image with a fine granularity. Figure 6.7 shows the concepts of micro- and macro-architecture, and their relation to each other.

2.3. Technology Issues

This section will deal with the technological background of the semicustom arrays, as far as it concerns the design of the micro- and macro-architecture and personalization characteristics. For reference purposes, the MOSIS design rule set [2] has been used. This design rule set can be seen as an example of a state-of-the-art technology interface. Although some of the features in the MOSIS rule set are not applicable to semicustom design, general constraints, as described below, are still valid for the semicustom environment.

The advances in the (CMOS) process technology have enabled the widespread use of semicustom arrays. The advances in process technology are mainly driven by the urge for larger memories and, as such are not completely portable to the VLSI (semi-) custom environment. Two sets of technology rules can be identified which

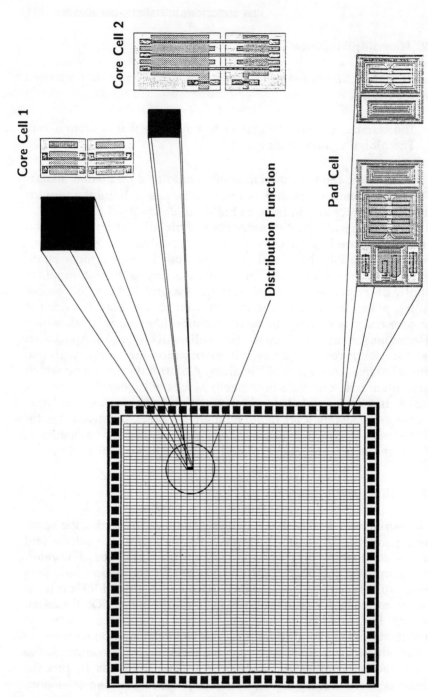

Core Cell 1

Core Cell 2

Distribution Function

Pad Cell

Figure 6.7. Micro- and Macro-Architecture.

have great impact on the design and personalization of semicustom arrays:

1. Contact rules: metal to metal, metal to poly and metal to diffusion
2. Metal pitch rules

An example of the influence of contact rules on the design of a core cell is illustrated in Figure 6.8. Current design rules do not allow stacked vias: metal2 to metal1, and metal1 to active or poly contact, stacked on each other. The designer is forced to use the inefficient staged via, which also blocks one or more route-through tracks. The micro-architecture of the core cell has to take this effect into account, otherwise large numbers of transistors will be rendered useless because of the lack of sufficient intermediate contact space. Another important constraint imposed by current design rules is via placement. Placement of a via on top of a poly gate, or on the edge of an active area is not allowed. Especially in channelless architectures, the micro-architecture of the core cell has to incorporate a number of locations where vias can be placed. The minimum metal pitch is as important as the minimum gate length that is specified for a certain process. The matrix that is built by creating rows and columns of metal wires, and where the space between rows and columns is based on the minimum pitch belonging to the metal layer, determines the design of the core cell. The denser this matrix will be, the denser will be the layout of the core cell. Another important characteristic of the metal layers used in a process is their current capacity. Older processes used to have a low limit on current capabilities of their metal, especially where the second level of metal was concerned. This limitation results in wide power and ground wiring channels, reducing the number of available transistors. Undersizing the power and ground wires could lead to reliability problems. Oversizing is also not attractive because of the waste in area and transistors. Low margins therefore force the designer to spend extra time on analyzing the switching behaviour of the circuit, after placement has been done. If necessary, the designer has to break up the circuit and reconfigure it in order to meet these power constraints. Last, but not least, the use of guard rings and substrate contacts has to be taken into account. The core cell must contain sufficient possibilities to place contacts on either guard ring, well-, or substrate contact. These contacts must be hooked up to either V_{dd} or V_{ss}, which will take away one or more routing tracks. Because of the extreme den-

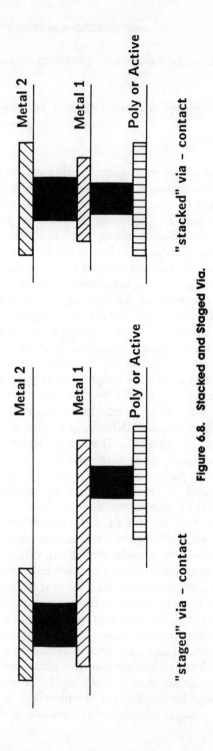

Figure 6.8. Stacked and Staged Via.

sities in semicustom arrays, the use of well- or substrate contacts is absolutely necessary to prevent latch-up.

3. FIRST GENERATION GATE ARRAYS

An example of the architecture of a typical first-generation gate array is shown in Figure 6.9. The core cell would usually consist of two to three transistors, with a common gate, and the core cells would be placed in geometrical isolation with a distribution function. No power routing had to be performed since power and ground were predefined. Standard cell libraries fitted well in this concept. Complexity of such gate arrays would reach up to about 4K gates, from which about 50% would be useable. Figure 6.10 shows a microphotograph of an older gate array. As can be seen, a channel architecture is incorporated in the array.

4. SECOND GENERATION GATE ARRAYS: SEA-OF-GATES

The introduction of the sea-of-gates concept, together with the use of gate isolation technique, marks the era of the second generation gate arrays. This new, more flexible implementation environment for ASICs was introduced in 1982 [3,1]. Gate arrays under the name of cell array, uncommitted logic array, continuous gate array, or structured array are also based on the sea-of-gates concept.

4.1. Overview of Sea-of-Gates Type Arrays

The introduction of the sea-of-gates concept, together with the use of gate isolation, marks the start of the second-generation gate arrays. This part will give an overview of the different developments that have taken place since the start of the new generation. It will describe a number of micro- and macro-architectures together with their advantages and disadvantages.

The developments in the gate array technology are illustrated by following the line of transistor packing densities, starting in 1982. This process is shown in Figure 6.11. Increases in density are not only caused by the improved fabrication technology but also by a denser design of the core cell and addition of special macro blocks, for example, memory blocks or processor slices.

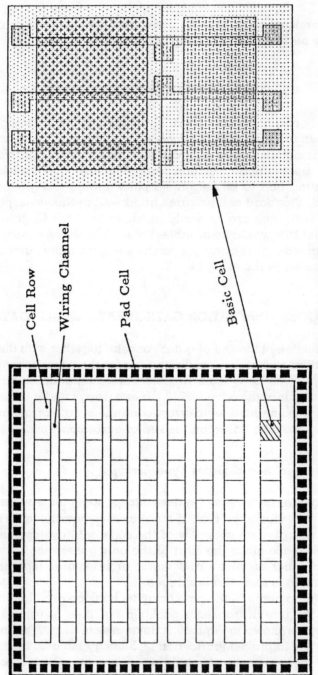

Cell Row

Wiring Channel

Pad Cell

Basic Cell

Figure 6.9. Conventional Gate Array with Basic Cell.

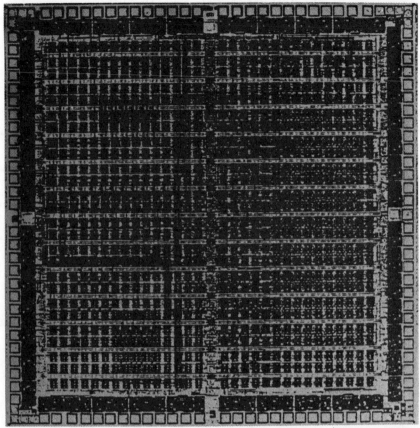

Figure 6.10.   Microphotograph First Generation Gate Array (source: CICC '87 educational sessions).

4.2. Basic Architectural Characteristics

Figure 6.12 shows three microphotographs of channelless type arrays. The arrays shown in Figure 12(a) and Figure 12(b) are based on one core cell using a uniform distribution function. The array shown in Figure 12(c) is based on five different core cells with block distribution functions. In the following sections a more detailed overview of the different characteristics will be presented.

4.2.1. Evaluating a Micro-Architecture

An important feature of any micro-architecture is its universality. How efficient can one implement different types of functions in a

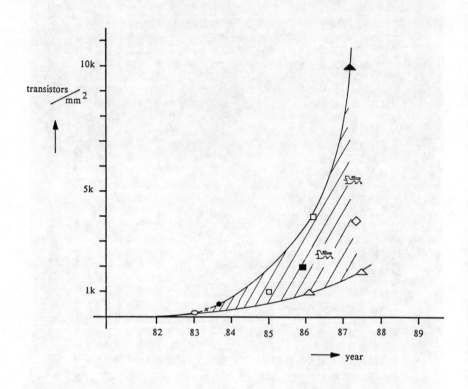

Figure 6.11. Transistor Densities for Sea-of-Gates Type Gate Arrays.

specific micro-architecture? These functions range from three-port RAM cells to PLA structures and flipflops.

Three functions were defined which were thought to cover an important part of the application area:

1. RAM cell, 2-port
2. D-flipflop
3. Four-input NAND

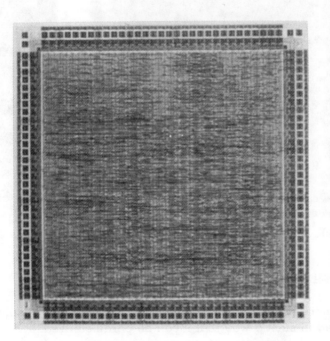

Figure 6.12(a).   Microphotograph Channelless Architecture with Core Cell.
Courtesy VLSI Technology Inc.

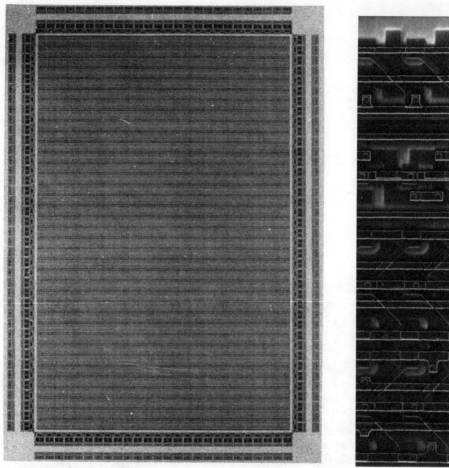

Figure 6.12(b). Microphotograph Channelless Architecture with Core Cell.

The RAM cell addresses two important aspects:

1. Parameterization of regular structures. The RAM cell should be designed in such a way that it can be parameterized.
2. Use of single transistors, for example, as read or write gate.

The D-flipflop was selected because it is on average the most used (placed) cell in custom designs [4]. The four-input NAND was selected as a representative of a normal logic function. The three functions have been used as a test vehicle during the evaluation of a

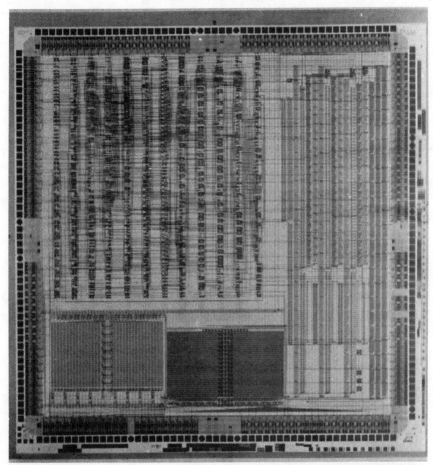

Figure 6.12(c). Microphotograph Second Generation Gate Array with Block Architecture.

number of alternative architectures. By working on a lambda grid instead of an absolute grid, some means of quality evaluation can be achieved when comparing the different implementations. It should be kept in mind that, apart from the area a function uses, the transparency of the resulting design is also very important.

4.3. Micro-Architectures

One of the most used micro-architectures is the "dog-bone" structure, shown in Figure 6.13. Because the dog bone structure is a commonly

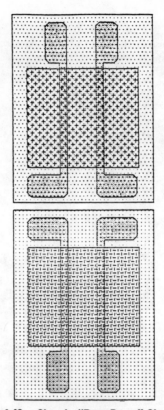

Figure 6.13.   Simple "Dog-Bone" Structure.

used micro-architecture, it will be discussed in more detail than other representatives. Figure 6.13 shows the structure in its basic configuration: two transistors with a shared drain/source area. The most important feature of this type of structure is the use in a channelless macro-architecture, and the fact that only geometrical isolation is used. Figure 6.14 shows an implementation of a D-type flipflop on the dog bone structure.

A further analysis of the dog-bone architecture reveals that although the connectability characteristics of the structure look favorable, a thorough evaluation reveals that for both data and control flow the horizontal and vertical access is equal to 1. Transparency is also marginal. Wiring such a cell will usually result in disabling a neighbor cell, which has to be used for wiring purposes. Exceptions are the implementation of low-complexity logic functions with short wiring distances. This actually reveals an important characteristic of the structure, and more generally macro-architectures based on

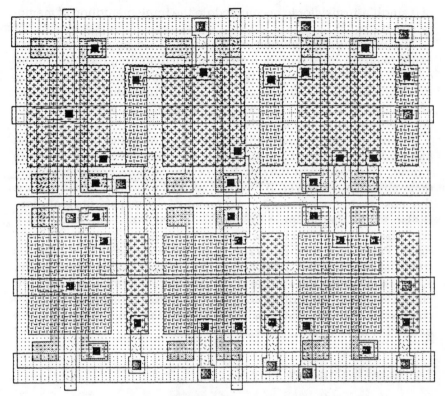

Figure 6.14.   Latch implementation (Sea-of-Gates/Dog-Bone).

the use of the structure: the micro-architecture is minimized in size, as to enable a maximum number of cells to be packed on the master.

Although the number of transistors per square millimeter could be seen as a quality mark of the master, it should be realized that the number of *used* transistors per square millimeter is a much better quality mark. Basic variations in the dog-bone micro-architecture are:

1. The use of gate isolation
2. The number of transistors in an active row
3. Common poly silicon gate for p,n transistor pair
4. Extending poly gate and/or active areas to improve the connectability characteristics of the structure.

Figure 6.4 (section 2.1.2) shows a number of variations on the basic dog-bone micro-architecture. An interesting variation is the addition of a small n-transistor to accommodate the implementation of memory structures [5].

The use of gate isolation in the unmodified dog-bone structure could result in extra wiring. Instead of just disabling its neighboring cell, it generates the necessity of isolation, resulting in an extra V_{dd} and V_{ss} connection to the respective gates. Variations in the number of transistors in an active row have no significant effect on the efficiency of the micro-architecture.

The use of common poly silicon gate p,n transistor pairs has as a main advantage the elimination of metal cross-overs from p-gate to n-gate. This results in the addition of one or more horizontal route-through tracks. However, it has also several negative consequences: the most severe one being the exclusion of the use of gate isolation. It also forces the designer to use the paired transistor, although it could be more efficient to use them on geometrically separated locations. Figure 6.4 also shows a micro-architecture which deviates from the usual dog-bone structure, a PLA specialized architecture.

Table 6.1 gives an overview of the different arrays, listing their characteristics, originating company, and (market) name. It is not a complete overview, but it is thought that the most representative examples have been included.

4.4. Macro-Architecture

Table 6.1, presented in the previous section, also listed the macro-architectural properties of each of the masters.

The macro-architecture is determined by the combination of distribution function(s) and core cell(s). A number of characteristic distribution functions can be identified:

1. Uniform distribution function,
2. Channel distribution function,
3. Block distribution function.

The first two distribution functions can be used in combinations with either one or more core cells. The last distribution function is almost solely used in combination with two or more core cells. Examples of the first type of macro-architecture can be found in [6,7,8]. The second type of macro-architecture is similar to the older gate array approach, where fixed wiring channels were defined. One reason for having fixed wiring channels could be the CAD tools used. A channelless router has to be sophisticated enough to accomplish a 100%

Table 6.1. An Overview of Sea of Gates Type Gate Array Architectures.

Origin[1]	Year	Name	Micro-Architecture	Macro-Architecture	Number of Gates	Technology	Reference
VLSI Technology Inc.	'86	Continuous Gate Technology	1p, 1n transistor; gate isolation; size approx. 138 × 13.5;	1 core cell; channel distribution function;	25–60K	1.5μ n-Well double metal CMOS	9
Sperry	'83	Hierarchical Logic Array	12n, 12p transistors; p and n transistor share poly gate; use of poly silicon jumpers for interconnect	1 core cell channel distribution function;	10K	1.2μ N-Well double metal CMOS	10
University of Bath	'83	Uncommitted Logic Array	NAND/NOR logic structure; prewired;	1 core cell; channel distribution function;		5μ isoCMOS	27
Bell Labs, Allentown	'83	CMOS Cell Array	1p, 1n transistors; gate isolation; also customized on poly level;	1 core cell; channel distribution function;		3.5μ CMOS twin tub; 2.5μ CMOS twin tub;	11
California Devices Inc.	'83	Advanced Architecture Channelless Gate Array	2p, 2n transistors; contacts already defined; "airy" cell design for vertical conn.	1 core cell; uniform distribution function;	4.1K	3μ double metal CMOS	6
Mitsubishi	'83		1p, 1n transistor; gate isolation;	1 core cell; block distribution function; (176 blocks in 44 rows and 4 columns)	10K	2μ n-Well double CMOS	28
LSI Logic Inc.	'85	Sea-of-Gates	2p, 2n transistors; with common drain-source areas; cells geometrical isol.; cell size: 41×38	1 core cell; uniform distribution function;	4.1K	2μ p-Well double metal HCMOS	7

(continued)

Table 6.1. *(Continued)*

Origin[1]	Year	Name	Micro-Architecture	Macro-Architecture	Number of Gates	Technology	Reference
NEC	'86	Macro Logic Array	2 core cells; 1-4p, 4n transis. 2–PLA dedicated structure: AND: 2p, 40n; OR: 1p, 18n;	2 core cells; uniform distribution function;	27K	1.6μ n-Well double metal CMOS	29
LSI Logic Inc.	'85	Structured Arrays LSA200X	more than one core cell used, some RAM, ROM, Multiplier ALU cells/slices; general core cell; 2p, 2n transistors; shared drain-source areas; cells geometrical isolated	more than one core cell; specialized cells are organized in macro blocks;	3K–5K	2μ p-Well double metal HCMOS	12
LSI Logic Inc.	'86	Variable Track Master Slice	1p, 2n transistors; gate isolation;	1 core cel; uniform distribution function;	135K	1.3μ double metal CMOS	30
Toshiba	'86	Compacted Array	2p, 2n transistors; common drain source area; cells are geometrically isolated	1 core cell; uniform distribution function;	100K	1.5μ double metal HCMOS	24
LSI Logic Inc.	'86	Compacted Array LCA 100XX	2p, 2n transistors; common drain source areas; cells are geometrically isolated	1 core cell; uniform distribution function	27K–129K	1.5μ double metal HCMOS	31 8 32

IBM Boeblingen	'87	Flexible Master	cell1: 3p, 3n transistors; common gate; geometrical isolation; cellx: RAM, ROM, PLA;	block distribution; not a true semicustom approach;	200K	1.0μ n-Well triple metal CMOS	13
NEC	'87	Analog and Digital Master Slice	cell1: 1p, 1n transistor; gate isolation, 4 routing tracks; cell2: 8 passive elements (double poly structures); 14 sensitive routing tracks;	2 core cells; uniform distribution function in alternating rows	4K; 7K pass.	1.6μ n-Well double metal, double poly CMOS	31
Motorola, Phoenix	'87		4p, 4n transistors; common drain-source areas; cell externally: geometric isolation;	1 core cell; channel distribution function;	6K	1.25μ twin well, double metal CMOS	33
Motorola, Phoenix	'87		4p, 4n transistors; gate isolation and geometrical isolation;	1 core cell; uniform distribution function;	150K	0.5μ triple metal CMOS	34

[1]This table does not pretend to be complete or exact. All figures were extracted from official publications or marketing announcements. Not all necessary data was available; sometimes data had to be extracted manually, which could have resulted in imprecise data.

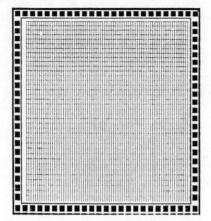

Uniform Distribution
Function

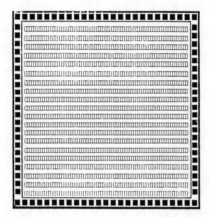

Channel Distribution
Function

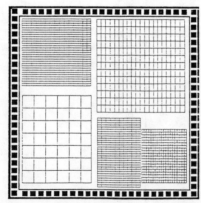

Block Distribution
Function

Figure 6.15. Macro-Architectures created with different distribution Functions.

routing completeness. It has to obey the constraints set by the design rules, for example, most technologies do not allow placement of vias on top of transistors, and so on. Examples of a channel approach can be found in [9,10,11]. Figure 6.15 shows the three different categories of macro-architectures. Most of the newer master designs do not use a channel distribution function. Block distribution functions are also widespread in use. Gate array masters which include memory macro blocks (RAM, ROM, EEPROM) or processor slices always use block distribution functions. Good examples of this type of macro-architecture can be found in [12,13].

5. THE CMOS GATE FOREST

As an extension of the existing sea of gates concept, the GATE FOREST concept will be presented, together with its implementation in CMOS technology. The CMOS GATE FOREST is an example of current developments taking place in the semicustom arrays. Because of its advanced architecture, it demands state-of-the-art design tools and technology. The efficiency of the GATE FOREST architecture will be demonstrated using a number of standard functions. Two more complicated design examples will be discussed: a five-input XOR and an 8×8 bit multiplier.

5.1. Introduction

The GATE FOREST distinguishes itself from the older sea-of-gates concept in its different architecture, which is based on a hierarchical view of both complex logic and design approach. Before discussing the micro- and macro-architecture of the GATE FOREST master in detail, the framework within which the GATE FOREST concept was developed will be described.

5.2. The GATE FOREST Philosophy

The philosophy behind the GATE FOREST architecture can be described by reviewing the different levels of complexity in logic structures. Starting on the level of a simple inverter, which can be designated as a leaf cell, a simple circuit of two complementary transistors can be distinguished. As the next step up in the complexity hierarchy, a five input dynamic AND structure could be taken as an example. Within this circuit a string of transistors can be distinguished (branch logic). Again the next step up in the hierarchy is a five input XOR function. Within this function several interconnected strings or branches of transistors can be distinguished, building the tree level logic. The top level of the hierarchy is the GATE FOREST level. The above described hierarchy is shown in Figure 6.16.

5.3. General Objectives

Apart from the fundamental reflections on the structure of the GATE FOREST, a number of general objectives have been identified, which were used to define the framework and rules for the implementation of the GATE FOREST concept:

1. *Design Considerations.* The support of dynamic circuit design for compact, high-speed applications was given a high priority. Support can be given on two levels:
   (a) Master level: tuning the micro-architecture to allow the efficient implementation of dynamic logic.
   (b) Design level: implementing dynamic cell libraries which are made available to the designer.
   The use of only dynamic logic would make the design environment inflexible and inefficient. Therefore two libraries were defined: a static version and a dynamic version. The dynamic cell library was divided into three sub-libraries: a domino logic-based [14], a cascode voltage switch logic-based [15], and a sample set differential logic-based [16] version. Another important aspect which influenced the design of the micro-architecture was the use of (distributed) memory. Already at the starting phase of the project, it was determined that no macro blocks with RAM, ROM, or EEPROM would be used. This influences the design of the core cell, since it must be possible to implement RAM or ROM on the core cell grid.
2. *Technology Considerations.* To increase the lifetime of both gate forest and cell libraries, a portable and scalable set of design rules was used for the development. As a base for this set, the MOSIS design rules [2] were taken and adapted to the European scene [17].
3. *Tool Considerations.* A number of tools were identified which were thought to be crucial for the realization of a design in the gate forest environment. The tools identified were: a custom place and route tool, a function router, a schematic and language interface, and simulation and optimization tools. With

Leaf Cell Logic

Branch Logic

Tree Logic

GATE FOREST

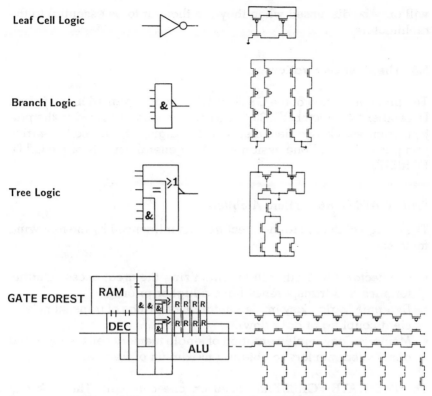

Figure 6.16.   From leaf cell logic to GATE FOREST.

function router, a tool is designated which "compiles" a logic
description and translates it in the equivalent layout. Main purpose of the function router is the realization of random logic
blocks.

As has already been stated under the technology objectives, a
close coupling between the implementation of the architecture and
the CMOS technology available at the IMS has been avoided in
order to maintain a high degree of portability and compatability
with other technologies. If strict IMS–CMOS technology rules had
been used for the implementation, a size reduction of 12% could have
been achieved.

The subsequent paragraphs will describe the implementation of
the first GATE FOREST master. They will concentrate on the technology and design aspects of the GATE FOREST. Tool considerations

will only be discussed when they are thought to be essential to the architecture.

5.4. The First Generation

The first generation of the GATE FOREST was designed in the period December 1985–October 1986. Three people were involved in the project, from which two designers were assigned to the cell libraries and pad cells, and one assigned to the general aspects of the GATE FOREST.

5.4.1. GATE FOREST Micro-Architecture

The design of the micro-architecture was influenced by the following factors:

* *Connectability*. Rather than minimizing the area, access characteristics and transparency have a higher priority.
* *Dynamic Logic*. Easy implementation of strings of transistors (efficient coupling of data flow).
* *Memory*. Easy implementation of single memory cells (supporting distributed memory to obtain a maximum of flexibility).

The IMS GATE FOREST is based on one core cell. The core cell contains a total of eight transistors: two p-transistors, four large n-transistors, and two small n-transistors. This p to n count of 1 to 3 demonstrates the specialization of the core cell towards the support of dynamic logic structures. The size relation is $4:2:1$, for the large p-, the large n-, and the small n-transistors, respectively. The core cell has a height of 107 lambda and a width of 34 lambda. The core cell uses both gate isolation and geometrical isolation. The small n-transistors are geometrically isolated from each other. The other p and n transistors are organized in a gate isolation configuration.

A schematic representation of the core cell is given in Figure 6.17.

Most important aspects of the core cell are its connectability characteristics, its access characteristics and its transparency. Optimal connectability of the core cell is supported by the following features:

1. The 45-degree orientation of the p- and large n-transistors allows internal track change without blocking a route-through track. The 45-degree orientation also enhances the access factor of the poly gates with a factor 2 (vertically 2, horizontally 3).

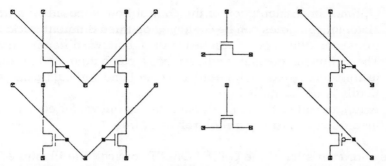

Figure 6.17(a).   Schematic Representation of the GATE FOREST Core Cell.

Figure 6.17(b).   Microphotograph of the GATE FOREST Core Cell.

2. Optimal implementation of the control flow is possible: n-transistor silicon gates can be contacted on three different tracks, p-transistor silicon gates can be contacted on two different tracks.
3. The diffusion geometry allows easy contacting of the same drain/source area on different horizontal and vertical tracks (vertically 2, horizontally 3).
4. Arrangement of the route-through tracks allows for easy implementation of serial/parallel transistor trees.

The characteristics of the GATE FOREST core cell are illustrated in Figures 6.18, 6.19, and 6.20.

5.4.2. GATE FOREST Macro-Architecture

As has already been stated, only one core cell has been used to generate the macro-architecture of the IMS GATE FOREST. No routing channels have been implemented (channelless architecture). In Figure 6.21 a corner of the GATE FOREST master is shown.

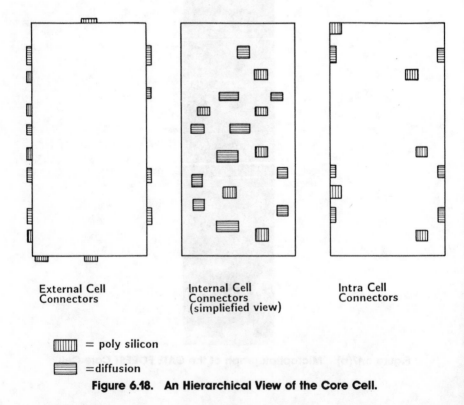

External Cell
Connectors

Internal Cell
Connectors
(simpliefied view)

Intra Cell
Connectors

▓▓▓ = poly silicon

▭ =diffusion

Figure 6.18.   An Hierarchical View of the Core Cell.

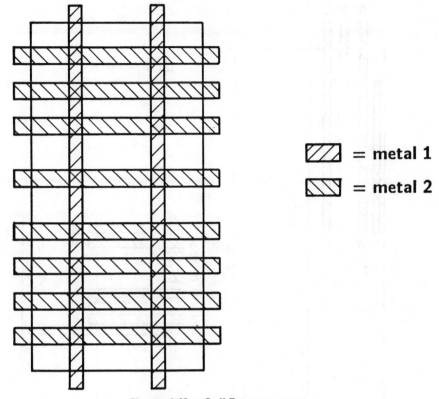

Figure 6.19.   Cell Transparency.

It was found that the use of more than one core cell would affect the general applicability of both micro- and macro-architecture. An important consideration was the influence of the core cell distribution pattern on the placement of actual function blocks (the use of the master in the design environment). Using more than one core cell creates the following possible realizations of the macro-architecture:

1. Using equal distribution functions for the core cells. This will result in a homogeneous grid.
2. Using different distribution functions. For instance, one could use one core cell with a general micro-architecture to generate the overall GATE FOREST structure. The second core cell, with a specialized micro-architecture could be concentrated in one or more dedicated (macro) blocks.

The first realization would result in a serious waste of transistors, since the dedicated cells would only be used in a small number of

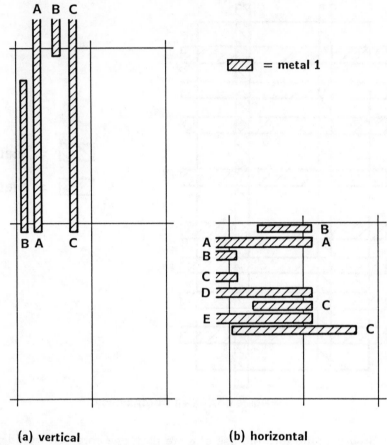

(a) vertical   (b) horizontal

Figure 6.20. Using the GATE FOREST Core Cell "Track Change" Capability.

function blocks. It has as advantage that the placement of the functions will not be determined by the distribution of the specialized cells, since these are a part of the general grid.

The second realization shows a reversal of the advantage and disadvantage noticed in the first realization. Normal function blocks can be implemented efficiently since only the general GATE FOREST grid is used. The disadvantage comes when a function needs such a specialized cell or cells. The function in question has to be placed close to the dedicated function block in order to prevent long interconnections. If more than one function is involved, congestion will be inevitable. This will result in longer interconnections. In general one could say that the use of a dedicated macro blocks bears the

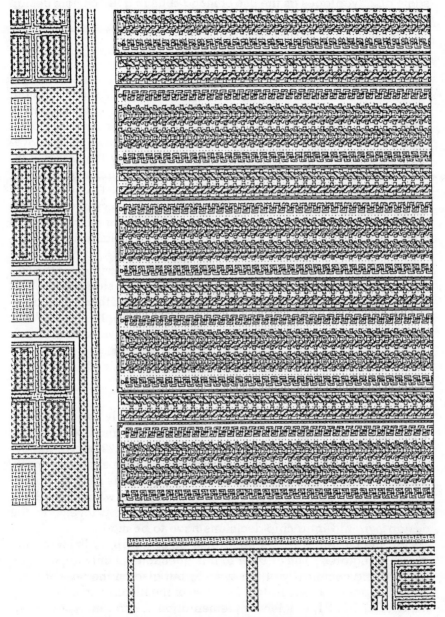

Figure 6.21. Corner of the GATE FOREST Master.

same disadvantages as the use of mega cells in a full custom design environment.

5.5. The GATE FOREST Design Environment

This section will describe the characteristics of a CAD environment which exploits all the aspects of the GATE FOREST silicon environment. Some parts of the described design environment have been realized, or are currently under development. Because of the novel architecture and the level of integration offered by the GATE FOREST, no existing design environment could be found which would match the ideal GATE FOREST design environment. To cover current needs, a number of available CAD tools were selected which performed satisfactorily. However, a part of the needs cannot be covered at all, since similar tools are not even available in the fullcustom world.

A large effort has been directed towards the realization of the cell and function libraries. Currently, a fully functional static cell library is available (NAND, NOR, AND, flip-flops, etc.), together with a number of function compiler modules (RAM, ROM, multiplier, etc.). Within the dynamic library a range of complex gates have been realized, using different dynamic design techniques [15,16,18].

5.5.1. The Design Hierarchy

Based on an hierarchical design approach, basically two main operation levels can be distinguished: (a) partitioning and floorplanning operations, and (b) mapping operations. Figure 6.22 shows the design path and some examples of partitioning and mapping operations. At the top of the pyramid, the actual system is located. Subsequent levels denote the components of the system which have been created with the decomposition process. At the top level(s) of the design pyramid intra chip decisions have to be made:

Can the current level be integrated on one chip, or is more than one chip required? The answer to this question not only depends on the size and complexity of the system, but also on the type of functions that are to be integrated. Because of the flexible architecture of the GATE FOREST, efficient implementation of different types of logic and memory is possible (the section on mapping will describe this in more detail).

In order to limit the scope of this chapter, important aspects of the design path such as simulation, design rule verification, and so on

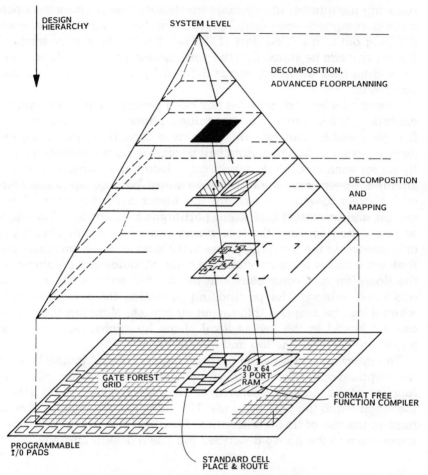

DESIGN
HIERARCHY

SYSTEM LEVEL

DECOMPOSITION,
ADVANCED FLOORPLANNING

DECOMPOSITION
AND
MAPPING

GATE FOREST
GRID

20 x 64
3 PORT
RAM

FORMAT FREE
FUNCTION COMPILER

PROGRAMMABLE
I/O PADS

STANDARD CELL
PLACE & ROUTE

Figure 6.22.   The GATE FOREST Design Hierarchy.

will not be discussed. For the same reason detailed discussions on
partitioning techniques and floorplanning operations have not been
included. For more detail, the reader is referred to [19,20].

5.5.2. Partitioning and Floorplanning

As in full-custom design, the partitioning and floorplanning operations on each level of the hierarchy are the key to efficient VLSI
system design. The importance of floorplanning in a semicustom
environment is even higher, since bad floorplanning will—apart
from other nasty effects—result in a larger wiring area, significantly

reducing the number of available transistors. The partitioning operation decomposes each module into a number of submodules, each carrying out a specified part of the function of the parent module. Basically it can be stated that the partitioning process deals with the three dimensional design space defined by area, concurrency and bandwidth.

After a new level of modules has been generated, a floorplanning operation takes place. In the initial phase of the design this floorplan will be sketchy, with inaccurate data. However, along the design path, the floorplan data will become more accurate and specifying for each module its aspect ratio, location of ports, power dissipation, speed, and so on. Iterative steps, backing up in the hierarchy, are necessary to explore the hierarchy/architecture of the design and to correct inefficient partitioning operations. The more accurate the floorplan, the less wiring is needed. Ideally, wiring is only needed in the mapping phase of the design, where modules are realized with for instance standard cells. Modules can be placed in the floorplan and connectors can be abutted without the need for additional wiring. The partitioning operation for a module ends when it can be mapped into layout structures. Mapping operations are not bound to the lowest level of the hierarchy, but can occur anywhere between the top and bottom level.

The information flow from partitioning and floorplanning level to the mapping operation contains functional data which describes the function of the module, geometrical data which specifies the size of the module and the port locations. The inclusion of geometrical data implies the use of flexible libraries. Flexible libraries are of crucial importance to the above described top-down design strategy.

5.5.3. Mapping

The mapping operation consists of transforming the functional and geometrical description of the module into layout. Four typical mapping "operators" are presented in Figure 6.23. The designer has basically the following options:

1. Using standard cells
2. Using parameterized cells
3. Using function compilers
4. Using handlayout

The important aspect of these possible realization methods is the flexibility of their implementation. Can they be adapted easily to the

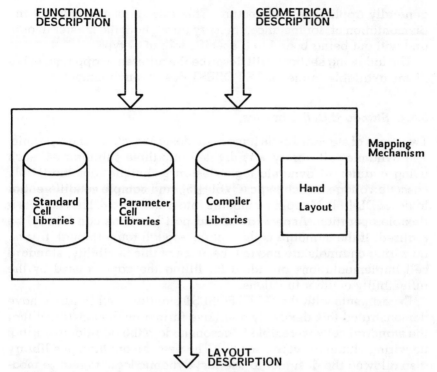

Figure 6.23. Mapping Mechanisms in the GATE FOREST Design Environment.

floorplan data? Although data on the "flexibility" of the module function should be available to the floorplanner, floorplan fitting based on the layout constraints of the implementing module is not desirable and should be avoided when possible. The flexibility of each of the implementation methods depends first of all on the underlying silicon environment. To demonstrate the effects of an inefficient architecture, a macro-architecture based on two core cells is taken as an example.

One core cell contains general applicable transistor structures, whereas the other contains a RAM cell. The macro-architecture consists of two blocks, one built with the general core cell, and the other built with the RAM cell. If decentralized memory is needed, one is forced to change the floorplan in order to be able to use the centralized RAM block. This will result in a significant wiring overhead, which again resulted in a reduction of the number of available transistors, longer delays, and so on.

As has already been described in section 5, one of the major design constraints during the design of the GATE FOREST was its generally applicable architecture. This allows for the efficient implementation of, for instance, memory throughout the master image, and without being bound to a specific format or type.

The following sections will describe the different mapping mechanisms available in the GATE FOREST design environment.

5.5.4. Standard Cell Libraries

Two types of standard cells have been designed: static and dynamic. The dynamic cell library was divided into three sublibraries, each using a different dynamic logic design technique (domino [14,18], cascode voltage switch logic (CVSL) [15], and sample set differential logic (SSDL) [16]). Mapping a module into a standard cell solution is a flexible operation. Aspect ratios and port locations can (easily) be realized. If the standard cells contain enough route-through tracks, no wiring channels are needed. Because of this flexibility, standard cell implementations are ideal for filling the gaps caused by the inflexibility of other functions.

Experiments with the GATE FOREST standard cell libraries have demonstrated this flexibility and have further on demonstrated that the standard cells were able to accommodate the additional wiring; no wiring channels were used [21]! The use of more than one library also allowed the designer to use fast dynamic logic to realize modules which had high-speed constraints.

Table 6.2 shows five different implementations of the same logic function, which is a five input AND. Figure 6.24 shows the personalization levels of a number of cells from the static library. Inputs and outputs are, on choice available on top, bottom, or both top and bottom side of the cell. Power and ground routing is done horizontally on second level metal. A footprint of a typical GATE FOREST standard cell is shown in Figure 6.25. A number of optimization steps

Table 6.2. Five Input AND Implementations.

Circuit	A[1]	t (ns)
SSDL	2	1.5
CVSL	2	4
Domino	1	4.5
Static	1	5
Handlayout	0.7	2.5

A: relative area factor ($136\mu \times 107\mu$)

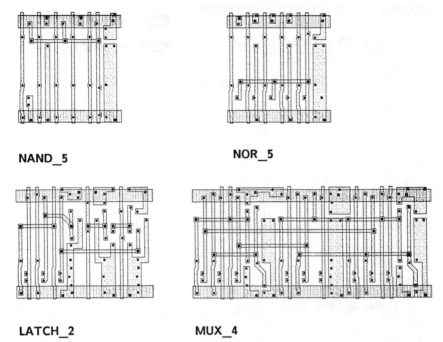

NAND_5   NOR_5

LATCH_2   MUX_4

Figure 6.24(a).   Examples of GATE FOREST Static Standard Cells.

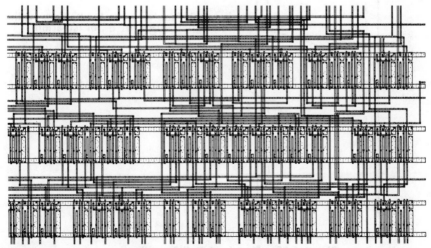

Figure 6.24(b).   Conventional Standard Cell Place and Route in Channel-less Architecture.

(STATIC) STANDARD CELL FOOTPRINT

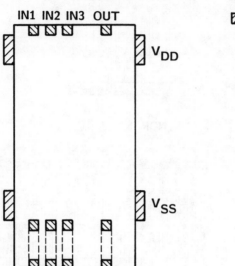

IN1 IN2 IN3 OUT

V_{DD}

V_{SS}

IN1 IN2 IN3 OUT

☒☒☒ = metal 1

▨▨▨ = metal 2

STANDARD CELL INTERNALS
(NORMAL ORIENTATION)

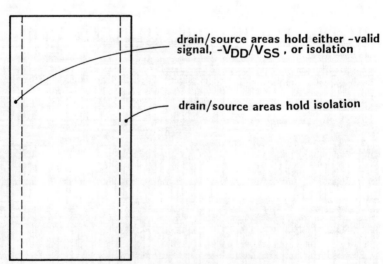

drain/source areas hold either –valid
signal, –V_{DD}/V_{SS} , or isolation

drain/source areas hold isolation

Figure 6.25. Standard Cell Specification.

are possible after the standard cell has been placed on the grid and has been wired.

First of all, during final placement, a cell could be shifted 17λ to the left—that is, it will cover 17λ of its left neighbor left edge—to share the isolation transistor, if present. The other optimization takes place after the routing phase. An extraction of the layout and a resimulation will show where driving capabilities can be optimized to minimize delay times. Two so-called regulator cells are available for this purpose. One will only increase n-transistor sizes, without increasing the cell area. The other regulatory cell will size both p- and n-transistor sizes at the output. This will result however in an additional 17λ wide cell being inserted in the cell row. Apart from these two possibilities it is of course also possible to insert different types of buffer cells (with a minimum width of 41λ).

5.5.5. Parameterized Libraries

Parameterized libraries contain functions such as memory, multipliers, adders, drivers, and so on. Modules can be implemented by specifying the appropriate parameters in a property sheet, and subsequently *assembling* the correct library building blocks. Important in this mapping operation is the flexibility of the building block library. Often, the use of these libraries *predefines* the module aspect ratio and the port locations. As has already been stated, layout should fit in the module as defined by the floorplan. Floorplan adaptation because of layout constraints should be avoided.

The GATE FOREST architecture allows the implementation of *format-free* parameterized libraries. Currently, the following functions are implemented, or under development:

1. RAM and ROM (1 and 2-port)
2. Standard logic functions (NAND, NOR,...)
3. CAM (1-port)
4. PLA

The implementation of format-free parameterized RAM and ROM cells with more than two ports is currently under study. Fixed-format multiport RAM and ROM cells are already available.

5.5.6. Compiler Libraries

Compiler libraries are able to generate layout, using a high-level functional description as input. One should make a clear distinction between the so-called compiler libraries from the "early" days, which were only able to *assemble* a function, and the compiler libraries currently available. The older compiler libraries should be classified under the parameterized libraries, which were described previously. The class of compiler libraries that is being discussed performs a number of intelligent operations, and is able to produce the layout description of a complex function. Logic synthesis, logic optimization, and timing analysis are operations which should be performed by the compiler. Functions can range from complex dynamic logic functions to datapath type functions.

The concept of compiler libraries within the GATE FOREST environment can be implemented using an underlying micro-library. The micro-library contains the different building blocks used for the micro-architecture. As opposed to the "conventional" concept of a micro-library (e.g., [22]), the GATE FOREST micro-library not just contains silicon cells (e.g., transistors, contacts, vias) but also "contactability" cells, allowing the compiler to use all routing capabilities offered by the GATE FOREST architecture. The use of such cells makes the software independent of the target image architecture, without introducing inefficiencies.

5.5.7. Hand Layout

Hand layout design is not an efficient way to design a VLSI system. Only in case of a function which is used frequently, has high performance demands, and cannot be efficiently implemented using one of the other three mapping methods, a designer can fall back on the basic layout editor. Hand layout design in a semicustom environment is restricted to the wiring of discrete transistors. Input to this operation are again the functional description and the geometrical specification of the module.

Since the degree of freedom in realizing the function is restricted to realizing the interconnections, it is clear that hand layout design will become obsolete. Currently some experiments with a function router have been carried out. Although still needing some manual editing, the results of these experiments were promising. The function router uses a transistor netlist as input, together with the aspect ratio and the port locations.

5.5.8. Design Efficiency

A short overview of a number of important functions implemented in the GATE FOREST is presented in Table 6.3. The relation between

Table 6.3. Efficient Implementation.

Efficiency Function	Area (λ^2)	No. of Trans.	Area per Trans.
Transmission Gate	1000	2	500
2-Input NAND	3600	4	900
3-Input AND/OR	7200	8	900
1 Bit SRAM	3600	6	600
1 Bit 2-Port SRAM	5400	8	675
1 Bit CAM	5400	9	600
4 Bit CLA Adder	104400	168	621
1 Bit ROM	500	1	500
1 Bit PLA	500	1	500
1 Bit Full Adder	12600	20	630
4 Bit Ripple Carry Adder	52200	82	636

area per transistor and the complexity of the function reveals an important characteristic of the GATE FOREST; increasing complexity causes a linear rise in the efficiency of the implementation, that is the area per transistor decreases (for the IMS GATE FOREST, the area per transistor will approach asymptotically the mean value of 450 square lambda).

5.6. Design Examples

Two design examples, implemented in the GATE FOREST environment will be discussed in detail. The first one is based on the use of dynamic logic, a five-input dynamic XOR. In order to be able to compare the efficiency of the chosen implementation, four different realizations will be discussed, each using a different logic design technique. As a standard, a standard-cell implementation, based on the same logic description has been implemented in a full-custom environment. The second example describes the implementation of an 8×8 bit multiplier using static logic.

5.6.1. A Five-Input XOR

To demonstrate the effectiveness of the GATE FOREST architecture, five different implementations of a five-input XOR function will be discussed. The five-input XOR was realized using the following implementation techniques:

1. Full-custom standard cell design (static)
2. IMS GATE FOREST standard cell design (static library)
3. IMS GATE FOREST standard cell design (dynamic library)
4. IMS GATE FOREST hand layout design (domino version)
5. IMS GATE FOREST hand layout design (SSDL version)

The results are summarized in Table 6.4. Three possible realizations are shown in Figure 6.26, 6.27, and 6.28. Figure 6.26 presents a conventional standard cell implementation. Figure 6.27 shows the personalization mask of the five input domino standard cell implementation of the XOR. Figure 6.28 presents the nonoptimized handcrafted design implementation of the XOR in the GATE FOREST. The handcrafted domino version is 45% faster and is 75% more efficient in silicon area. The tradeoff against the static version is, of course, the extra clock signal that is needed for the precharge and evaluation phase.

5.6.2. An 8×8 Bit Multiplier

The choice of a multiplier as a test vehicle of the GATE FOREST was based on the following grounds:

Table 6.4.   Five-Input XOR Implementations.

| | 5-Input XOR | | |
Realization Method	Area (λ^2)	Speed (ns)	Area/ Trans.
Full Custom Standard Cell	410×450	11	915
GATE FOREST Static Standard Cell	428×510	11	1080
GATE FOREST Dynamic Standard Cell	428×408	8	895
GATE FOREST Domino Hand Layout	275×178	6	815
GATE FOREST SSDL Hand Layout[1]	275×356	3	815

[1]The SSDL version was constructed using the domino version as building block. Design time was approximately three hours.

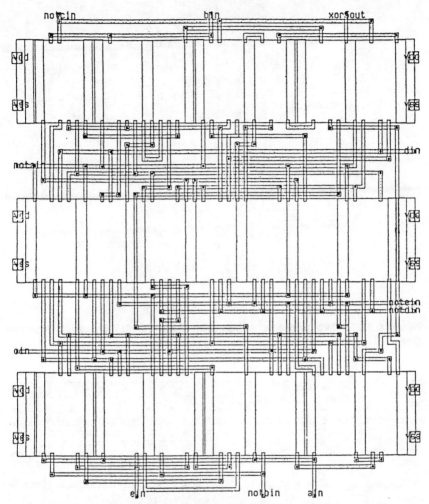

Figure 6.26.   XOR5 Implementation with Full Custom Standard Cells.

1. Parameterization aspects—Equivalent to memory cell design. The parameterization aspects are important qualifiers for the flexibility and efficiency of the implementation environment.
2. A fast multiplier is an important building block for ASIC's
3. Comparison with a dynamic version is possible.

For the implementation of the test vehicle, only a few architectures were reviewed. It should be realized that the main purpose of the design was the evaluation of the GATE FOREST architecture, and

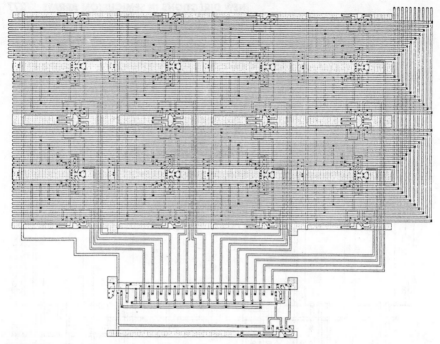

Figure 6.27. XOR5 Implementation with GATE FOREST Dynamic Standard Cells.

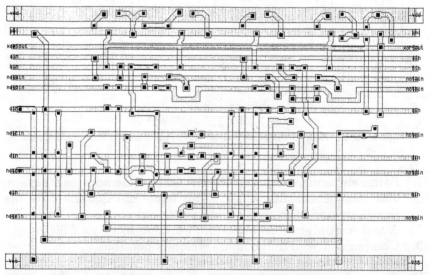

Figure 6.28. GATE FOREST Domino Logic XOR5 Implementation, "Handcrafted" Design (Experimental Function Router was used).

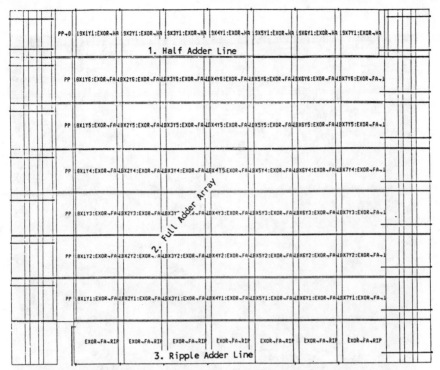

Figure 6.29.   Architecture of 8×8 Bit Multiplier.

not the design of a high-speed multiplier. The implemented version has a parallel architecture [23], and operates on two eight-bit words. The architecture can be divided into three levels:

1. Half Adder Line,
2. Full Adder Array,
3. Ripple Adder Line.

The composing cells of these levels are AND, NAND, NOR, XOR, and complex logic gates for carry generation. The XOR function has been realized with transmission gates. The architecture of the multiplier is shown in Figure 6.29. A microphotograph of the multiplier is shown in Figure 6.30. Transistor utilisation for the multiplier is 93%. This transistor count includes the isolation transistors.

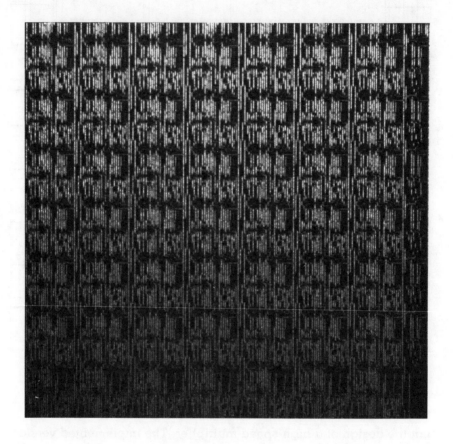

Figure 6.30. Photograph of a part of the 8×8 bit multiplier.

6. FUTURE DEVELOPMENTS

This section will describe some of the current activities concerning the development of the next generation of semicustom arrays. It is expected that the importance of semicustom arrays will continue to grow. Developments in technology will enable the fabrication of semicustom arrays with more than 500K gates. However, apart from higher integration densities, both technology and CAD tools need to improve in essential areas. A number of these areas are identified in the following sections.

6.1. Technology Perspectives

Most of the technological bottlenecks have been identified in section 2.3. A number of these technology constraints will be discussed in more detail in this section.

Apart from the natural desire for smaller feature sizes (smaller λ values), the following items are important:

1. Use of metal 3 as an additional routing layer
2. Use of "stacked" via1 (and via2) instead of the "staged" via, which consumes more area and blocks more tracks
3. No limitations on via placement
4. Higher current capacity of metal layers

The use of a fabrication process with a smaller minimum feature size, for example, $\lambda = 0.5\mu$, would first of all result in a reduction in gate delays. A significant increase in packing density depends on the shrinkage behaviour of metal and contact layers. Decreasing metal pitches must be compensated with an increase in the maximum current density of the metal layers (reduced typical resistance values). This is necessary to cope with metal migration problems and excessive voltage drops on long interconnections.

Another interesting development is the introduction of direct-write facilities. The introduction of direct-write facilities will reduce both turn-around time and fabrication costs. More important, however, is the impact on the customer interface. It will allow for easy breadboarding by system designers because they can work with single wafers at low fabrication costs. Together with emerging silicon-on-silicon bonding techniques, system designers can use the wafer as a "silicon bread-board" to implement their system.

6.2. Design Perspectives

Current semicustom arrays offer integration densities up to a 100K gates [24,25,26], and semicustom arrays with more than 500K gates are expected within two years from now. The demands imposed on the design environment are massive, and cover practically the whole spectra of computer-aided design tools.

Starting at the top of the design path, the designer needs full support during the decomposition of his design into lower levels of complexity. The partitioning results on each level of the hierarchy must be evaluated by the design system. The design system must provide the designer with enough data to enable a reliable quality evaluation of the partitioning results. It must support the evaluation of a number of alternative decomposition paths, the comparison of different paths, and easy "backtracking" c.q. review of partitioning decisions. Furthermore, the design system must provide means to match current behavior and system (customer) specifications. This should enable quick and early correction of out-of-spec behavior of the design.

This system level support not only serves the designer during the design process, but should also be capable of producing the correct documentation that is needed for production tests, interface specifications, and so on.

The first phase of the design is often referred to as the so-called "exploratory" phase, during which the designer experiments with different partitioning operators to explore the architectural possibilities. Architectural variations can consist of the addition of more parallelism, the use of redundant functions, different algorithms, pipelining constructs, and so on. Analysis of partitioning results will be based on a number of tools:

1. Floorplanner (placement and routing)
2. Timing estimator
3. Behavioral simulator
4. Power estimator

The "partitioning assistant" must be able to advise the designer on how to improve, for instance, the timing behavior of his design. This could be possible, for instance, by adding more parallelism to his design or reiterating his previous partitioning step. Also, it should be possible to evaluate the effects of adding redundant functions to improve both yield and reliability of the design.

Accurate simulation of designs with more than 100K gates is currently only possible on expensive hardware accelerators. These accelerators can also be used for testability analysis, fault grading, and automatic test pattern generation. Since the simulation problem is more or less a problem bound by the available "raw" computer power, it is not thought to be a major obstacle in the application of ULSI type arrays.

Another important aspect is the testability of a design with a complexity of more than 500K gates. The testability of a design must be forced upon the designer by the design system. As has already been mentioned in the previous paragraph, hardware accelerators will enable a testability analysis of a design. Current advances in design for testability shows progress in the areas of signature analysis, BILBOs, and level-sensitive scan design. These types of test strategies should be supported by the hardware accelerators (pattern generation, extended fault grading, etc.). Level-sensitive scan design will be important to test the circuit on timing errors (clock skew, critical path, process variations, races, etc.), which become more and more a source of concern with decreasing gate delays. Production testing of such devices will require the development of test equipment capable of testing more than 400 pins at frequencies over 200 MHz.

6.3. System Integration

The expected increase in transistor packing densities, together with improved packaging technology, will lead to an urge for true system integration. This will generate, among other things, the desire to integrate digital and analog functions into the *semi-custom* world. Some developments that are currently taking place indicate such a growth of the application area. For the GATE FOREST these developments include the design of modular A-to-D and D-to-A converters, which will be located in the periphery of the array. Less complex modules such as comparators have already been implemented in the GATE FOREST environment.

REFERENCES

1. I. Ohkura, "Gate Isolation—A Novel Basic Cell Configuration for CMOS Gate Arrays," *Proceedings of the Custom Integrated Circuits Conference*, May 1982.
2. A. Mukherjee, *Introduction to nMOS and CMOS VLSI Systems Design*, Prentice-Hall, Englewood Cliffs, NJ, 1986.
3. H. Fukudu, "A CMOS Pair Transistor Array Masterslice," *Symposium on VLSI Technology*, 1982.
4. S. Sunter, "Designing a CMOS Standard Cell Library," *Proceedings of the Custom Integrated Circuits Conference*, May 1987, pp. 237–240.
5. M.A. Beunder, J.P. Kernhof and B. Hoefflinger, "Effective Implementation of Complex and Dynamic Logic," *GATE FOREST Environment*, *IEEE Proceedings of the Custom Integrated Circuits Conference*, May 1987, pp. 44–47.
6. R. Lipp, "Advanced Architecture (Channel-less) Dual Layer Metal CMOS Gate Array," *IEEE Proceedings of the Custom Integrated Circuits Conference*, May 1983, pp. 71–73.
7. A. Hui, C. Delloca, D. Wong and R. Szeto, "A 4.1K Gates Double Metal

HCMOS Sea of Gates Array," *IEEE Proceedings of the Custom Integrated Circuits Conference*, May 1985, pp. 15–17.

8. LSI Logic Inc., LCA10000 Compacted Array™ Series, Preliminary Information, Milpitas, CA, June 1986.

9. VLSI Technology Inc., "Continuous Gate Technology," San Jose, CA, 1986.

10. N.E. Preckshot, W.W. Heikkila and D.E. Schultz, "A 10,000 Gate Hierarchical Logic Array," *IEEE Proceedings of the Custom Integrated Circuits Conference*, May 1983, pp. 10–13.

11. M.A. Brown, M.J. Gasper, J.W. Eddy and K.D. Kolwicz, "CMOS Cell Arrays–An Alternative to Gate Arrays," *IEEE Proceedings of the Custom Integrated Circuits Conference*, May 1983, pp. 74–76.

12. LSI Logic Inc., LCA2009 HCMOS Structured Array, Advanced Information, Milpitas, CA, November 1985.

13. H. Schletter and G. Koetzle, "A Processor Chip Set on a 60K Master Image Chip," *Proceedings of the ISSCC*, 1987.

14. R.H. Krambeck, "High Speed Compact Circuits with CMOS," *IEEE*, Vol. SC-17, No. 3, June 1982.

15. L.G. Heller, "Cascode Voltage Switch Logic: A Differential CMOS Logic Family," *Proceedings of the ISSCC*, February 1984.

16. T.A. Grotjohn and B. Hoefflinger, "Sample-Set Differential Logic (SSDL) For Complex High-Speed VLSI," *IEEE*, Vol. SC-21, No. 2, April 1986.

17. M.A. Beunder, "The IMS Lamba Design Rules," Technical Report, Institute for Microelectronics, Stuttgart, West Germany, August 1987.

18. N. Weste and K. Eshraghian, *Principles of CMOS Design, A System Perspective*, Addison-Wesley, Reading, MA, 1985.

19. M.A. Beunder, "A Partitioning Strategy for VLSI Design Based on the Use of Quality Factors," Technical Report, Philips Telecommunications Industry, Hilversum, The Netherlands, 1985.

20. S. Goto, *Design Methodologies*, North Holland, Amsterdam, 1986.

21. M.A. Beunder, J.P. Kernhof and B. Hoefflinger, "Efficient VLSI Implementation," *Proceedings of CompEuro*, May 1987, pp. 1022–1025.

22. S.G. Smith, P.B. Deneyer, M. Keightly and S. Nagara, "Second: A VLSI Function Library Compiler," *Proceedings of the EESCIRC*, September 1987.

23. S. Wasser, "High Speed Monolithic Multipliers for Real-Time DSP," *Computer*, Vol. 8, October 1978.

24. T. Kobayashi, H. Suzuki, K. Yamasaki, T. Wong, A. Hui and D. Wong, "A High Performance 100K Gates CMOS Array," *Proceedings of the Custom Integrated Circuits Conference*, 1986.

25. LSI Logic Inc., LCA100K Compacted Array Plus Series,™" Advance Product Information, Milpitas, CA, October 1987.

26. J.R. Lineback, "Probing the News: LSI Logic's Giant Array Breaks the Record for Useable Gates," *Electronics*, Vol. 55, No. 56, October 1987.

27. S.L. Hurst and P. Jennings, "Layout and Design Criteria for Routable Masterslice Gate Arrays," *IEEE Proceedings of the Custom Integrated Circuits Conference*, May 1983, pp. 322–326.

28. K. Sakashita, T. Arakawa, M. Takagi, K. Sugizaki, S. Asai and I. Ohkura, "A 10K Gate CMOS Gate Array with Gate Isolation Configuration," *IEEE Proceedings of the Custom Integrated Circuits Conference*, May 1983, pp. 14–18.

29. Y. Kitamura, K. Furuki, N. Sugiyama, M. Minowa and T. Yamada, "A CMOS Macro Array," *IEEE Proceedings of the ISSCC*, February 1986, pp. 68–69.

30. Y. Kuramitsu, Y. Akasaka and I. Ohkura, "A 540K-Transistor CMOS Variable Track Masterslice," *Proceedings of the Custom Integrated Circuits Conference*, 1986.

31. S. Masuda, "A CMOS Analog and Digital Master Slice LSI," *Proceedings of the ISSCC*, 1987.

32. LSI Logic Inc., "LC10038Q Compacted Array™," Product Information, July 1986.

33. F. Anderson, R. Brzozwy and S. Metzgar, "A 6K Gate Array with Self-Test and Maintenance," *Proceedings of the ISSCC*, February 1987, pp. 150–151.

34. F. Anderson and J. Ford, "A 0.5 Micion 150K Channelless Gate Array," *Proceedings of the Custom Integrated Circuits Conference*, May 1987, pp. 35–38.

7

VLSI and CAD/CAM Applications

JAMES D. FACTOR

McDonnell Douglas Corporation-MDAIS
St. Louis, MO

CHAMAN L. SABHARWAL

University of Missouri-Rolla
St. Louis, MO

1. INTRODUCTION

The emergence of high-performance hardware for computer graphics and specialized algorithmic computations will have a profound effect on scientific and engineering problem solving for CAD/CAM in the 1990s. Developments in application-specific integrated chips (ASIC) are the future of interactive computing, benefiting both display and analysis. This is particularly true due to the yearly decrease in cost of each MIPS (Million of Instructions Per Second) and each MFLOPS (Million of double precision Floating Point Operations Per Second), and to the improvement in VLSI design tools. The emerging systems, which are primarily in the form of workstations, provide powerful sets of primitives in a combination of custom VLSI circuits, conventional hardware, firmware, and software. An example of such a system is the IRIS (Integrated Raster Imaging System), which is based on the Geometry Engine developed by James Clark [1]. The more recent version of the IRIS is the IRIS 4D/60 (with the Turbo Option) which is considered a superworkstaton performing at 10 MIPS (10 times a Vax 11/780) and at 1.1 MFLOPS. Systems like the IRIS have primarily used VLSI technology to enhance graphic display capabilities of CAD systems. The question becomes: Which area in an integrated mechanical CAD/CAM environment would benefit most by migration to VLSI technology?

CAD/CAM areas that would benefit greatly from VLSI technology are those requiring computationally intensive algorithms. An important area where this is particularly true is the area of solid modeling. Interactive solid modeling is the real-time creation, display, and analysis of objects individually and in relation to each other. Such operations as creation (e.g., Boolean set operations of union, intersection, and difference, solid swept out by a surface), display (e.g., color shading, hidden surface removal, translation, rotation, scaling) and analysis (e.g., interference detection, mass properties, finite element analysis) are all useful operations for a variety of application areas in CAD/CAM. Some applications of solid modeling in CAD which can benefit from these kinds of operations are part design, finite element mesh generation (FEM), and strength/structural analysis. Examples of applications in CAM that can benefit from the use of a solid representation are assembly, robotics, tooling, quality assurance, process planning, and numerical control (NC) tool-path generation and verification [2].

It is widely supported that the solid model will become the dominant form of geometric representation for CIM (Computer Integrated Manufacturing) within the next decade [3]. The solid model will be a major link in creating an integrated CAD/CAM environment and interactive solid modeling will be the fundamental method for part design, providing a complete unambiguous model for manufacturing.

Historically, solid modelers have suffered from inadequate algorithms for the required analysis, limited kinds of solid objects (due to difficulties in extensibility), and the inability of general purpose hardware to meet solid modeling performance requirements. The purpose of this chapter is to propose a solution depending on VLSI technology that will address, at least in part, each of these deficiencies.

The first step toward this solution is to analyze each of the basic approaches to solid model representation and determine which approach is most suited to a mechanical CAD/CAM environment.

1.1. Solid Model Representations

A solid model is an informatively complete, unambiguous geometric representation of a three-dimensional object. The representation is complete in the sense that any geometric analysis that can be theoretically performed on an actual object can be performed on the solid representation automatically. It is unambiguous in the sense that it does not suffer from the misinterpretations inherent in "wire-frame" geometry. Note in wire-frame geometry only the curves of the object are stored and several objects can have the same set of lines as edges. As a consequence, it is not clear which object is being represented (Figure 7.1). Thus wire-frame geometry does not provide enough information to define an object completely.

There are three basic approaches to representing a solid object. These are the CSG (Constructive Solid Geometry) representation, the B-rep (Boundary Representation), and the Voxel element (or Octree) representation (Figure 7.2).

The CSG representation approach is based on the use of simple objects (e.g., the block, sphere, cylinder, etc.) as building blocks to construct more complicated solids. These complicated solids are constructed by applying the Boolean set operations of union, difference, and intersection to the primitive solid objects, taking them two at a time. In the CSG representation a tree structure is used to define the solid object, with leaf nodes corresponding to primitive objects, branch nodes representing set operations, and the root node representing the object being generated. One of the disadvantages of this method is the limited number of primitive building blocks. The CSG approach generally requires less storage but more computation to reproduce the model and its image. In fact, a boundary evaluation

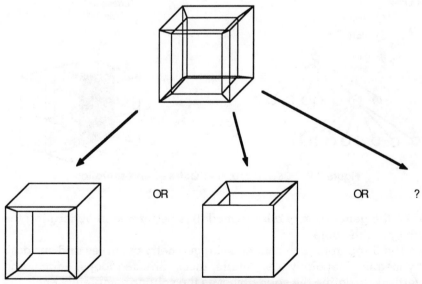

Figure 7.1 The Ambiguity of the Wire-Frame.

CSG Tree

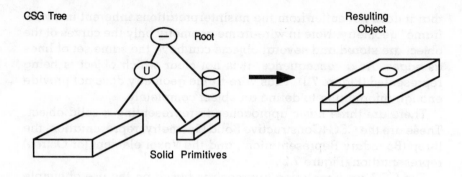

Resulting
Object

B-rep

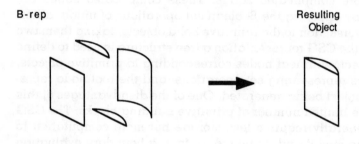

Resulting
Object

Octree

- ○ Empty
- ◓ Partial
- ◉ Full

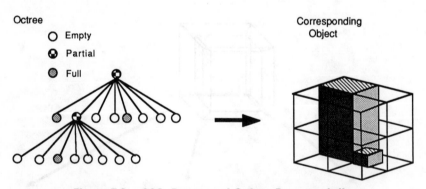

Corresponding
Object

Figure 7.2. CSG, B-rep, and Octree Representations.

(i.e., the generation of a B-rep model) is performed in generating the image of the object.

The B-rep approach connects the geometry of curves and surfaces by means of topology (i.e., shells, faces, directed loops, edges, and vertices) to define the solid object as the volume completely enclosed by its geometry. Thus separating the space inside the object from the space outside of the object and precisely defining the surface of the object. The approach stores an explicit definition of the model boundaries (i.e., the topology). This requires more storage space but does not require the amount of computation needed to reconstruct the model as does the CSG approach. The added advantage is that it is relatively easy to convert a B-rep model to a wire-frame model and back, due to the similarity of their definitions. This makes B-rep systems compatible with most CAD systems, which are wire-frame based [4].

The Voxel representation is a relatively new approach to solid modeling, breaking with the earlier approaches of CSG and B-rep representations. This approach is based on the technique of octree encoding which was proposed by Jackins and Tanimoto [5]. This work was then extensively analyzed and expanded on by Meagher [6]. An octree is a representation of a solid object by hierarchically organized cubes of different sizes. The advantage of the hierarchical structure is that it allows search time to be reduced by skipping small cubes included in a large one. The octree representation is used to approximate the object by a collection of three types of cubes: a cube totally out of the object (i.e., empty), a cube entirely in the object (i.e., full), and a cube only partly in the object (i.e., partial). If the cube is partly in the object, then that cube is divided into eight smaller cubes which are each again one of the three types. This process is applied recursively allowing any degree of accuracy to be achieved.

The CSG approach is useful for designing an object that requires for its construction only simple geometric shapes such as the cylinder, sphere, block, or torus. An example of such an application would be the design of piping and flow systems in process plants. The Voxel approach is making inroads into the area of medical analysis (e.g., CT (Computed Tomograghy) scan), but has not had significant impact in the mechanical CAD/CAM industries. Of the three kinds of solid modeling approaches, the B-rep is the most natural fit in terms of the legacy of curve and surface representations (i.e., wire-frames) that have been used for design and manufacture in the aerospace and automobile industries over the last 25 years. Solid objects with aircraft or automotive free-form (i.e., sculptured) surfaces are very difficult, if not totally impractical, to design with the CSG building block approach. And again, as mentioned earlier, a CSG model must be converted to the B-rep form for display purposes.

In an environment in which all surfaces and curves are parametrically defined and accessed through a single parametric evaluator interface, the B-rep solid model representation can model the largest variety of solid objects. The reason for this is that the parametric evaluator approach will allow complete flexibility in adding any curve or surface definition to the system. And in turn the topology will guarantee the connectivity of this geometry in the B-rep solid representation of the object.

As a consequence, the B-rep approach can be identified as a major technology where progress will be a significant benefit to the mechanical CAD/CAM area, especially those fields in mechanical CAD/CAM which have inherited a legacy of wire-frame and surface definitions. And VLSI based processors can greatly aid in facilitating this progress.

1.2. VLSI in Solid Modeling

Each of these three methods could benefit from VLSI-based technology. In fact, at the time of this writing, work at Cornell University is being applied to the PADL-2 solid modeler (probably the most widely used and known CSG based system) to exploit special computer accelerator technology to attain real-time performance [7]. In addition, the Voxel representation has already taken advantage of VLSI technology. The solid modeling system INSIGHT (by Phoenix Data Systems. Inc. - Albany, NY), developed by Donald Meagher, has addressed the hardware inadequacy issue by implementing simple algorithms in parallel, high-bandwith VLSI processors. To the knowledge of the authors, at the time of writing, no one has introduced VLSI technology to improve the performance of B-rep solid modelers.

Because solid models require so much processing power to create, manipulate, and display objects, they have been too slow for general production use to date. During such analysis, performing operations such as Boolean operations, hidden-surface removal, and interference detection, quadratic growth of the associated data occurs. At the core of this analysis are the system's intersection algorithms no matter whether the solid modeling system is using a CSG, a B-rep, or a Voxel representation. Consequently, efficient intersection algorithms are required.

1.3. Intersection

The problem of intersection between two objects arises naturally in the design of CAD/CAM geometric applications, ICs, graphics, and operations research. If the two objects do intersect, questions such as the following must be answered: what is the type of intersection? What is the representation of the intersection? For example, in designing a system for integrated circuits or printed circuit board, it is important that two wires do not overlap to make a short circuit. In an industrial application for designing layouts to be executed by numerically controlled machines, it is important to know that no two parts of the layout intersect, or if they do intersect, to be able to detect that intersection. In computer graphics, the problem of determining which set of objects is obscured from a particular viewpoint can be formulated as a geometric intersection problem. The problem of ray tracing is another example of geometric intersection. In operations research, the mathematical formulation of many important problems leads naturally to the geometric intersection problem [8]. Given N objects, the running time of the intersection problem is of the order N^2. The question arises as to whether the formulation can be revised to have a running time of order N or $NlogN$.

In the area of solid modeling, the problem of intersecting two B-rep solid objects reduces to the case of determining which corresponding surfaces of the two objects intersect. Certain considerations as surface type and representation play an important role in determining the intersection. This consideration coupled with the algorithmic approach is used to achieve the intersection, effect the accuracy, robustness, and speed of the resulting software. It is the authors firm belief that careful consideration must be given to the efficiency of an algorithm before it can be considered as a candidate for implementation in hardware micro-code. These considerations will be addressed in what follows.

2. TYPES OF SURFACES

First consider the types of surfaces available for intersection and the kind of intrinsic constraints imposed on them. An implicitly represented surface suffers from the following drawbacks: there is no way to identify the boundary of the surface, and there is no way to distinguish one side from the other. Such a surface is not suitable for B-rep modelers. Parametric curves and curved surfaces are a common form of surface and object representation. A surface may be represented parametrically with the parametric domain normalized to a unit square. Parametric representation has the advantage that a point in the parametric space directly leads to the determination of a position vector on the surface or a tangent vector to an isoparametric curve on the surface. A surface is said to be C^k if the k-th order partial derivatives are continuous. The C^k, $k > 0$, surfaces are not only useful in many calculations, but are necessary for any significant analysis of the problem. For example [9], a C^2 surface can be easily approximated linearly by utilizing the bounds on the second derivatives. Triangular approximation may also be obtained by using the normals and tangents to the isoparametric curves of C^1 surfaces [10, 11]. C^0 surfaces are currently handled by considering them as piecewise C^1 surfaces, which is a severe constraint, particularly in B-rep modelers. There is scope for research for handling the C^0 surfaces directly.

Currently, parametric surfaces are treated in three ways with respect to intersection. The first class of methods are those methods which depend on the intrinsic properties of the surfaces for evaluation purposes, for example, such surfaces as specific Bezier, B-spline, and so on. Evaluation is fast but surfaces are very specialized. General parametric surfaces do not have this intrinsic evaluation property. The other two classes for general purpose parametric surfaces tend to be "evaluator based". Given a point in the parameter space, the evaluator provides the position values and the derivative values. C^1 and C^2 surfaces are examples of such surfaces frequently used. The second class of methods involves C^2 surfaces which require not only knowledge about the second-order derivatives, but also knowledge about the bounds on these derivatives. For parametric bicubic surfaces, such computations are extremely simple because the second-order derivatives reduce to linear terms, but for reasonably complex parametric surfaces computing the second order derivatives and the norms on these derivatives can prove to be a nightmare, "in general these norms are not used in CAGD" [9]. The third class of methods involves general purpose parametric C^1 surfaces whose first-order derivatives provide the necessary tangent vector and normal vector information for planar approximation of the surfaces. Since C^0 surfaces are treated as piecewise smooth surfaces, if two surfaces consist of M and N smooth subsurfaces, respectively, then the computational complexity of intersection is of order MN, whereas the complexity may be reduced to be of order one by appropriate use of numerical analysis. Numerical intermediate calculations may be substituted for exact calculations to speed up the process without loss of robustness.

2.1. Divide-and-Conquer Paradigm

Perhaps the most important, most widely applicable technique for designing efficient algorithms is a strategy known as "divide-and-conquer." The divide-and-conquer (i.e., selective subdivision) paradigm is chosen here as a method for solving the intersection problem for a number of reasons. It is widely accepted that this method can be very robust and efficient provided the simplicity conditions can be reliably and cheaply recognized [12]. Some divide-and-conquer algorithms are based on specific composite surfaces (such as Bezier, B-spline, Rational B-Spline, or Beta-Spline), while others are more general purpose in nature, allowing the intersection of any two arbitrarily defined surfaces. Sophisticated divide-and-conquer algorithms depend on decisions involving dynamic refinement on internal algorithms to improve the accuracy of the overall results. The consequence of such refinement is often an exponential growth of data structures and a corresponding increase in computational time. To process the large quantity of information resulting from such recursive subdivision requires VLSI technology. In fact, recursive subdivision algorithms have been shown to be naturally suited for support by VLSI hardware. This was demonstrated by Don Meagher's work in the INSIGHT solid modeler. In this case, the simplicity condition was addressed by the design of algorithms by using only simple arithmetic operations (i.e., $+$, $-$, magnitude comparison and shift) and attaining linear growth by a one-time spatially presorted data structure (the octree).

A divide-and-conquer method that culls and then locally subdivides would be an effective algorithm for intersection of any two sculptured surfaces. Such a method is presented in the next section.

3. GENERAL INTERSECTION PHILOSOPHY

The objective here is to illustrate and suggest a method for hardware implementation, a very simple but versatile architecture for intersection between two parametric surfaces for real-time interactive computing. There are four steps to the general parametric surface/surface intersection method proposed, namely, subdivision, intersection, sorting, and refinement. A detailed discussion of the four steps for surface/surface intersection algorithm will be given. The main objective is to suggest an architecture for hardware implementation of this algorithm.

3.1. Subdivision

Recursive subdivision is a powerful approximation technique in computer-aided geometric design (CAGD) for intersection and rendering of free-form surfaces. Adaptive subdivision methods have been applied to parametric piecewise bicubic Bernstein-Bezier surfaces. The advantage of such a technique is that computations are local, reducing the computational requirements on evaluator-based systems. One may refer to [13] for a history of subdivision approaches used for curves and surfaces.

As a prescreening step to reduce subdivision, cull all surface pairs which do not intersect, thus eliminating unnecessary computation. The culling process is done by first enclosing the two surfaces in bounding volumes and determining if the bounding volumes intersect. The cost of intersecting the bounding volumes is significantly lower than the cost of intersecting the surfaces. An important and much debated issue is how to calculate the enclosing volume. The bounding volumes of the surfaces can be computed in several ways: (a) axis-oriented parallelepipeds [10], (b) surface-oriented parallelepipeds [11], (c) convex hulls [14], (d) ellipsoids [15], and (e) spheroids [16]. The desire is to minimize the difference between the minimal geometric volume enclosing the surface and the computed bounding volume enclosing the surface. It is the authors's experience that (b), (c), (d), and (e) are poor choices for one or more of the following criteria: the poor computation time for the calculation of bounding volumes, the convex hull property of the surfaces, the poor performance time for intersecting the bounding volumes, and the deviation between the minimal geometric volume enclosing the surface and approximate bounding volume enclosing the surface. The torus represents an example of a surface where none of the above-mentioned bounding volume methods works well. There is a need to strike a balance to achieve the best out of this situation. The simplicity of box calculation with axis-oriented parallelepipeds and the associated simplicity in box intersection makes (a) more acceptable than other methods.

First of all, the subdivision of surfaces for finding the common intersection is discussed. Recursive subdivision requires a data structure, which grows selectively rather than exponentially, to store information needed at each level in order to eliminate recomputing the information at lower levels, or even at the sibling levels. This approach is feasible both for economical use of computer resources with respect to internal memory and run-time. Unlike nonsystematic exhaustive search, this method is both exhaustive and systematic.

In order to apply subdivision to the surface/surface intersection problem, one needs to determine a subdivision criteria: (a) where to subdivide, which parts of the surface to subdivide, (b) how to subdivide, in one or both parametric directions; and (c) the subdivision stopping criteria, when to stop subdividing with respect to stopping tolerance. In general it is advantageous to work with surfaces with smaller curvature than surfaces with larger curvature.

Whatever the subdivision criteria, one needs to detect the surface curvature and then subdivide where the curvature is high; subdivide only along a parametric direction in which the curvature is unacceptable; and stop when the surface is sufficiently planar. Planar approximation may be achieved by utilizing the properties of the surface, that is, C^2, C^1, C^0. Only the latter two types, which are least constrained, will be considered. Several methods may be employed to estimate the surface curvature. These computations may be analytical or sampled. For curvature computation, one needs derivative data. In the absence of derivative data, derivative data must be generated from the existing positional data. A mathematically well-founded method for deriving such information as applicable to the surface/surface intersection problem can be found in [13, 17, 18]. The computation of the size of the surface piece may be a by-product of the curvature computations. Once a surface piece has been subdivided, a flag may be set to avoid recalculating the curvature and size information.

3.2. Intersection

A central idea of this divide-and-conquer process is that it begins with a rough overall estimate of "possibly" intersecting surfaces and it converges to a final structure of surface pairs that "actually" intersect.

However any algorithm using numerical approximation techniques for intersection of surfaces can be frustrated by creating sufficiently unrealistic examples. For reasonably realistic surfaces, the intersection between two surfaces may consist of (a) no intersection for disjoint surfaces, (b) single isolated points (e.g., the points of intersection where corners of a surface are coincident on a planar surface), (c) one or more continuous curves (e.g., the intersection of a cone and a cylinder), and (d) surfaces (e.g., the intersection of two coplanar planes). The first three cases are most significant, since they arise naturally in cross-intersection problems [18, 10].

Some techniques, for intersection, require the determination of a startpoint. Subdivision technique is used to determine the start point, and the Newton-Raphson technique is used to trace the path until a complete curve has been obtained. This estimate is detrimental to the determination of the entire curve of intersection, since the accuracy of the resulting curve depends on the accuracy of the starting point [19, 20]. In addition an extra effort is required to define the meaning of the termination criteria in such a case. In this strategy, care must be taken to ensure that a curve is not computed twice. Barnhill's [19] method avoids the use of the divide-and-conquer strategy, until the Newton-Raphson technique fails to generate a start point, and then it returns to the divide-and-conquer strategy.

There are other techniques which utilize the flatness of the surfaces to calculate approximate intersection curves [9, 11, 10]. The approximately flat surfaces are treated as planar surfaces and are subdivided into triangles. Then pairs of triangles are intersected to calculate approximate intersection segments. Again the accuracy of the intersection curves depends on the tolerance of flatness criteria for the surfaces. However this criteria does not affect the determination of the approximate curve of intersection. The accuracy of the approximate intersection curve can be improved by a refinement step [11, 10].

3.3. Sorting

The amount of computer time spent on sorting is enormous. There are sorting techniques with a wide variety of timing characteristics. The literature is full of sorting algorithms, both internal and external sorting. Such algorithms are normally based on some kind of linear ordering, for example, natural ordering, lexicographic ordering, ordering based on the representation of data. Unlike these sorting algorithms, the sorting in the surface/surface intersection problem is geometric in nature and is based on the concept of "nearness" relation between objects. None of the simple or complex algorithms helps to do the geometric sorting at hand. Some ideas may be borrowed from Heapsort and Mergesort algorithms [21], but none of these is directly applicable. In the surface/surface intersection problem, all the computed intersection segments are unorganized as far as the curves of intersection are concerned. One must thread the intersection segments in a way that the net outcome is presentable as continuous curves of intersection. Thus the objective of sorting, in this case, is to rearrange the intersection segments so that the end points of the segments are "near" each other according to some well-defined "nearness" criteria.

Sorting is the process of linking the points of intersection into curves of intersection. This process is facilitated by the proper choice of data structures for the problem of subdivision and intersection. The points are connected in a hierarchical manner such that closer points are considered for linking first, and distant points are linked later [10].

3.4. Refinement

Refinement is the process which is desirable when all the intersection points have been calculated. Since the computed points are approximations, they are not necessarily on the surfaces. These approximations can be refined to points on the surfaces or points closer to the surfaces. Since the curves are in the object space, their corresponding curves can be found in the parameter space of the two surfaces. A criteria must be used to find points on the surfaces or close to the surfaces within a given tolerance [12].

4. A VLSI SOLUTION TO SURFACE/SURFACE INTERSECTION

For a general-purpose, divide-and-conquer surface/surface intersection algorithm, some architectural decisions must be made at the VLSI components level to take advantage of the high-level technology. A Surface/Surface Intersection Processor Architecture (SSIPA) is proposed which can be configured with an arbitrary number of identical processors operating in parallel. Each of the parallel processors can be programmed identically as if it were a single processor system. Such an architecture can be used to achieve extremely high performance. Multiprocessor architectures have been used for several years to meet the demanding needs of interactive graphics. Although parallel processors have been used for drawing operations, little work has been done to take advantage of parallel processing for front end geometric and arithmetic operations. The SSIPA architecture proposes to employ an arbitrary number of identical processors for culling, intersection, linking, and refinement steps.

Since high-speed hardware capable of rendering vectors and polygons is widely used, high-speed curve and surface rendering is usually done by subdividing and rendering them as straight lines and planar polygons. Research has been focused on subdivision methods for rendering and modeling. Recursive subdivision for curve and surface rendering is expensive to implement in hardware due to high-speed stack memory requirements. But the added cost to develop such hardware can be well worth it, provided an efficient, robust, general-purpose algorithm is being implemented. Such an architecture will be proposed in the remainder of the section.

4.1. Surface/Surface Intersection Processor Architecture (SSIPA)

The SSIPA is described as consisting of four components derived from the four steps of the surface/surface intersection algorithm. These four components are: the Subdivision Processor (SUBDP), the Intersection Processor (INTEP), the Sorting Processor (SORTP), and the Refinement Processor (REFNP). The precedence of these four processors is described graphically from left to right in Figure 7.3.

4.2. Subdivision Processor

A surface is subdivided into at most four subpieces, and thus a surface pair can result in at most 16 pairs of surface pieces. It is proposed that SUBDP consists of 16 parallel identically programmed subprocessors such that each processor is endowed with the following functionality:

1. It computes the bounding volume for each surface piece and uses this bounding volume criteria to determine whether a surface pair is a candidate for further subdivision. Nonempty intersection of the bounding volumes is an indicator of such candidacy.
2. It uses a flatness criteria on a pair of possibly intersecting surfaces. One of the simplest flatness criteria is to determine the "approximate" curvature of the surface and check it against the "varying" curvature tolerance. If a surface is not flat enough then subdivide it into 2, 3, or 4 subpieces depending on the degree of curvature of the surface.

Thus each subprocessor inputs a pair of surface pieces, it examines them for possible intersection, and outputs a list of up to 16 subpairs

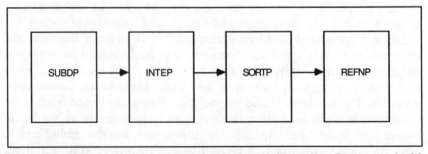

Figure 7.3. Block diagram of Surface/Surface Intersection Processor Architecture (SSIPA).

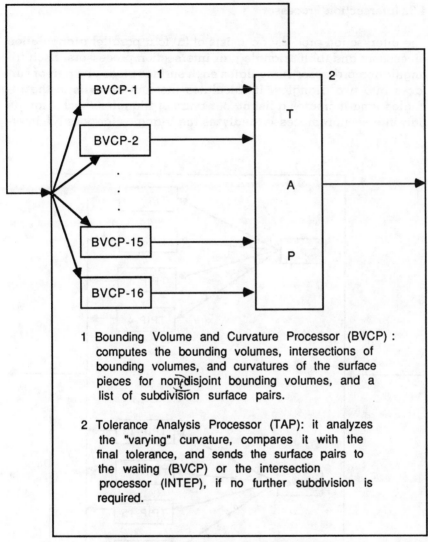

1 Bounding Volume and Curvature Processor (BVCP) : computes the bounding volumes, intersections of bounding volumes, and curvatures of the surface pieces for non-disjoint bounding volumes, and a list of subdivision surface pairs.

2 Tolerance Analysis Processor (TAP): it analyzes the "varying" curvature, compares it with the final tolerance, and sends the surface pairs to the waiting (BVCP) or the intersection processor (INTEP), if no further subdivision is required.

Figure 7.4.   Subdivision Processor (SUBDP).

of surfaces. Then these subpairs of surfaces are distributed over the 16 subprocessors. This process continues until the surfaces are flat within "varying" curvature tolerance. Then the tolerance is revised and the above steps are applied recursively until surfaces are flat within final tolerance. This process is described in Figure 7.4.

4.3. Intersection Processor

The intersection processor consists of (a) four parallel triangulation processors and (b) 16 triangle pair intersection processors. Each triangulation processortriangulates each surface piece of a pair of surfaces into two triangles, it calculates the unit normals to the triangles, and it creates a list of four pairs of triangles. Each triangle pair intersection processor analyzes the triangles for possible inter-

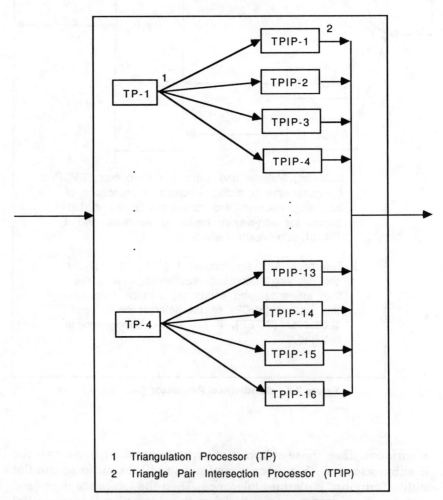

Figure 7.5.   Intersection Processor (INTEP).

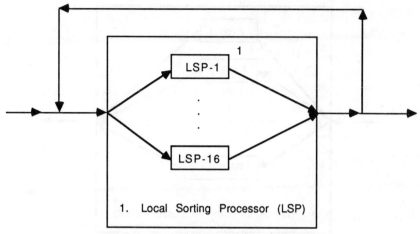

Figure 7.6.   Sorting Processor (SORTP).

section. If an intersection is found, it returns the intersection segment, or else no intersection is found. Each surface pair results in at most four intersection segments. This processor is described in Figure 7.5.

4.4. Sorting Processor

The sorting processor consists of 16 parallel subprocessors for sorting locally. Sorting is a polyphase process. Each processor first links initial runs of segments at the lowest level nodes in the tree structure and then these curves are backed up to the parent level nodes, one level at a time. The curves at the parent level nodes are then sent to the processors. This process is repeated until the root node is reached. This processor is described in Figure 7.6.

4.5. Refinement Processor

For realistic and practical curves of intersection, on the average there are about 100 points on the intersection curves. It is reasonable to have a refinement processor with 64 identically programmed components. Each component starts with an approximate computed point and brings it closer to the two intersecting surfaces. This processor is described in Figure 7.7.

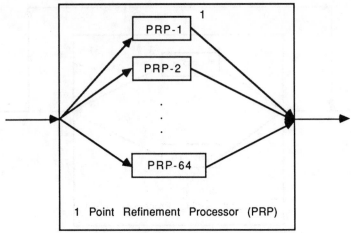

Figure 7.7.   Refinement Processor (REFNP).

5. CONCLUSION

This chapter identified the area of solid modeling as a key technology in CAD/CAM that would greatly benefit from the use of application specific VLSI-based hardware. In particular, it determined that the B-rep solid model representation would be a focal point for integrating (especially, in the automobile and aerospace industries) the legacy of wire-frame and surface representation systems of the past with the advanced surface definitions of the present and future. It was noted that the intersection problem of any two B-rep solid objects could be reduced to determining the intersection of two surfaces of the two objects. A general purpose surface/surface intersection algorithm was proposed as a solution to this problem, and a suggested hardware architecture for this algorithm was presented.

REFERENCES

1. J.H. Clark, "The Geometry Engine: A VLSI Geometry System for Graphics," *Proceedings of the SIGGRAPH 82*, 1982, pp. 127–133.
2. R.N. Stover, *An Analysis of CAD/CAM Applications With an Introduction to CIM*, Prentice Hall, Englewood Cliffs, NJ, 1984.
3. P. Marks, "CAD/CAM Databases...Six Steps Toward Control," *CAD/CAM Database Strategies*, Vol. 1, No. 1, 1987.

4. M.P. Groover and E.W. Zimmers, Jr., *CAD/CAM: Computer-Aided Design and Manufacturing*, Prentice Hall, Englewood Cliffs, NJ, 1984.

5. C.L. Jackins and S.L. Tanimoto, "Oct-trees and Their Use in Representing Three-Dimensional Objects," *Computer Graphics and Image Processing*, Vol. 14, 1980, pp. 249–270.

6. D. Meagher, "Geometric Modeling Using Octree Encoding," *Computer Graphics and Image Processing*, Vol. 19, 1982, pp. 129–147.

7. S. Sheridan, "The Scions of a Solids Modeler Move into Industry," *Mechanical Engineering*, Vol. 109, 1987, pp. 36–41.

8. R. Sedgewick, *Algorithms*, Addison-Wesley, Reading, MA, 1983.

9. D. Filip, R. Magedson and R. Markot, "Surface Algorithms Using Bounds on Derivatives," *Computer Aided Geometric Design*, Vol. 3, 1986, pp. 295–311.

10. C.L. Sabharwal, "A Divide-and-Conquer Method for Curve Intersection Between Two Parametric Surfaces," Advanced CAD/CAM Technology Research Technical Note 25-010, McDonnell Douglas Corporation, St. Louis, MO, 1981.

11. E.G. Houghton, R.F. Emnett, J.D. Factor and C.L. Sabharwal, "Implementation of a Divide-and-Conquer Method for Intersection of Parametric Surfaces," *Surfaces in Computer Aided Geometric Design Vol. 2*, R.E. Barnhill and W. Boehm (eds.), North Holland, Amsterdam, 1985, pp. 173–183.

12. M.J. Pratt and A.D. Geisow, "Surface/surface Intersection Problems," *The Mathematics of Surface*, J.A. Gregory (ed.), Oxford University Press, Oxford, UK, 1986, pp. 117–142.

13. J.M. Schmitt, B.A. Barsky and D. Wen-Hui, "An Adaptive Subdivision for Surface-Fitting from Sampled Data," *SIGGRAPH 86 Conference Proceedings*, Vol. 20, Dallas, TX, 1986, pp. 179–188.

14. R.N. Goldman and T.D. Derose, "Recursive Subdivision Without the Convex Hull Property," *Computer Aided Geometric Design*, Vol. 3, 1986, pp. 247–265.

15. B.V. Herzen and A.H. Barr, "Accurate Triangulation of Deformed, Intersecting Surfaces," *Computer Graphics*, Vol. 21, 1987, pp. 103–110.

16. C.L. Sabharwal and T.G. Melson, "Survey of Implementation of Bounding Volumes for Parametric Surfaces," McDonnell Douglas Report MDC B0820, McDonnell Douglas Corporation, St. Louis, MO, 1988.

17. H. Akima, "On Estimating Partial Derivatives for Bivariate Interpolation of Scattered Data," *Rocky Mountain Journal of Mathematics*, Vol. 14, 1984, pp. 41–52.

18. A. Preusser, "ALGORITHM 626 TRICEP: A Computer Plot Program for Triangular Meshes," *ACM Transactions on Mathematics Software*, Vol. 4, 1984, pp. 473–475.

19. R.E. Barnhill, G. Farin, M. Jordan and B.R. Piper, "Surface/surface Intersection," *Computer Aided Geometric Design*, Vol. 4, 1987, pp. 3–16. M.S. Casate and E.L. Staton, "An Overview of Analytic Solid Modeling," *IEEE Computer Graphics and Applications*, Vol. 5, 1985, pp. 45–56.

20. G.A. Sachs, A.J. Schwartz and F.B. Sleator, "Determining the Intersection of Parametric Surfaces by Solving the Ordinary Differential Equations," *Proceedings of the SAE/ESD International Computer Graphics Conference*, Detroit, MI, 1987, pp. 27–30.

21. D. Harel, *Algorithmics: The Spirit of Computing*, Addison-Wesley, Reading, MA, 1987.

8

A CMOS 16 × 16 Parallel Multiplier

H.A. NIENHAUS
D. STEISS

Electrical Engineering Department
University of South Florida

1. INTRODUCTION

A parallel multiplier which can perform multiplications in one clock cycle is an essential component in digital signal processing architectures. This chapter describes the design of a CMOS 16 × 16 parallel two's complement multiplier which was developed for the University of South Florida's CMOS cell library. The multiplier combines two of the most popular algorithms to enhance its speed. These are Booth's algorithm [1,2,3] which minimizes the number of adders required, and the carry save algorithm, which provides carry propagation free addition in all but the final adder (decoder). Propagation delays in the final adder were minimized by using carry select over four bits. A similar multiplier [4] which combines Booth's and the carry save algorithms uses an extra row of carry save adders and differs in its circuit implementation.

Since radix 2 signed digit (SD) numbers have also been used for carry propagation free addition [5], this technique was considered instead of the carry save technique. Advantages of the SD technique are simpler complements, simpler decoder (complexity is between that of an adder and an incrementer), fewer carry propagation free adders (if 3 × n partial product generators are used), and the ability to use a binary addition tree to enhance speed. These advantages become more significant as the number of multiplier bits increases. The major disadvantage of the SD technique is that twice as many bits are required. This increases the size and complexity of the full adder arrays and doubles the size of the shifters, which consume much of the multiplier area. In our opinion, the disadvantages outweigh the advantages for a 16 × 16 multiplier.

2. DESIGN METHODOLOGY

A behavioral simulation of the multiplier was written in C before layout began. Layout was done using MAGIC. A switch level simulation using ESIM was performed on the circuit from the extracted layout. A test pattern generation program was written in C for simulation and test. A timing simulation of the critical paths using FACTS indicates a worst-case delay of 108 ns using the MOSIS scalable CMOS 3u P-well process nominal parameters. The multiplier has been fabricated by MOSIS in this process and has been tested. The speed of the multiplier should be significantly less in a high-performance, state-of-the-art CMOS process.

3. SYSTEM ARCHITECTURE AND LOGIC

A block diagram of the multiplier is shown in Figure 8.1. It consists of a two's complement generator, a top-row partial product generator (TPPG) which multiplies the two LSBs of the multiplier A by the multiplicand B, seven additional 2×16 partial product generators (PPG), six carry save adders, a most significant word (MSW) adder which decodes the 16 MSBs of the product, a least significant word (LSW) adder which decodes the next 14 LSBs of the product, and Booth decoders. The first three partial products are added together in the top carry save adder row. Each of the remaining partial products is added to the two outputs of the carry save adder above it. Although carry save tree addition [6] was considered, it was not evident that this could significantly improve the speed of the multiplier. This is because the critical path in the multiplier includes the carry propagation in the LSW adder and MSW adder. A tree-type structure is also more difficult to lay out. A description of each of the major blocks in the multiplier follows.

3.1. Two's Complement Generator

The block diagram of the two's complement generator, which generates the two's complement of the multiplicand for the PPG's, is shown in Figure 8.2. This is essentially an incrementer with inverted inputs. It has full look-ahead carry in every block of four bits and carry select over each four bit block to minimize carry propagation delays. In an incrementer the sum is the XOR of the input bit and the

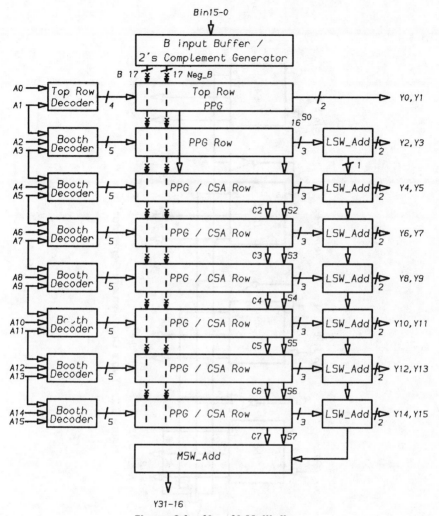

Figure 8.1.   16 × 16 Multiplier.

carry-in, and the carry-in is simply the AND of all of the next LSBs of the input. Note that the two's complement of a 16-bit number is 17 bits wide.

The logic block diagram of the four LSBs of the incrementer is shown in Figure 8.3. The block diagram of the other 4-bit slices is shown in Figure 8.4 and that of the MSB is shown in Figure 8.5.

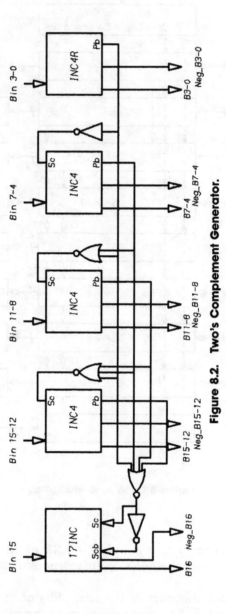

Figure 8.2. Two's Complement Generator.

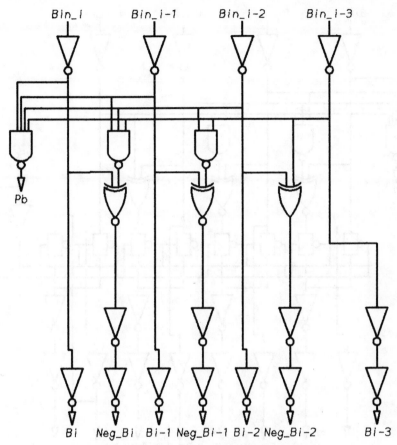

Figure 8.3.   Right Complement Generator.

3.2. Top Partial Product Generator (TPPG)

The top partial product generator generates the product of the two LSBs of the multiplier (a1 a0) and the multiplicand (B). Table 8.1 lists what these products are for a Booth multiplier. Note that the only operations required in this cell are conditional inhibit, pass, two's complement, and/or shift.

The block diagram of this cell is shown in Figure 8.6. The logic block diagram of a one-bit slice is shown in Figure 8.7. The operation of this cell is as follows. The two's complement of the multiplicand is either passed (a0 = 1) or shifted (a0 = 0) to the left one-bit by a shifter made up of an array of two input pass gate muxes. The shifter output is the correct output if a1 = 1. An array of AND cells is used to

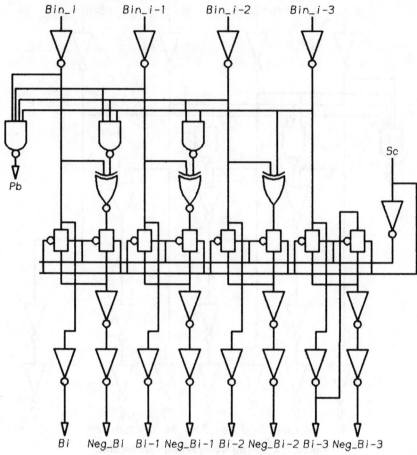

Figure 8.4.   4-Bit Complement Generator.

generate the correct output if $a1 = 0$. Finally a second array of two input pass gate muxes selects the correct output.

Note that the two muxes are not required for the LSB of the product since this is simply the AND function of $a0$ and $b0$ for any multiplier.

Table 8.1.   2 × n TPPG.

$a1$	$a0$	Product
0	0	$0 \times B$
0	1	$1 \times B$
1	0	$-2 \times B$
1	1	$-1 \times B$

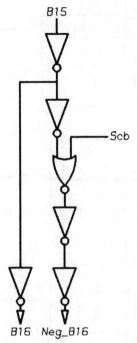

Figure 8.5.   Bit 17 of Complement Generator.

Also, the shifter mux is not required for the MSB of the product since the sign bit is extended if it is not shifted.

3.3. Multiplier Row

The block diagram of the general 2 × 16 multiplier row is shown in Figure 8.8. The block diagram of a 4-bit slice of this cell is shown in Figure 8.9. It consists of a 2 × 16 partial product generator (PPG) which produces the 18-bit product of 2 multiplier bits and the multiplicand. This is added to the previous partial products by a carry save adder array. For a Booth multiplier the product of the two multiplier bits ($ai + 1$, ai) and the multiplicand is given in Table 8.2.

Note that the only operations required in the PPG are conditional inhibit, pass, two's complement, and shift. The logic block diagram of a one bit slice of the PPG is shown in Figure 8.10. In this circuit, an array of two input muxes selects either the multiplicand or its two's complement. This corresponds to a multiplication by +1 or −1. A second array of two input muxes either passes this straight ahead or shifts it one bit to the left. This corresponds to a multiplication by 1 or

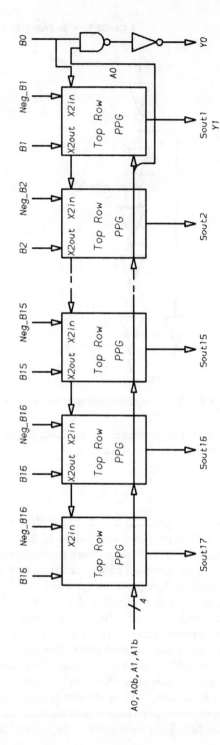

Figure 8.6. Top Row.

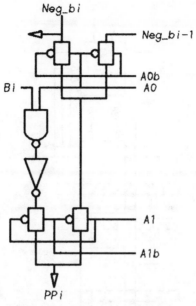

Figure 8.7.   Top Row P. P. G.

2. The shifter output is either inhibited or passed to the carry save adder by a NOR gate. This corresponds to a multiplication by 0 or 1.

Since the LSB of the PPGs is simply the AND function of b0 and the X2′ output of the Booth decoder, the two muxes are not required for this. Also, the shifter is not required for the MSB of the PPG, since this is extended if it is not shifted.

Table 8.2.   2 × n PPG.

a_{i+1}	a_i	a_{i-1}	Product
0	0	0	$0 \times B$
0	0	1	$1 \times B$
0	1	0	$1 \times B$
0	1	1	$2 \times B$
1	0	0	$-2 \times B$
1	0	1	$-1 \times B$
1	1	0	$-1 \times B$
1	1	1	$0 \times B$

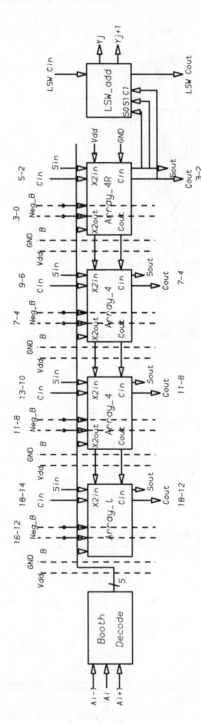

Figure 8.8. General Multiplier Row.

316

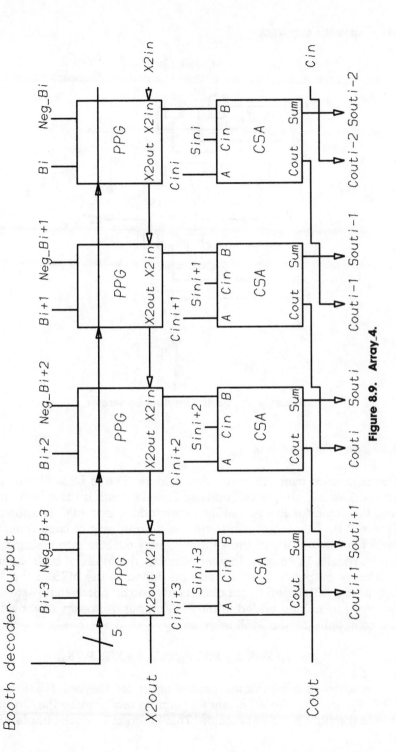

Figure 8.9. Array_4.

317

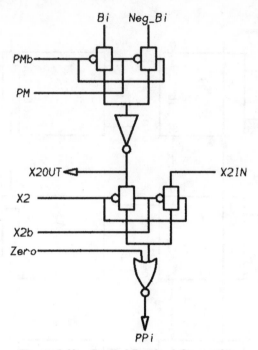

Figure 8.10. Partial Product Generator.

3.4. Carry Save Adders

The multiplier uses six carry save adders. The 15 LSBs of the carry save adder are simply full adders. The sixteenth bit is a half adder and the logic for the two MSBs of the adder and PPG is shown in Figure 8.11. This logic results from a unique way of combining the most significant bits of the sum and carry outputs into a single bit, which results in simpler logic. Normally, the MSBs of both the sum and carry outputs are extended and added to the MSB of the PPG output in a full adder. In our circuit only one bit needs to be extended left two places and added to the PPG output. It is easy to show that the composite output MSB is given by

$$S_{o17} = P_{17} \text{ XOR } S_{i17} \text{ XOR } P_{16}S_{i17} = P_{17} \text{ XOR } P_{16}{'}S_{i17}$$

Since the 10 combination cannot occur for the two MSBs of the PPG, P_{17} and P_{16}, the XOR function can be replaced by the OR function in the right hand expression. This function is much simpler than

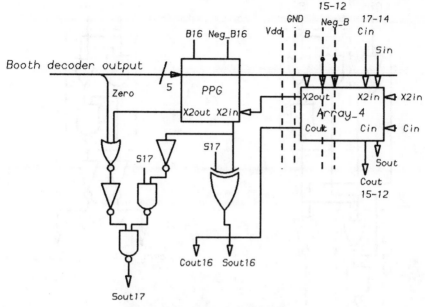

Figure 8.11.   Sign Extend Logic.

a full adder. The composite MSB also means that the full adders, normally used for the next two LSBs of the carry save adder, are replaced by an XOR gate and a half adder, respectively.

The logic block diagrams of the full adder and half adder are shown in Figure 8.12. Except for the top CSA, the inputs to each full adder are the sum and shifted carry bit outputs from the higher row CSA and the output bit of the PPG. The fast and slow inputs of the full adders were alternated from row to row to equalize delays.

3.5. Booth Decoder

The Booth decoder determines the multiplication required in the PPGs as a function of the two multiplier bits and the next least significant multiplier bit. The logic design of the Booth decoder for all but the TPPG follows directly from Table 8.2. The logic block diagram is shown in Figure 8.13. A major concern in the design of this cell is providing enough buffering to drive the 18-bit PPG. The Booth decoder for the TPPG consists simply of a pair of buffers for the two multiplier bits. This follows directly from Table 8.1.

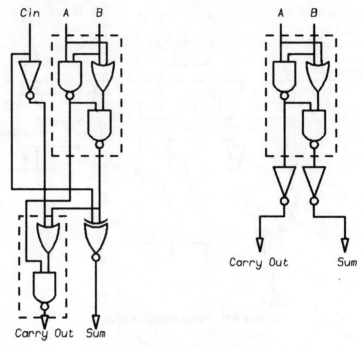

Figure 8.12.   CSA and Half Adder.

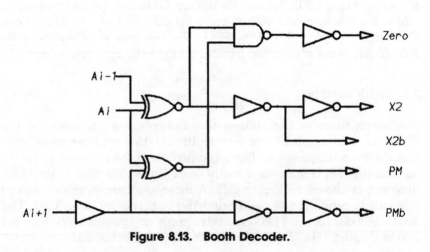

Figure 8.13.   Booth Decoder.

3.6. Least Significant Word Adder

The two LSBs of the product are obtained directly from the TPPG. The next 14 LSBs of the 32-bit product are obtained from the least significant word (LSW) adder. Each 2-bit slice of the LSW adder combines two sumbits and two carry bits to produce two product bits and the carry to the next 2-bit slice. The block diagram of a 2-bit slice of the LSW adder is shown in Figure 8.14. It consists of a half adder with a carry out to a full adder. The carry propagation for this cell is a two gate delay, which is important since the LSW adder is in the critical path for the multiplier. The carry output of the LSW adder is the carry input to the MSW adder.

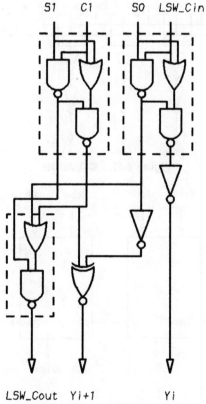

Figure 8.14.   LSW Adder.

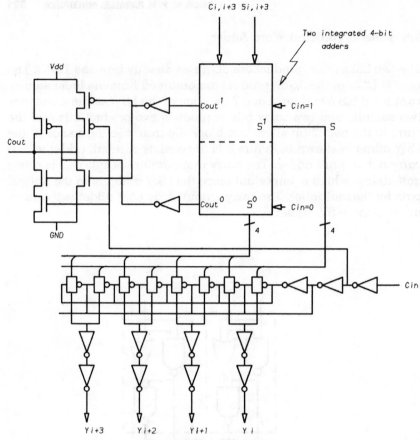

Figure 8.15. CSL Adder.

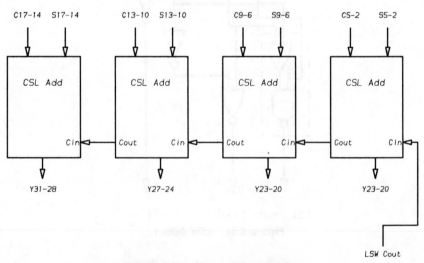

Figure 8.16. Upper Word Adder.

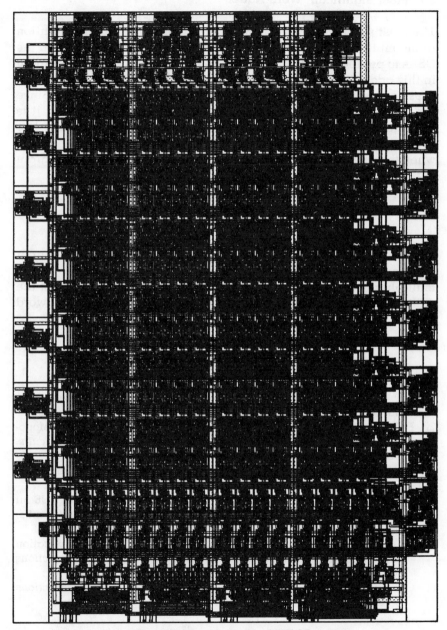

Figure 8.17. Multiplier CIFPLOT.

3.7. Most Significant Word Adder

The most significant word (MSW) adder performs the final addition in the multiplier as it combines the sum and carry streams from the CSAs to produce the 16 MSBs of the 32-bit product. Carry propagation in this adder is part of the critical path for the multiplier. This adder uses carry select over every 4-bit slice, as shown in Figure 8.15. Since the carry propagation over the 4-bit slice is a two gate delay, it is extremely fast (approximately 5 ns). Internally, the 4-bit adder has two ripple carry chains to generate the carry output for the case when the carry input is 0 and when it is equal to 1. The block diagram of the entire 16-bit adder is shown in Figure 8.16.

4. SUMMARY

The multiplier contains 6350 transistors including input and output buffers. Layout size is 2042 lambda × 1465 lambda. The cifplot of the multiplier is shown in Figure 8.17. Because of array structure of the multiplier, it is relatively easy to create versions with different word sizes.

REFERENCES

1. A.D. Booth, "A Signed Binary Multiplication Technique," *Quarterly Journal of Mechanical Applied Mathematics*, Vol. 4, 1951, pp. 236–240.
2. F. Ware, W. McAllister, J. Carlson, D. Sun and R. Vlach, "64 Bit Monolithic Floating Point Processors," *IEEE Journal of Solid State Circuits*, Vol. sc-17, October 1982, p. 898.
3. M. Uya, K. Kaneko and J. Yasi, "A CMOS Floating Point Multiplier," *IEEE Journal of Solid State Circuits*, Vol. sc-19, October 1984, p. 697.
4. D.A. Henlin, M.T. Fertsch, M. Mazin and E.T. Lewis, "A 16 Bit × 16 Bit Pipelined Multiplier Macrocell," *IEEE Journal of Solid State Circuits*, Vol. sc-20, No. 2, April 1985, pp. 542–547.
5. N. Takagi, H. Yasuura and S. Yajima, "High Speed VLSI Multiplication Algorithm with a Redundant Binary Addition Tree," *IEEE Transactions on Computers*, Vol. c-34, No. 9, September 1985, pp. 789–796.
6. C.S. Wallace, "A Suggestion For A Fast Multiplier," *IEEE Transactions on Computers*, February 1964, pp. 14–17.

9

Design and Simulation of a Reduced Instruction Set Computer*

HARRY W. TYRER

Dept. of Electrical and Computer Engineering
University of Missouri-Columbia

1. INTRODUCTION

Reduced Instruction Set Computer (RISC) architectures evolved quite naturally from the requirement to provide a "flexible" microcode in Complex Instruction Set Machines (CISC). Microcode provides an easily extendable instruction set so that simpler (hence cheaper) machines with upward compatibility can be constructed. Improved throughput should be expected if the control store could be changed to implement frequently-used sequences of instructions. However, the very nature of microprogramming precludes the flexibility so conveniently accessible by software programming. Hence RISC architectures, which implements only a few simple but fundamental instructions, could provide the tradeoff between flexibility and speed by providing hardware instructions with small numbers of cycles.

---

* The author wishes to acknowledge the gifts provided to the University of Missouri-Columbia, College of Engineering by Apollo Computers, Inc. (Chelmsford, MA) and Mentor Graphics, Inc. (Beaverton, OR). Their gracious and generous university gift programs provided equipment without which this chapter could not have been written.

Tom Howell, Patty Hayden, and Lo-Kan (Bill) Yu, participated as a class to design and construct MizzouRISC. Their hard work and effort resulted in the correct operation of the MizzouRISC components. Tom Howell undertook to debug the fully connected circuit and to implement the Fibonacci program in the system.

The author gratefully acknowledges the work of Jeffrey A. Brown, for the graphics, Rom Ramakrishnan, for his technical assistance, and Pam Willett for typing. Furthermore the availability of resources provided by the Engineering Computer Network is also gratefully acknowledged.

RISC philosophy produces machines with interesting characteristics: the instructions are executable in one clock cycle and a tradeoff between software and hardware is exploited. The software, because of its flexibility becomes more extensive than with a comparable CISC machine. Consider these two characteristics more closely.

The single cycle instruction allows RISC computers to produce very high throughputs. Indeed five to 10 million instructions per second (MIPS) is not uncommon in these machines. Since each instruction consists of a Fetch and Execute cycle, requiring at least two clock cycles, pipelining is usually employed.

If in the Execute portion of the cycle an operand fetch is required, an increase in the number of cycles per instruction results, violating RISC design philosophy. Arithmetic instructions are either unary or binary, requiring one or two operand fetches, respectively. Furthermore, if the destination of the result is a memory location, an additional clock cycle is required. Variable numbers of clock cycles increases the complexity of a design by either increasing the number of opcodes or by increasing the complexity of the memory access modes. Consequently in RISC machines only LOAD and STORE operations provide memory fetch and the remaining instructions operate from data previously stored in registers.

That RISC computation is performed within registers has been made possible in part by the technology advances in optimized compilers: the majority of compiled operations take place within registers. A recent review [1] provides some interesting insights.

Reduced instruction set computers provide a tradeoff between software and hardware. Since software is flexible, infrequent and complex instructions should be so implemented. Hardware can implement simple, atomic instructions which are not changeable and form a suitable set of instructions for general purpose computing.

Studies have shown that simple instructions such as LOAD, STORE, and BRANCH are the most frequently employed [2]. A more complex instruction set, for example, the CASE instructions in superminicomputers, is implemented in RISC computers by software. Furthermore, optimized compilation with these most frequently used instructions can assure high-speed execution. The resulting hardware design is much simpler, reducing cost and VLSI design complexity.

It is presumed that a compiler will be used in preference to an assembler since high-level languages (such as C or ADA) can be used for system design. As a result, it is possible to consider tradeoffs between hardware design costs and compiler design costs.

These tradeoffs include the cost of design, complexity, system cost, and training and implementation costs.

The design discussed in this chapter features a 32-bit word. Memory access if provided by LOAD and STORE instructions with 12 memory access modes. An unusual feature, a hardware stack, was included to promote rapid context switching. Since this device was to be designed and simulated on a Computer Aided Electronic Design (CAED) system for pedagogical purposes, neither pipelining nor privileged instructions for system operation were included.

This processor, called MizzouRISC, was designed in a classroom setting by three graduate students and the instructor. The class followed a project management model. The design tradeoffs were discussed and each person was made responsible for a particular part of the design. In the end the components were brought together, and final debugging was performed so that the system could be simulated. RAM memory was added so that a program could be stored for performance evaluation.

This chapter demonstrates that RISC architecture is a superb teaching tool because of its simplicity and completeness. Indeed a working CPU with only 12 instructions was designed and implemented by carefully organized students. Nevertheless this design incorporates a highly complex addressing scheme and an unusual architecture for handling critical instructions. Perhaps more importantly, the architecture is expandable so that future classes can stamp MizzouRISC with their creative personalities.

2. MizzouRISC ARCHITECTURE

The MizzouRISC architecture features an address bus (ADDBUS) and data bus (DATBUS), each 32 bits wide. External control is provided to the processor by means of a 2-bit priority bus, clock, and reset lines. The processor responds externally with interrupt acknowledge, read memory, and write memory signals. No separate I/O instructions were provided; I/O is implemented by memory polling using LOAD or STORE instructions. Figure 9.1 shows a diagram of the MizzouRISC processor and its external connections.

The architecture divides the 32-bit word into eight 4-bit nibbles. Each nibble division is adhered to rigorously for ease of the design of the data path. The architecture of the word organization is shown in Figure 9.2.

Each instruction has the opcode in the seventh nibble, and 12 of

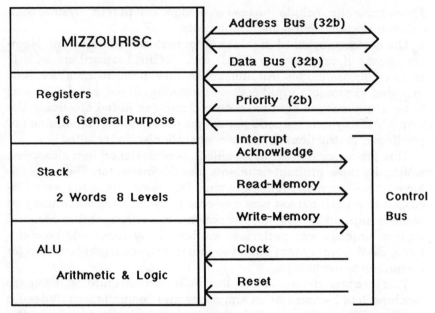

Figure 9.1. The MizzouRISC device features 16 general-purpose registers and an ALU. It also has an unusual module, a hardware stack providing two words of storage and eight levels of depth.

the 16 possible opcodes were implemented (Table 9.1). The rest of the nibbles identify either 16 source or 16 destination registers, 16 memory addressing modes; remaining space in the word was used for either immediate data or unused (reserved).

In the Data Translation Instruction Word, only one nibble was required for mode since data progressed either from memory to register (LOAD) or from register to memory (STORE). The memory access modes implemented are shown in Table 9.2. In Data Translation Instructions, the first four nibbles (16 bits) are used for immediate data.

The Arithmetic And Logical Word supports binary (ADD, subtract, logical AND, logical OR) and unary (SHIFT TO MOST SIGNIFICANT BIT, logical NOT) instructions. The binary instructions feature two source registers and a single destination register, all three of which may be different. The unary instructions feature a source and destination register. Again, the last 16 bits were not used.

The Control Word instructions provide the implementation for program jumps. Each of the four instructions has 16 condition codes and

WORD ORGANIZATION

32 BIT INSTRUCTION WORD

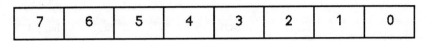

7	6	5	4	3	2	1	0

DATA TRANSLATION WORD

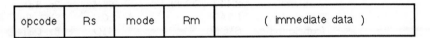

opcode	Rs	mode	Rm	(immediate data)

ARITHMETIC AND LOGICAL WORD

Binary Operations

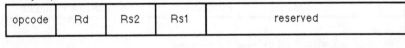

opcode	Rd	Rs2	Rs1	reserved

Unary Operations

opcode	Rd	reserved	Rs	reserved

CONTROL WORD

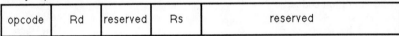

31		22 21		0
opcode	condition	Pri	label	

PROCESSOR STATUS WORD

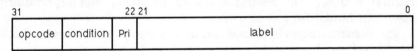

	9	5	2	0
reserved	C Z V N	stk depth	Pri	

Figure 9.2. The word organization of various instruction types and the Processor Status Word.

24 bits of space for a label. It became useful to provide two of those label bits for priority.

Finally the Processor Status Word.Priority PSW(1:0), the condition code status bits (carry, zero overflow and negative, PSW (5:8), and three bits for stack depth (4:2) are the only occupied fields.

The hardware stack is implemented by two registers, one for PSW

Table 9.1. Instructions.

OP Code (H)	Type	Instruction		Syntax	
0		—			
1		—			
2	Logic	NOT	NOT	Rs, Rd	
3	Logic	AND	AND	Rs1, Rs2, Rd	
4	Logic	OR	OR	Rs1, Rs2, Rd	
5	Arithmetic	ADD	ADD	Rs1, Rs2, Rd	
6	Arithmetic	SUBTRACT	SUB	Rs1, Rs2, Rd	
7	Arithmetic	SHIFT TO MSB	STM	Rs, Rd	
8	Translation	LOAD	LOD	SRC, Rd	
9	Translation	STORE	STO	Rs, DST	
A		—			
B		—			
C	Control	BRANCH	BRN(CC)	LABEL	
D	Control	SUBROUTINE CALL	CAL(CC)	LABEL	
E	Control	HOP	HOP(CC)	LABEL	
F	Control	RETURN	RNT(CC)	LABEL	

Notes
Rs, Rs1, Rs2 source; Rd destination registers.
SRC, DST are source and destination for addressing modes.
CC condition codes.

and the other for the current PC. As Subroutine_call, HOP, or interrupt instructions occur, it is possible to nest them to a depth of 8. Further nesting can be implemented by using memory, trading speed for hardware complexity.

The 12 instructions implemented in this design are shown in Table 9.1. This lists the opcode number in hexadecimal, the instruction type, and the typical syntax employed with each instruction.

Arithmetic and Logic instructions for binary operations have two source registers. The syntax of the operation shows that the RS1 and RS2 are combined and the result placed in the right-most register. For the unary operations the direction of the syntax is the same.

To implement multiplication and division a single shift instruction was provided. This instruction (shift to most significant bit) changed the nature of the data path so that a second type of register was required. However once a shift operation has been defined it is reasonably convenient to perform additional other shift instructions such as shift to least significant bit, rotate to the left, and rotate to the right.

An interesting feature of this design is the use of program control instructions. The four control instructions are defined according to the module level of the program. It is convenient to discuss each

Table 9.2.   Addressing Modes.

Mode	Mode Number	Implementation Syntax
Immediate	0	L #⟨data⟩
Immediate indirect	1	(L #⟨data⟩)
Immediate high	2	H #⟨data⟩
Immediate high indirect	3	(H #⟨data⟩)
register direct	4	Ri
register indirect	5	(Ri)
Displacement	6	⟨data⟩#Ri
Displacement indirect	7	(⟨data⟩#Ri)
PC	8	PC
PC indirect	9	(PC)
PC offset	A	⟨data⟩#PC
PC offset indirect	B	(⟨data⟩#PC)

instruction in the singular even though each individual instruction contains 16 of its corresponding counterparts according to the 16 possible condition codes (See Table 9.3).

The BRANCH instruction is intended to be used within a single module. The compiler will resolve the references from the calling to the serviced variable. The SUBROUTINE_CALL instruction is intended to call separately compiled modules. This instruction has its variables resolved by a loading utility. The HOP instruction provides dynamic linkage to anywhere in memory. Specifically this instruction is intended to provide access to the operating system supervisor. The SUBROUTINE_CALL instruction and the HOP instruction

Table 9.3.   Condition Codes.

Condition	Syntax	Number
GREATER THAN	GT	1
LESS THAN OR EQUAL	LE	2
GREATER THAN OR EQUAL	GE	3
LESS THAN	LT	4
HIGHER	HI	5
LOWER OR SAME	LOS	6
LOWER	LO	7
HIGHER OR SAME	HIS	8
PLUS	PL	9
MINUS	MI	A
NOT EQUAL	NE	B
EQUAL	EQ	C
NO OVERFLOW	NV	D
OVERFLOW	V	E
ALWAYS	ALW	F

increase the depth of the stack. Finally the RETURN instruction provides a return for both the HOP and SUBROUTINE—CALL instructions by reducing the depth of the stack.

The translation instructions (Table 9.1, Figure 9.2) use the mode nibble which provides for 12 of 16 possible addressing modes. The unused four nibbles of these two instructions provide 16 bits for either immediate or immediate high data to facilitate the construction of a 32-bit immediate data word. Addressing modes, register indirect and displacement (for indexing), allows access to arrays; use of the program counter provides for relative addressing.

The standard 16 condition codes were implemented (Table 9.3). Tests for zero results are implemented by the equal and not equal conditions. The unsigned conditional branches are implemented by the higher, lower or same, higher or same, and lower conditions. On the other hand, signed conditional branches are implemented by less than, less than or equal, greater than, and greater than or equal. Tests for negative results is minus or plus, and for overflow results are no overflow and overflow. Finally, unconditional program control instruction is implemented by the *always* condition.

This architecture can be used to perform integer arithmetic calculations, for example, the generation of the Fibonacci series. A high-level language representation of the program to be implemented on the reduced instruction set computer is shown in Figure 9.3, a design program written in ADA. The Fibonacci series is given after initializing. The first number is found in R6 (0) then R1 contains

```
$ type fib_risc.a
-- Calculate Fibonacci numbers to test RISC.
with INTEGER_IO; use INTEGER_IO;
procedure fib_risc is
        R1, R2, R5, R6, ONE : INTEGER;
begin
ONE:= 1;                           --Initialize storage to one.
R5:= 1;                            --Initialize registers.
R6:= 0;                            --1st number.
R1:= R6 + 1;                       --2nd number.
R2:= ONE;                          --3rd number.
        for   index in 1..15
        loop
                R1:= R2 + R1;      --R1=Fn-1.
                put(R1);
                R2:= R2 + R1;      --R2=fn-2.
                put(R2);
        end loop;
end fib_risc;
$
```

Figure 9.3. The design program (in ADA) to generate the Fibonacci series.

SAMPLE PROGRAM
Fibonacci Number Generator

Machine Language			Assembler		
Address	Instructions	Label	Instruction		;Comments
1 0000	CFC0	0000	RSET	BRN(3) #4#RSET	;Set Priority
2 0004	8F20	FFFF		LOD H#FFFF,R15	;Initialize Condition
3 0008	2E0F	0000		NOT R15,R14	;flags
4 000L	EF00	0014		HOP(0) FIB	;Begin Program
5 0010	0000	0001	ONE	.DW 1	;Data
6 0014	8500	0001	FIB	LOD L#0001,R5	;Set Reg 5 to "1"
7 0018	8600	0000		LOD L#0000,R6	;Set Reg 6 to "0"
8 001L	8120	5555		LOD H#5555,R1	;High byte PORT/2
9 0020	8200	5555		LOD L#5555,R2	;Low byte PORT/2
10 0024	5021	0000		ADD R1,R2,R0	;PORT/2 Address
11 0028	7000	0000		STM R0,R0	;PORT Address
12 002C	8166	0001		LOD #1#R6,R1	;Initialize F_0-1
13 0030	8210	0010		LOD (L#ONE),R2	;Initialize F_1-1
14 0034	9150	0000		STO R1,(R0)	;Save F_0
15 0038	9270	0001		STO R2,(#1#R0)	;Save F_1
16 003C	5121	0000	LOOP	ADD R1,R2,R1	;Calculate F_{n+1}
17 0040	9150	0000		STO R1,(R0)	;Output F_{n+1}
18 0044	5221	0000		ADD R1,R2,R2	;Calculate F_{n+2}
19 0048	9270	0001		STO R2,(#1#R0)	;Output F_{n+2}
20 004C	DF80	FFB0		CAL(2) ROUT	;Call Subroutine ROUT
21 0050	6654	0000		SUB R4,R5,R6	;Clear Reg 6, Set flags
22 0054	CC3F	FFE4		BRN(EQ) LOOP	;Loop forever
23 0000	5456	0000	ROUT	ADD R6,R5,R4	;Set Reg 4 to "1"
24 0004	FF00	0000		RTN(0)	;Return to FIB

Figure 9.4.   The listing of the Fibonacci number generator using MizzouRISC assembler.

the second number and R2 is given the third number (in each case 1). Finally the loop is entered where the fourth number is calculated in R1 and the fifth number is calculated in R2. The remaining numbers are generated successively in R1 and R2.

The MizzouRISC assembler sample program performing the Fibonacci number generation is shown in Figure 9.4. This listing shows the machine language equivalent as well as the assembler instruction. The design language program in Figure 9.3 actually implements lines 5 through 22. In addition, lines 20 and 21 were inserted not for the purpose of generating Fibonacci numbers but for testing the subroutine call capability of the system. This program tests every instruction and addressing mode in the architecture.

3. LOGIC DESIGN OF THE MIZZOURISC PROCESSOR

The logic design consists of the data path and implementing control algorithms in the control circuit. Essentially a top-down design was employed, in which the larger logical subunits defined the connections of the smaller units and control signals were passed to a common control circuit.

To save execution cycles some control operations were implemented within the data path. Nevertheless, the control circuit consists of gates and a ROM which was addressed according to the instruction opcode. The extensive use of gate logic saves cycles but control store provides ease of implementation. RISC architecture is highly amenable to design with logic gates which is considered a characteristic.

The MizzouRISC CPU consists of six modules, including control circuit, and the appropriate buses. A block diagram of the overall data path is shown in Figure 9.5. The databus (DATABUS) connects the instruction decoder, memory module, arithmetic logic unit, register stack, and register module. The address bus (ADDBUS) connects the memory module and the register stack. The memory module produces the read and write signals. The remaining external signals emanate from the I/O module: interrupt acknowledge, reset, and priority. Consider now a brief description of each module; further detail is provided when the instructions are discussed.

The Instruction Decoder receives each instruction word and apportions each nibble to the appropriate location. The opcode is passed to the control circuit and the arithmetic logic unit. The register number is passed to the register module. Data and mode nibbles are passed to the memory module. Condition codes are passed to the control circuits and the priority and data of the control transfer instructions are passed to the memory module.

The arithmetic logic unit performs all of the arithmetic and logic instructions using the registers in the register module. The register module maintains the 16 registers and decodes the register number to determine the appropriate register.

The memory module, which determines the next address, contains the program counter, and the processor status word. The decoding for the memory access mode takes place in this circuit.

The register stack contains the 16 registers, two at eight levels deep. The intent of the register stack is to store the current program counter and processor status word to speed context switching for rapid nesting of subroutines.

The I/O module provides interrupt access to the processor. The final operation in each instruction is to check for interrupts. The interrupt check microroutine (INT_CK) tests the priority bits to see if they are set. If so, the priority is compared against that of the PSW and the interrupt is serviced if the priority exceeds or is equal to the

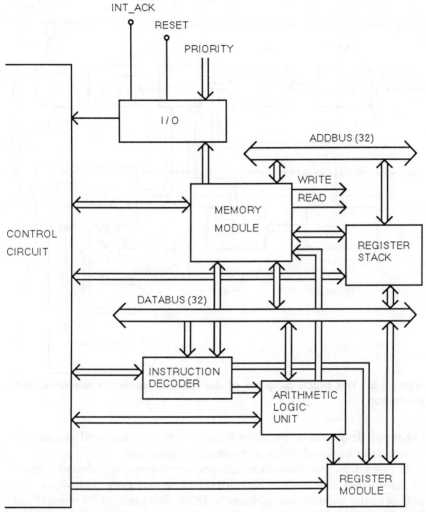

Figure 9.5. The block diagram of the data path for the MizzouRISC processor.

current running priority. If the interrupt is to be serviced the acknowledge is returned to the device. Finally the RESET signal is
entered through this circuit so that the system can start at the micro-
program address of 2 (FETCH).

Signals from each of the six modules go into the control circuit to
provide next-state data. Figure 9.6 shows a block diagram of the
control circuit.

Inputs to the control circuits are the reset, opcode, processor sta-

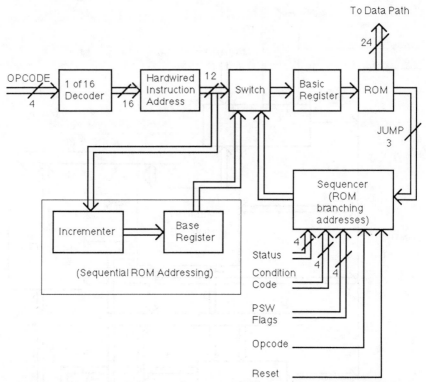

Figure 9.6. The block diagram of the control circuit for the MizzouRISC processor.

tus word flag, condition code bits, and four additional status bits. These data determine the sequencer information.

In operation the control circuit receives the opcode, decodes one of 16, identifies one of the 12 hardwired instruction addresses, and points to the instruction address in ROM. For each ROM word (Table 9.4), 24 bits go to the data path, and the next three bits provide for branching among the ROM instructions. Sequential ROM instructions use the incrementer which is switched in (or out) by the ROM instructions.

A close examination of the microcode of the ROM (Table 9.4) shows that the FETCH instruction and the RESET micro-instructions require one cycle, seven micro-instructions require two cycles, and the remaining micro-instructions (3) require three clock cycles. So a maximum of six cycles is required for three instructions, achieving a substantially reduced number of cycles per instruction. The compro-

Table 9.4. Microcode for ROM

Micro Instruction	Cycle Number	Contents (Hexadecimal Nibbles)								
INT_CK	00	1	0	2	0	0	0	0	8	0
	01	0	0	0	4	0	0	0	8	1
FETCH	02	0	0	0	C	0	0	0	8	0
NOT	03	1	0	3	0	0	0	9	4	0
	04	2	0	0	1	0	0	2	1	0
ALU's	05	1	0	5	0	0	0	9	4	0
	06	0	8	0	0	0	0	5	2	0
	07	2	0	0	1	0	0	2	1	0
STM	08	1	0	8	0	0	0	9	0	8
	09	0	8	0	0	0	0	0	8	4
	0A	2	0	0	1	0	0	2	0	2
LOD	0B	0	8	0	0	0	8	0	8	0
	0C	2	0	0	0	0	8	2	0	0
STO	0D	0	8	0	0	0	8	0	8	0
	0E	2	0	0	0	0	8	3	0	0
BRN	0F	1	0	0	0	4	0	0	8	0
	10	2	0	0	1	0	5	0	8	0
CAL	11	1	0	0	0	F	0	0	8	0
	12	2	0	0	1	0	5	0	8	0
HOP	13	1	0	0	0	F	0	0	8	0
	14	2	0	0	1	0	3	0	8	0
RTN	15	1	0	0	0	4	0	0	8	0
	16	0	8	0	0	1	0	0	8	0
	17	2	0	0	3	0	1	0	8	0
RESET	18	2	0	2	0	0	0	0	8	0

mise not to meet the one cycle per instruction was predicated by practical considerations.

MizzouRISC has FETCH, EXECUTE, INTERRUPT_CHECK instruction cycle. The next sections describe the logic and control required to implement the FETCH, INT_CK (interrupt check), and the execute segments of the instructions.

3.1. Fetch and Interrupt_Check Micro-instructions

The data path segment which performs the FETCH and INTERRUPT_CHECK portions of the instruction cycle are shown in Figure 9.7a. The instruction decoder, memory module, and I/O module obtain signals from the control circuit. The I/O module is also connected to the external device through the address bus and priority bits of the control bus.

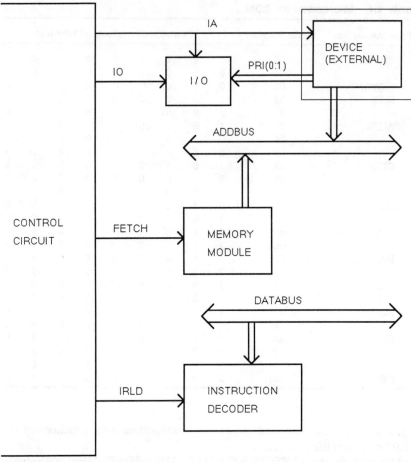

Figure 9.7a. The modules involved in the FETCH and interrupt check (INT _CK) micro-instructions.

In performing a FETCH (Figure 9.7b) the program counter value is placed into the address bus. In the memory module the program counter is increased by four and the contents of the data bus (as defined by address bus contents) is placed into the instruction decoder.

The INTERRUPT_CHECK makes up the last part of each instruction and tests to see if the interrupt bits have been set. If so, the device vector address is also placed on the address bus and the instruction decoder receives the first instruction of the interrupt service routine. If not, then FETCH is called again and the next instruction cycle begins. In the remaining figures of the pseudocode de-

```
Process (FETCH)
    Begin
            ADDBUS ← PC              (FETCH)
            Cobegin
                  PC ← (PC + 4)   (IRLD)
                  IR ← DATABUS
            CoEnd
      End (FETCH)

(Execute Instructions)

Process (INT. CK)
      Begin
            If (I0 = 1) Then
            then ADDBUS ← DEV. ADDRESS    (IA)
            IR ← DATABUS                  (IRLD)
            End If
            CALL FETCH
      End (Process INT.CK)
```

Figure 9.7b. The pseudocode for the microcode of the FETCH and the interrupt check (INT_CK) micro-instructions.

scriptions of the instructions (Figures 9.7b, 9.9b, 9.10b, 9.11b, 9.11c), the letters in parenthesis define the asserted signals that are sent by the control circuit to the required module.

3.2. Load and Store Execution Segment

The overloading of the definition of nibbles of each instruction word requires that multiplexers route these signals according to the opcode (Figure 9.8). This device, to save cycles, requires the processor to decode the opcode to provide signals for the appropriate routing of data in the nibble.

Shown in Figure 9.9a is the data path segment for the modules used in the LOAD and STORE instructions. Shown in Figure 9.9b is the pseudocode for the LOD and STO micro-instructions. Since the FETCH portion of the instruction has been executed the instruction is in the instruction decoder. Examining the pseudocode in Figure 9.9b the addressing mode is identified using combinatorial logic to reduce instruction cycles. Signal MMOE, set by the decoding of the opcode in the control circuit, signals that the instruction requires address decoding. The addressing mode defines that the operation

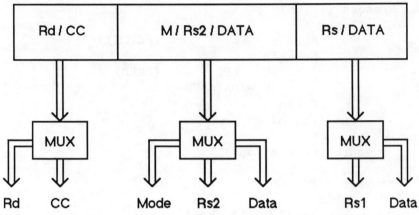

Figure 9.8. Multiplexed outputs of the various fields of the instruction word.

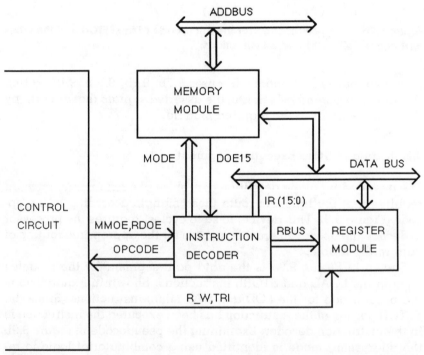

Figure 9.9a. The modules involved in LOAD or STORE instruction's execution segment.

LOD/STO

```
Process (LOD)
     begin
          addressing mode implemented combinatorially (MMOE)
          Rd ← DATBUS (MMOE, RDOE; TRI, R_W = 0)
          CALL INT.CK
     end(LOD)
Process (STO)
     begin
          Addressing mode implemented combinatorially (MMPE)
          DATBUS ← Rd (MMPE, RDOE, R_W; TRI = 0)
          CALL INT.CK
     end.
```

Figure 9.9b. The pseudocode for the microcode implementation of the execution segment of LOAD and STORE instructions.

is on either immediate data, in a register, or to be calculated. Once the particular memory address is obtained from a LOAD instruction, the contents on the databus are passed to the destination register; the STORE operation implements the reverse, and data in the destination register is released to the data bus.

3.3. Arithmetic and Logic Instruction Execution Segment

The arithmetic logic unit is the central module for the execution of arithmetic and logic instructions. Each instruction contains the source and destination registers pointed to by RBUS (Figure 9.10a), according to the cycle of the instruction. The Register Module passes register data to ALU through the databus. The condition code signals are passed to the memory module; the opcode is provided to the ALU for combinatorial decoding.

The description of the arithmetic and logic instruction are basically given in three sets: The NOT instruction, the instructions labeled ALUS (ADD, SUB, AND, OR), and the STM instruction. If either the NOT or the ALUS instructions is to be executed then RS1 (Source 1 register) is loaded; furthermore if either an ADD, SUB, AND, or an OR instruction is executed then RBUS provides also RS2 (Source 2 register) in the second cycle of the instructions. On the other hand the STM instruction requires that the RBUS information go to a shift register in the ALU. The microcode in Table 9.4 shows the additional

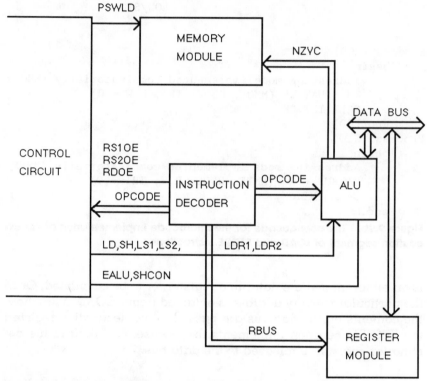

Figure 9.10a. The modules involved in the execution segment of the arithmetic and logic instructions.

cycle required for RS2 in the ALUS (binary) instructions and the two cycles required for unary instructions.

3.4. Program Control Instruction Execution Segment

The program control instructions make use of the memory module and register stack as shown in Figure 9.11a. The instruction register contents (bits 23:0) are placed into the memory module to provide immediate label data. This provides the number of bytes to be jumped. The pseudocode for the BRN micro-instruction (BRANCH) and for the CAL micro-instruction (SUBROUTINE_CALL) are shown in Figure 9.11b.

The BRANCH instruction is intended for loops within a single compilable module. The BRN microcode implements the following. If the condition code is satisfied then the BRANCH occurs, if not, the instruction completes by calling the interrupt check.

```
Process (NOT, ALUS, STM)
     begin
         IF non-shift instruction (EALU)
             THEN Load Source 1 Register (LS1)
                 Obtain reg# (RBUS, RS10E)
                 CASE <opcode>OF
                 1. NOT: continue

                 2.  ADD, SUM, AND, OR:
                         RBUS determines Source 2 register (RS20E)
                         Load Source 2 register (LS2)
                 END CASE
                 enable carry and bus driver (LDR1)
                 enable destination register (RDOE)
                 load PSW flag bits (NZVC, PSWLD)
                 Shift Instruction (SHCON)
             ELSE
                 RBUS determines operand register (RS10E)
                 Load shift register (LD)
                 Shift to Msb(SH)
                 Enable carry and bus driver (LDR2)
                 Enable destination register (RDOE)
                 Load PSW flag bits (NZVC, PSWLD)
     end (NOT, ALUS, STM).
```

Figure 9.10b. The pseudocode for the microcode of the execution segment of the arithmetic and logic instructions.

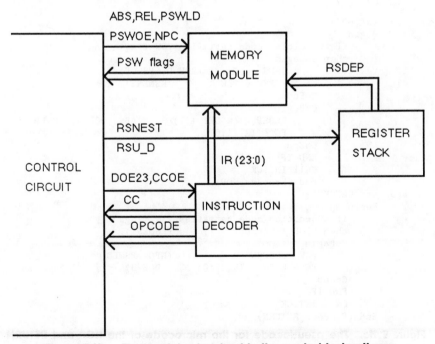

Figure 9.11a. The modules involved in the control instructions.

```
Process BRANCH
     Begin
          If <Condition code satisfies PSW flags>
          then PC ← (PC) + IR(21:0)
          END IF
          Call INT.CK
          End (Process Branch)

Process (SUB-CALL)
     Begin
          If <Condition code satisfies PSW flags>
               then CoBegin
                    RSPSW ← PSW      (RSU_D, PSWOE,
                    RSPL ← PC           RSNEST)
               CoEnd
               CoBegin
                    RSDEP ← (RSDEP + 1)
                    PC ← (PC + IR(21:0))          (REL, DOE23, PSWLD)
               CoEnd
               END IF
               Call INT.CK
          End (Process SUB_CALL)
```

Figure 9.11b. The pseudocode for the microcode for the BRANCH instructions and the SUBROUTINE_CALL instructions.

```
Process (HOP)
     Begin
          If <Condition code satisfies PSW flags>
          then CoBegin
                    RSPC ← PC      (RSU_D, PSWOE)
                    RSPSW ← PSW        RSNEST)
               CoEnd
               CoBegin
                    RSDEP ← (RSDEP + 1)     (ABS, DOE23, PSWLD)
                    PC ← IR(21:0)
               CoEnd
               END IF
               Call INT.CK
               End (Process HOP)
Process (RETURN)
     Begin
          If <Condition code satisfies PSW flags>
          then RSDEP ← (RSDEP - 1)     (RSNEST)
          CoBegin
               PSW ← RSPSW            (NPC, PSWLD
               PC ← RSPC + IR(21:0)       DOE23)
          CoEnd
          END IF
          Call INT.CK
     End (Process RETURN)
```

Figure 9.11c. The pseudocode for the microcode of the HOP and RETURN instructions.

Additionally the SUBROUTINE—CALL instruction requires that, if the condition codes are satisfied, the processor status word and program counter value are stored in the register stack. The register stack depth is incremented and the program counter is adjusted to the desired value. CAL microcode saves the PSW and PC, increments the stack depth, and obtains a new PC value.

Dynamic linkage to access the operating system supervisor is implemented by the HOP instruction. HOP (microcode HOP) requires that the condition codes be satisfied, and if so, essentially implements a CALL—SUBROUTINE instruction. The difference is that the signal ABS for absolute address is set rather than the REL signal as with the case with the SUBROUTINE—CALL. At the conclusion of the instruction the interrupt check is called.

Both the HOP and INTERRUPT—CALL instructions require a RETURN (microcode RTN) instruction to restore the register stack depth and to return the program counter value and processor status value of the original calling task. This RETURN instruction has two unique features, a conditional return and an offset from the return location by an instruction label.

4. DESIGN AND SIMULATION OF THE MizzouRISC PROCESSOR

Simulation of the MizzouRISC processor was accomplished with a Computer Aided Electronic Design System (Mentor Graphics, Beaverton, Oregon) housed on a token ring computer network (Apollo Computers, Chelmsford, MA). The simulated processor was interfaced to simulated RAM memory for program control.

Logic devices (analogous to chips) were constructed from a library of generic devices (such as NAND, LATCH, etc.) and connected together to form the processor. These devices included basic, load, and shift registers. In addition bus drivers, switches, and ROM were built up from the elements in the generic library.

The hierarchical development of the logic devices is shown in Figures 9.12a and 9.12b. The basic register (Figure 9.12a) is made up of individual D flip-flops which are elements in the generic library. From the basic register a load register (Figure 9.12b) was developed. The load register allows the input to be reflected on the output when the load is high and the clock makes a 0 to 1 transition.

Each of the blocks of the MizzouRISC discussed (Figure 9.5) were constructed by connecting these mathematically defined elements, including RAM for program storage. Each block was designed and

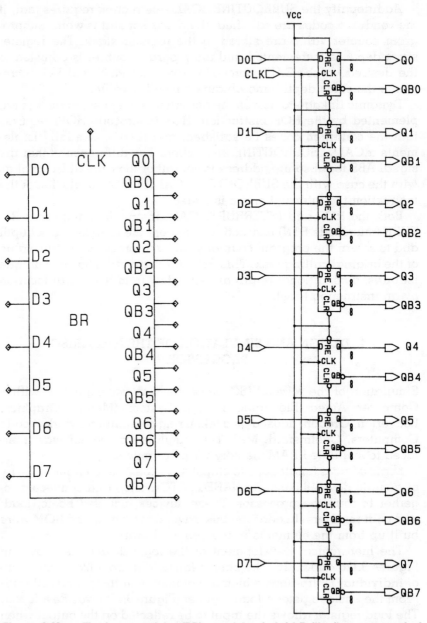

Figure 9.12a. The base register (BR) consists of eight D flip-flops connected in parallel.

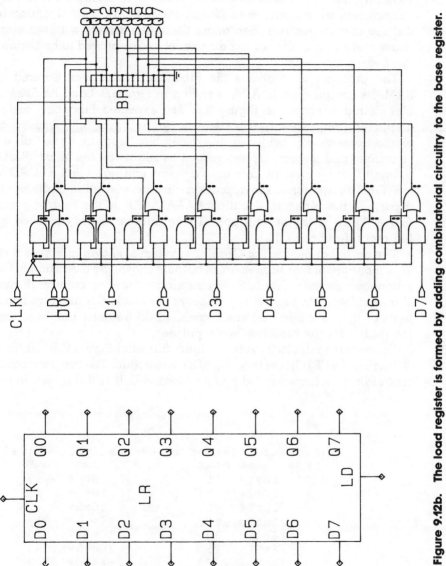

Figure 9.12b. The load register is formed by adding combinatorial circuitry to the base register.

tested individually against its specifications. The blocks were then connected and each instruction tested. Originally, the bus drivers were switches but this unfortunately resulted in multiple simultaneous sources on the bus, re-enforcing the need for careful timing in the use of a shared bus. Replacing these bus drivers with registers while maintaining the correct number of cycles proved to be tedious but necessary.

The program to generate the Fibonacci series was entered in RAM. Its design code in ADA is shown in Figure 9.3 and its Assembler listing is shown in Figure 9.4. The expected Fibonacci series displayed from two output ports is shown in Figure 9.13. Additional instructions were provided in the assembler program to test all instructions and memory access modes available on the MizzouRISC.

Input/Output from the chip uses memory polling so that a LOAD or a STORE instruction to the appropriate memory location implements a port. In the program, location AAAA AAAA is the first port and AAAA AAAB is the second port. These addresses are accessed by indirect reference to R0.

The output of the Mentor Graphics system is shown in Figure 9.14. This montage of five sequences of outputs shows the execution of the Fibonacci program (Figure 9.4) beginning at location counter 18 (machine address 44). Figure 9.14 displays the clock, the time, and contents of the data and address busses, RBUS (register number), and the timing for the read and write pulses.

Following each clock cycle in Figure 9.14 (and Figure 9.4), address 44 begins the FETCH cycle of the ADD instruction. The program counter (addbus) is incremented by four (second half of the cycle). In the

```
$ run fib_pap

                Fibonacci series in Hexadecimal(Decimal)
                PORT AAAA AAAA              PORT AAAA AAAB
                   16#1#(   1)                 16#1#(   1)
                   16#2#(   2)                 16#3#(   3)
                   16#5#(   5)                 16#8#(   8)
                   16#D#(  13)                 16#15#(  21)
                   16#22#(  34)                16#37#(  55)
                   16#59#(  89)                16#90#( 144)
                   16#E9#( 233)                16#179#( 377)
                   16#262#( 610)               16#3DB#( 987)

$
```

Figure 9.13. The Fibonacci numbers generated by each port in the sample program in Figure 9.4.

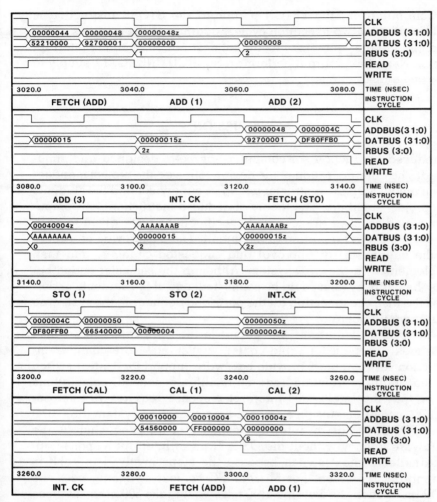

Figure 9.14. The output of the MizzouRISC address bus, data bus, register bus, clock, and read write lines in the execution of lines 18, 19, 20, and 23 of the sample program in Figure 9.4.

next clock cycle, ADD (1), the value D(16) is placed in the data bus, RBUS references R1 and the address bus is set to z, the tristate high; thus placing D from R1 to the ALU source 1 register. Similarly, in the next cycle, 8 is placed from R2 to source 2 register in the ALU. In the fourth cycle 8 and D are combined to form the result 15, another Fibonacci number, which is placed from the ALU destination register to R2. The instruction concludes with the interrupt check portion of the cycle.

Continuing on, the FETCH portion of the STORE instruction is followed by its two execution cycles, adding 1 to the contents of R0, and placing the contents of R2 at that destination, then the interrupt check. Next, the program performs a SUBROUTINE_CALL simply to test these instructions.

5. DISCUSSION

A reduced instruction set computer has been designed and simulated. The administration of the design followed the project management model with the instructor acting as supervisor and the students the project members. The theory of Reduced Instruction Set Computers was discussed in class and specifications were given to each student to design a portion of the circuit. The design was presented to the supervisor for approval and suggested changes, and then implemented in the CAD system. Although the semester ended before the entire system could be connected, one of the students undertook the task of connecting all the parts and debugging the system so that it would operate.

An unusual feature of this circuit is the hardware stack which presages a system for rapid context switching. More complex instruction set computers provide hardware support for context switch so that multiprogramming can be facilitated. Indeed, calculations show that the Intel 80386 interrupt response requires 70 microseconds, measurements [3] on a real time operating system (RSX-11M) on a PDP 11/60 has an interrupt response of 160 μsec whereas the hardware latency without the OS is 11 μsec. Interrupt response approximates context switch because the steps involved in each is essentially the same. For MizzouRISC context switching uses the HOP instruction. Its 5 cycles at 10 mhz would take 500 nsec, 22 times faster than the minicomputer processor above.

In this design, as multiprogramming increases, nesting depth also increases. This system performs best under conditions of non-preemptive scheduling: high throughput will be achieved with processes that rarely access the supervisor. To completely provide for context switching in this design, each stack level requires an associated set of registers.

The MizzouRISC does not strictly meet all the RISC philosophy requirements. Indeed [4] and [2] point out, practical considerations will force RISC philosophy compromises so that economically useful processors can be developed. In this design, pipelining and context switching were compromised due to practical considerations of time.

An interesting philosophical aside is the simulation of MizzouRISC with nonreal components. The components used in this design are based upon a generic library of nonreal devices which are defined according to their mathematical properties. Consequently, clock rise times, heating losses, and fanout (for example) did not become issues of consideration. Fortunately, circuits constructed with nonphysical devices can be simulated with computers and the value of the realizability of the devices assessed.

The MizzouRISC performance has been examined with a simple algorithm and improvements are in order. The absence of privileged or kernel instructions (or a HALT instruction) is necessary if the device is to be constructed since an operating system supervisor for rudimentary control would be required. Future developments call for the simulation of an operating system and construction of the chips. Furthermore 32-bit address space implies that segmented or paging system supporting virtual memory management should be implemented in the system.

RISC applications are just emerging. An interesting variation is to provide a RISC subset of instructions in a CISC computer. Thus compilers could take advantage of the highly optimized but atomic instructions and even gain further speed by putting onto hardware more frequently used complex instructions. In a second application one can imagine a floating point device with a reduced instruction set to support the floating point operations. Third, special purpose processors might be optimized for computer networking, and so on. Interestingly, the evaluation of processors for these applications is made possible not only by VLSI technology advancements but by the advancement in design and simulation, and in compiler technology.

REFERENCES

1. D.A. Patterson, "Reduced Instruction Set Computers," *Communications of the ACM*, Vol. 28, 1985, pp. 8–21.
2. M.G.H. Katevenis, *Reduced Instruction Set Computer Architecture for VSLI*, MIT Press, Cambridge, MA, 1984.
3. H.W. Tyrer and N.J. Pressman, "Strategies for Automated Placements of Cells for Microscopy," *Applied Optics*, Vol. 26, No. 16, 1987, pp. 3308–3314.
4. G. Radin, "The 801 Minicomputer," *IBM Journal of Research and Development*, Vol. 27, No. 3, 1983, pp. 237–246.

Author Index

Subject Index